'Essential Agony'

The Battle of Dunbar 1650

Arran Johnston

Helion & Company

To my son Archer, who celebrated his first birthday as I wrote this book.

Helion & Company Limited
Unit 8 Amherst Business Centre
Budbrooke Road
Warwick
CV34 5WE
England
Tel. 01926 499 619
Email: info@helion.co.uk
Website: www.helion.co.uk
Twitter: @helionbooks
Visit our blog at http://blog.helion.co.uk/

Published by Helion & Company 2019
Designed and typeset by Mach 3 Solutions Ltd (www.mach3solutions.co.uk)
Cover designed by Paul Hewitt, Battlefield Design (www.battlefield-design.co.uk)
Printed by Henry Ling Limited, Dorchester

Text © Arran Paul Johnston 2019
Monochrome illustrations © Author's collection unless otherwise noted
Colour plate images © as individually credited
Maps drawn by Dr Lesley Prince © Helion & Company 2019

Every reasonable effort has been made to trace copyright holders and to obtain their permission for the use of copyright material. The author and publisher apologise for any errors or omissions in this work, and would be grateful if notified of any corrections that should be incorporated in future reprints or editions of this book.

ISBN 978-1-912866-58-8

British Library Cataloguing-in-Publication Data.
A catalogue record for this book is available from the British Library.

All rights reserved. No part of this publication may be reproduced, stored in a retrieval system, or transmitted, in any form, or by any means, electronic, mechanical, photocopying, recording or otherwise, without the express written consent of Helion & Company Limited.

For details of other military history titles published by Helion & Company Limited, contact the above address, or visit our website: http://www.helion.co.uk

We always welcome receiving book proposals from prospective authors.

Contents

List of Illustrations		iv
List of Maps		vi
Acknowledgements		vii
Introduction		viii
Prologue		xvii
1	A Bitter Engagement	31
2	Kings and Covenants	46
3	The Storm Gathers	61
4	Cromwell Comes	75
5	Retreat	94
6	"Sensible of our Disadvantages", Monday, 2 September	114
7	"The Wrestle of Death", Tuesday, 3 September	142
8	All the King's Men	165
Epilogue		187
Colour Plate Commentaries		199
Appendices		
I	Instructions from the Scottish Parliament to the commissioners going to the King's Majesty, 8 March 1650	204
II	Orders of Battle for the Armies at Dunbar	207
III	Scottish Officers taken at the Battle of Dunbar	209
IV	Letter from David Leslie to the Marquess of Argyll	216
V	Cromwell's Proclamation Concerning Wounded Men	217
Bibliography		218

List of Illustrations

1.	Cromwell at Dunbar, 1897	xvi
2.	Preston Bridge	xx
3.	The Red Bank, Winwick	xxiv
4.	Winwick Church	xxvi
5.	Duke of Hamilton and his brother the Earl of Lanark	36
6.	Roman Bridge, Musselburgh	39
7.	Stirling Town Walls	41
8.	Mar's Wark, Stirling	42
9.	Coldingham Priory	44
10.	Mercat Cross, Edinburgh	47
11.	King Charles II in 1650	52
12.	Oliver Cromwell	58
13.	David Leslie	62
14.	George Monck	70
15.	Berwick Old Bridge	76
16.	Mordington	77
17.	Road from Ayton to Coldingham Moor	79
18.	Cockburnspath Tower	80
19.	Sparrow Castle, Cockburnspath	81
20.	Dunglass Old Bridge	82
21.	Dunbar from the Old Harbour	86
22.	Gladsmuir	90
23.	Hoylroodhouse and St Anthony's Chapel	91
24.	Musselburgh	96
25.	Dunbar Townhouse	98
26.	Redhall Castle	102
27.	Scene of the artillery duel at Gogarburn	104
28.	Site of the English camp at Galachlaw	106
29.	St Mary's Church, Haddington	109
30.	The area in which Cromwell deployed on arriving at Dunbar	115
31.	Dunbar Harbour	117
32.	Doon Hill from the Brox Burn	119
33.	Detail of Fisher's plan showing the church and English camp	121
34.	Doon Hill from Dunbar Parish Church	122
35.	The reverse slope of Doon Hill, where the Scots camped	124

LIST OF ILLUSTRATIONS

36. Leslie's view from the summit of Doon Hill — 128
37. The ridge between the hill and the burn — 129
38. Broxmouth Lodge, possible site of the 'poor house' — 131
39. Detail of Fisher's plan showing Broxmouth, the ford, and the poor house — 131
40. Spott House — 135
41. Broxmouth House and Cromwell's Mount — 137
42. Site of the ford at Broxburn village — 145
43. Detail of Fisher's plan showing Pride's brigade fording below Broxmouth — 147
44. The 'pass' of the road between the folding ground — 148
45. Area of the cavalry engagement — 150
46. Detail of Fisher's plan showing the battle on the Scots right — 153
47. The artillery salient, viewed from Doon Hill — 154
48. Little Pinkerton and the surrounding area — 156
49. Fisher's plan of the Battle of Dunbar — 161
50. Grave of Sir William Douglas — 164
51. Memorial plaque dedicated to the Scottish prisoners of war who perished in Durham — 169
52. Satirical print showing the Covenanters pressing the King's nose to the grindstone — 171
53. View of Stirling from the north — 174
54. The Coronation of Charles II at Scone — 185
55. Powick Bridge, Worcester — 188
56. MacLean monument, Inverkeithing — 189
57. Fort Royal, Worcester — 192
58. Statue of Charles II, Parliament Square, Edinburgh — 196
59. The Battle of Dunbar Monument — 197

List of Maps

1. Scotland — xxx
2. The English reach Dunbar for the first time — 84
3. The English march from Preston to Edinburgh — 93
4. Cromwell's attempt to strike west of Edinburgh — 103
5. Cromwell's contested retreat — 111
6. Dunbar, 1 September 1650: the armies arrive — 113
7. Dunbar, 2 September 1650: redeployment — 134
8. Dunbar, 3 September 1650: opening moves — 143
9. Dunbar, 3 September 1650: the crisis point — 159
10. South-Central Scotland — 178
11. The Worcester campaign, 1651 — 190
12. The Battle of Worcester — 193

Acknowledgements

This book has been a labour of love, but it would not have been possible without the support of my wife. Fiona is also the reason I have made Dunbar my home, which is no small contribution to facilitating this book! My young children deserve praise for their endurance, as they have been enthusiastic participants in long drives around the country to explore and photograph the locations of the great events I have attempted to describe. Most of these places barely get a mention in the final text, let alone an image; but visiting them was essential in helping me to build my understanding.

I am of course grateful to Helion & Company, particularly to Charles Singleton, for encouraging me to undertake this project. They have arranged the commissioning of the fantastic new illustrations and maps which accompany my own words and photographs, which I hope readers will agree help to enhance our visual understanding considerably.

For other images in the book, I thank the National Library of Scotland's excellent map services, the Scottish National Portrait Gallery, and the Royal Collection. In particular I would like to thank the Ashmolean Museum in Oxford for their enthusiastic support in facilitating my use of the Fitz-Payne Fisher plan of the battle. I am also grateful to the owners at Broxmouth and Mordington for allowing me to visit and photograph the relevant locations.

Introduction

At this "pass," on and about the present London road, as you discover after long dreary dim examining, took place the brunt or essential agony of the Battle of Dunbar long ago. Read in the extinct old Pamphlets, and ever again obstinately read, till some light rise in them, look even with un-military eyes at the ground as it now is, you do at last obtain small glimmerings of distinct features here and there, which gradually coalesce into a kind of image for you; and some spectrum of the Fact becomes visible; rises veritable, face to face, on you, grim and sad in the depths of the old dead Time. Yes, my travelling friends, vehiculating in gigs or otherwise over that piece of London road, you may say to yourselves, Here without monument is the grave of a valiant thing which was done under the Sun; the footprint of a hero, not yet quite undistinguishable, is here!

Thomas Carlyle, 1845

It was 174 years ago, almost half of the distance back between our present selves and the Battle of Dunbar, that Thomas Carlyle wrote the above summary of that historic encounter. It first appears in his remarkable edited volume of the *Letters and Speeches of Oliver Cromwell* (1845). Although Carlyle was a Scotsman and could clearly sense the pain of his country's defeat, his eyes were dazzled by the brilliance of the Cromwell which he conjured out of the archives and animated for his readers. Such was Carlyle's esteem that when William Scott Douglas wrote *Cromwell's Scotch Campaigns* in 1898, he demurred from describing the battle in detail since he felt certain not only that all his readers would have read Carlyle, but that the earlier synopsis was unbeatable. This does not prevent Douglas from pointing out the occasional flaw, but he does so with a self-conscious lightness of touch as if the criticism is somehow close to sacrilege. Perhaps it is hardly surprising then that it was the words of Carlyle – 'here took place the brunt or essential agony of the Battle of Dunbar' – that were carved into the soft sandstone of the new monument erected to commemorate the tercentenary in 1950. Then from the monument they make their way onto the cover of this unworthy little text.

Carlyle's influence still holds strong, often unrecognisably, over the popular understanding of the Battle of Dunbar. He rings a chime which still echoes today: Cromwell, Cromwell, Cromwell. Carlyle believed in the Great Man of History, the overwhelming influence of individuals over the course of affairs and the essential truth that great men exist to steer the state on our behalf. When they arise, these figures are deserving of our respect and obedience, and future generations should study, admire and emulate their qualities even when accepting their uniqueness. It was in this light that Carlyle presented Cromwell to his readers, and since it seemed to the philosopher-historian wholly inadequate to contain Cromwell within the bounds of mere biography, only the subject's own words would suffice. Thus, and I for one am immeasurably grateful for it, Carlyle painstaking collated most of the surviving letters and proclamations of Oliver Cromwell and used them to bring him into our immediate presence. The letters are linked by the editor's engaging if partisan narrative summaries, keeping up a pacey chronology and bringing in supporting sources. The occasionally acerbic commentary appeals as much to modern readers as to Carlyle's original Victorian audience, even if it is not how most historians would choose to present their case today.

But to Carlyle, Oliver Cromwell was the man his times demanded; there is an overt sense in his presentation of him that modern Britain owes him a reverential gratitude. Even so, this is not a Cromwell presented as the champion of parliamentary democracy, but rather as an antidote to it; the great man cannot be restrained by mere mediocrities. As with every treatment of Cromwell Carlyle's is contentious, but it is certainly not balanced. The trickier issues which mar his reputation are glossed over or ignored, and little empathy is given to Irish or Scottish perspectives in the chapters devoted to those theatres. For audiences of his own time, Carlyle was challenging the inherited prejudices of a post-restoration (and therefore largely pro-royalist) historiography; but the move from supervillain to superhero misses out the man in the middle.

Most importantly for our purposes here, Carlyle's very influential framing of Cromwell is one of the roots of our difficulty of separating a discussion of the events at Dunbar in early September 1650 from the name of Oliver Cromwell. Obviously the victorious commander of any battle is going to hog the limelight, but at Dunbar it comes at the cost of casting his adversaries into total darkness. Even modern treatments of the battle cannot resist attaching the victor's name to their titles: *Cromwell's Masterstroke* (Reese, 2006), *Cromwell Against the Scots* (Grainger, 1997); *Dunbar 1650: Cromwell's Most Famous Victory* (Reid, 2004). Something like *Leslie's Disaster* would presumably be less attractive commercially!

This is not, of course, Carlyle's fault; or at least not entirely. Cromwell is the ultimate heavyweight personality of British history, a colossus with an immensely long and sometimes dark shadow. His name is known across the British Isles and beyond, his face (warts and all) instantly recognisable and his politics neatly distilled into a familiar caricature which inspires fear and admiration in equal measure. Cromwell polarises, and I have encountered serious-minded folk who either loathe him with an intensity I have hardly ever seen for figures so far into our past, or who hail his manifold virtues and long for his second coming. From both sides of this often fruitless debate, however, there is an acceptance of his massive significance and his exceptional abilities. And like all such figures, about whom so many volumes have been written by so many eminent scholars, and whose characters have also been interpreted for us in art, fiction, film and television, it remains difficult to get to grips with the living, breathing human being that they were. But that does not mean we do not owe it to our audiences to try.

Fortunately, however, it is not the purpose of this book to dissect Oliver Cromwell's politics or his personality, or at least only to do so insofar as it impacted the military operations we are considering. It is not my role either to judge nor to defend, only to piece together events and present the most likely explanations for how and why they panned out the way that they did. I am inclined to agree with Carlyle's great man theory only so far as to accept that individual personalities can determine the course of history, and that those who do are worthy of our respect and study. Whatever my own personal instincts, Cromwell was one of those men. But for the most part life is not made up of great men, and they are rarely representative the everyday experience of the everyman and everywoman of the past.

In the particular and peculiar context of the historic battlefield, whilst the generals can plan the finest tactical operations their minds can devise it is still the plain old soldier who has to execute them. Whether such men are tired or unhappy, angry or enthused, can alter the direct of affairs. The influence of the man who first runs away from his regiment, to be followed by his friends, or of the man who storms through the unassailable breach and proves that it can be done, can change the course of history. So too can a failed harvest, a ship lost at sea, or a badly constructed sentence. History is not all about great men, significant though they undoubtedly are in the military context which preoccupies us here. So this is not the story of Oliver Cromwell, however important he is as one of our central players; and although I have given him the modest honour of opening this book, Cromwell is neither its hero nor its villain.

Nor, it must be said, is his opponent David Leslie. The Scottish commander at Dunbar is a considerably less familiar figure to most casual readers than Cromwell; especially in the context of his defeat, his decisions and abilities therefore require a little more consideration. It is easy to conclude that at Dunbar Leslie was outgeneralled, and he was. But that was by no means inevitable, nor is it a representative picture of the preceding campaign. It is immensely frustrating that Leslie's correspondence is so spartan compared to Cromwell's fulsome and energetic reports. It leaves us with far less to conjure with. The military and political situation in Scotland at the time was complex and fluid, and Leslie's place within that context does require discussion for the events of the battle to be understood in their entirety. I have attempted therefore to bring Leslie into a little more focus than he is accustomed to. In some ways the result is an unsatisfactory compromise: David Leslie cannot emerge from analysis of the battle unscathed or with all the obvious questions answered, but he can at least be better understood. But this book is no more about presenting the battle simply as Leslie's defeat than as Cromwell's victory. These rivals knew one another, had served beside one another, observed their rival and responded accordingly. Both made mistakes; both stories need to be told.

The imbalance of source material is not limited to the commanders. It is cliché to remark that history is written by the victors, and my studies of the

INTRODUCTION

Jacobite rising of 1745-6 have made clear to me how failure can be a powerful muse for comprehensive narratives, memoirs, and self-justifications. In the case of Dunbar however the best accounts are the English ones, satisfying both the appetite for detailed reporting back in London and the need for the experimental republic to prove itself as stable, formidable, and triumphant. It is too easy not to recognise how high the stakes were for the new republic of England. Cromwell, emerging into a position of dominance within it, also had a clear incentive to ensure the right narratives of his victory were in ready circulation. By contrast, word of the defeat of the Scots army would spread quickly and organically, and as there was still a war to fight and an enemy inside the kingdom, there was little immediate incentive to circulate descriptions of the defeat. The result of this imbalance is that, unsatisfied by the fragments in the Scottish record, we are drawn to interpreting Scottish actions through the observations of their opponents. Such an approach requires obvious caveats to be applied.

The Battle of Dunbar comes in what proved to be the closing phases of a wider series of conflicts across the British Isles which had already lasted for over a decade. This context has to be understood, but it would be beyond our scope here to draw back to the birth of the National Covenant and the crises it went on to trigger. We do however need to go back at least as far back as the Engagement of 1648. This helps us to understand the political situation in Scotland, the animosities and fears motivating England, and the makeup of the cast for the Dunbar campaign. I have opted to close the narrative at the end of 1650, by which point the immediate impacts of Dunbar had been revealed. It is also important to acknowledge that, militarily at least, Dunbar was not a decisive engagement and it certainly did not end the war. Whilst its single most important outcome may have actually been the survival, military and political, of Oliver Cromwell – cold comfort for the thousands who died to achieve it – the psychological impact of the defeat changed the political landscape within Scotland. The fact that the Scottish resistance survived and managed to revitalise in a relatively short time, just as it had after Pinkie Cleugh a century before, should not be underestimated. For that reason I have taken the narrative through the beginnings of that recovery up to the end of the year, and although I do not go beyond the coronation of Charles II, I felt it necessary to close with reflections of the Battle of Worcester in 1651 to give a rounded sense of closure.

The thought of the men who marched and fought in these great events is rarely far from my mind. Battles must not, however inviting the trap and however inevitable that we draw the maps in exactly that form, be viewed only as two-dimensional landscapes with neatly labelled blocks following the smooth courses of directional arrows. They must be presented instead from the ground; as thousands of individual men, with all their various motivations and emotions, stumbling across obstacles or losing their footing in the mud, finding the courage to hold their nerves and slay their fellow man whilst the air around them fills with noise and smoke and lethality. This book will therefore attempt to bring something of the realities of that experience to the fore. Sometimes that means painting pictures, and where I feel a more descriptive tone can be enlightening, I hope you will indulge me even if it is not naturally to your taste.

'ESSENTIAL AGONY'

In getting closer to the men of the battle, I have been immensely aided by Durham University's Scottish Soldiers Project, which followed the discovery of a grave pit on university ground during building works. After extensive archaeological investigation and analysis, it was demonstrated that the bodies recovered represented a small but significant sample from the mass burial of Scottish prisoners who perished in captivity there in 1650. The resulting studies have shined unprecedented light onto the Scottish soldiers of the Dunbar campaign, bringing not only greater understanding but also empathy. Forensic reconstruction work by Liverpool John Moores University then provided that most tangible of connections to the past: a face. It is a face which has since looked down from above my desk whilst I write, a simple but evocative reminder of the human cost of war. That face once gazed down from the heights of Doon Hill, across the very land on which this book has been written. Somewhere hereabouts many of those who fought beside him still lie in the ground. The work of the Scottish Soldiers Project to date, both in relation to the prisoners who died and tracing those who surived, is presented in the remarkable book *Lost Lives: New Voices* (2018). As this volume is both comprehensive and authoritative, I have no intention here of attempting to rival its presentation of the story of the prisoners taken at Dunbar.

I have been fortunate in being able to communicate in recent months with descendants of some of those Scottish prisoners who lived on beyond their captivity. Fascinating as their individual genealogies are, it is the collective sense of a common heritage which I have found most striking. My doctoral thesis explored contemporary engagement with historic identity in the global Scottish diaspora, and this is a particularly fascinating case of that. There is a real sense of immediacy in their connection between past and present which makes the intervening centuries seem far shorter. The work of groups like the Scottish Prisoners of War Society is not only important but enlightening: it reminds us that battlefields can be connecting points in our historical experience. Out of the bloodshed can come community, even hundreds of years on.

Today there are around 9,000 people living in Dunbar and the area surrounding the battlefield. If every current Dunbar resident left their home and mounted a horse, that would be the size of the cavalry fight on the eastern side of the battlefield. The town has of course grown considerably since 1650, especially in recent years as the easy commuting distance to Edinburgh has fuelled a housing boom. The broad High Street, with two museums and a range of independent shops, the historic twin harbours and castle ruins, and the pleasant combination of rolling farmland, beaches and clifftop walks, make Dunbar an attractive destination for both residents and visitors. Connected to the Scottish capital by motorway and rail, there are also several big local employers in the area as diverse as power generation and brewing. Dunbar is a wonderful town in which to live; although I am a recent incomer, my wife was born and raised here. At its core is a confident and engaged community, enjoying the benefits of the parks and beaches whilst contributing to the festivals, clubs and activities which keep Dunbar feeling alive.

Dunbar's relationship with its battle is however understated: there is a 1650 Coffee Shop, a Leslie Way, and a Cromwell Harbour (the name deriving from a repair grant for the seawall during the Protectorate). An image of Cromwell appears on the banners hung from lampposts during the annual Civic Week. There has been a stone monument on the battlefield since 1950, which was later moved from Oxwell Mains to its current location to accommodate the growth of the cement works. It was erected by the Cromwell Association and its design is unobtrusive. Not until 2019 did the first interpretation panels appear beside it, as part of a project I had the privilege to lead on behalf of the Scottish Battlefields Trust. There have been major re-enactments of the battle in the 1970s, 1990s, and in both 2016 and 2019. An active local history society includes the battle in its many broad interests. So whilst the battle might be a low-key feature of the community, there is wide awareness and considerable interest.

The 1650 battlefield has, overall, survived the centuries well. Most remains as open farmland, its contours the same as those climbed in the seventeenth century, with the mighty mass of Doon Hill rising to the south and the ravine of the Brox Burn carving through towards the rocky coast. However the intervention of the A1 motorway – the main road between Edinburgh and London – and the East Coast Mainline railway running parallel to it, has split the battlefield into two halves. The pedestrian explorer has difficulty passing between the two. The worst damage has been done by the cement works and its quarry, changing the landscape on the coastal (north-eastern) side of the battlefield and introducing an artificial loch over the site of the cavalry battle. Fortunately, on a battlefield so large and benefitting from the lofty viewpoint of Doon Hill, these interventions do not significantly reduce our ability to interpret the events of the engagement.

Gaining a clear understanding of those events is the key objective of this book. My aim is to present a plausible interpretation of how the rival forces moved into and across the battlefield area, allowing those fortunate enough to visit the site to imagine the flow of events around them. For those not able to reach Dunbar, I hope the narrative and landscape descriptions can combine with enough power to help them visualise the scenes just as clearly. To build that interpretation I have sought to overlay the details described in the primary evidence onto the landscape which I have so often looked upon and explored.

The great advantage of living within the registered battlefield area, gazing on the slopes of Doon Hill from my street every day and imagining the serried ranks upon its summit, is that I have a constant opportunity to explore and observe the landscape and its moods. Every walk across the battlefield raises new questions and provides fresh opportunities to evaluate. These explorations are important, as the deployments at Dunbar are far from uncontentious and some of the contemporary description can feel confused. Most modern plans of the battle are fairly consistent and, overlooking the occasional directional arrow which betrays a lack of first-hand knowledge of the battlefield by sending soldiers over improbable obstacles, they agree that the final Scots deployment aligned with the south side of the burn.

There is however an alternative suggestion which pivots the whole battle and brings the Scots army into alignment with the motorway rather than the ravine. This interpretation is based primarily on a reading of Firth's analysis (1900) of Fitz-Payne Fisher's contemporary illustration of the battle. Firth did not himself illustrate his article with a new deployment plan, and his interpretation therefore gains significance primarily from its adoption by Historic Environment Scotland (HES), the national heritage agency, who *have* chosen to redraw the battle lines.[1] By including this in the official designation record, the revised deployment has been given an instant authority in the planning system, although its adoption as an official interpretation appears to have gone largely unnoticed. The battlefield's designation record mentions that this new interpretation, citing Firth as its basis, has not been expressly challenged. In fact, the weaknesses of relying solely on Fisher's illustration have indeed been highlighted, including by Reese (2006). Although the HES interpretation post-dates Reese and Reid (2004), both of these authors have considered Fisher's plan and Reid's more recent work (2012) explicitly cites Firth's article in his bibliography so has presumably weighed its conclusions. The fact that neither have chosen to adopt the interpretation which places the battle-lines at right angles to the Brox Burn, a decision with which I concur, should now be taken as a rejection of that argument.

I have taken considerable effort to weigh the relative merits of the alternative possibilities, and although my conclusion is that I concur with the mainstream, I hope my analysis provides an important contribution to our understanding of the battle since that does not preclude disagreement over other issues. For example, I agree with Firth's placement of the 'poor house' around which skirmishing occurred, whereas Reese follows Douglas in placing it at Brand's Mill. This moves the 'pass' which is fought over away from the fords, meaning we need to find an alternative geographical feature on which to centre the preliminary fighting.

My proximity to the battlefield and the relatively limited range of Cromwell's campaigning range in 1650 have also allowed me to carry the principle of seeking understanding through first-hand exploration into the wider theatre of the war. I have endeavoured to trace the English army's invasion route as closely as possible, and although there are some questions that cannot be answered definitively a more detailed picture has hopefully emerged than is usually presented. This process is the aspect of my work which gives me the greatest joy, taking me in search of crumbling bridges, forgotten castles, and lost road courses. All help to bring the soldiers of the past back into the landscape of the present, presenting an opportunity to follow in the very footsteps of armies of 1650. I hope the resulting photographs also help in the visualisation of that landscape. I have occasionally come across local traditions which I cannot reconcile with the military situation

I have attempted to present the tangled political and ideological webs of the mid 1600s in an accessible form, without either over-simplifying or becoming bogged down in the narrower factional debates. For simplicity and variety, I sometimes refer to the Scottish Committee of Estates or the English Council of State as the government, at which purists might bridle. I have also tried to make clear which national parliament I am referring to

---

1   Firth, C. 'The Battle of Dunbar', *Transactions of the Royal Historical Society*, Vol. 14, (Cambridge: University Press, 1900), p. 19-52. For the HES interpretation, see: http://portal.historicenvironment.scot/designation/BTL7

at a given moment, since some recent texts appear to forget that there was more than one. I have made a distinction between "pure" royalists and the Engagers, whilst the label Covenanter, which I have tried to use sparingly, usually refers inclusively to the full spectrum of Remonstrators, Kirk Party and the Engagers. For clarity I tend to refer to Cromwell's army as the English, and to remember that despite the more confusing picture of the civil wars it should not be forgotten that this part of the conflict was a war between two independent states. Too often the presentation of this subject comes across as Anglo-centric, even if that is not the intention; I have seen modern works which accept the narrative that the Scots were planning an invasion of England in the summer of 1650 without challenge, for example. I have hopefully avoided any overt bias, seeking to maintain a balanced picture of the rival causes and present the perspectives of those who were there.

I have tried not to judge either causes or individuals, to allow the reader to decide whether the Archibald Strachans of our story are traitors or men of consistent principle; whether Charles II was a selfish cynic or a pragmatic leader trying to build unity out of faction; whether Cromwell's victory was planned genius or the seizure of opportunity; if Leslie was wrong to come down from his hill. I do not pretend to know the answers, but I think we can get close. The events described in these pages were momentous, devastating, and formative. They can trigger emotional responses on both national and personal levels, which can both distract us from the historical truth and allow us to engage with it more deeply. On both sides of this conflict there was suffering and heroism, justice and ignorance, reason and radicalism. On both sides there were real people like you and I.

A note on spelling and dates

To aid in clarity of expression, since I try as frequently as possible to blend the primary accounts into the text, I have modernised most of the seventeenth century spelling when quoting directly. I have however tried to retain the original punctuation and capitalisation.

Until 1752, the English new year officially started on 25 March. Since 1600 however, the Scottish year had begun on 1 January just as we are accustomed to it doing today. This means that January 1649 in Scotland was January 1648 in England. The confusion this can create was highlighted at a recent exhibition featuring letters apparently written before the events they were describing! I have opted to present all dates in their "Scottish" form, since this correlates with how they would be presented today. This obviously only affects dates in the first three months of the year: the battle was fought on 3 September 1650 according to both nations.

Both Scotland and England were still using the old Julian calendar. Many European (particularly Catholic) countries such as France, Spain, and the Holy Roman Empire, had already adopted the Gregorian calendar. Britain would only change to the Gregorian in 1752, during which the dates had to leap forward to catch up. To a contemporary French observer therefore, the Battle of Dunbar was fought on 13 September 1650. I have kept to the Julian dates throughout.

'ESSENTIAL AGONY'

1. A typical nineteenth century illustration of the Battle of Dunbar, concentrating on Cromwell and the religious zeal of his troopers. This example is from an 1897 edition of *The Boy's Own Paper*, which aimed to inspire schoolboys through stories with fitting protestant messaging.

Prologue

Preston, Lancashire, 17-19 August 1648

Oliver Cromwell could not afford to waste time, sensing the opportunity before him, so the forlorn was ordered forward. When Major Pownell and Captain Hodgson raised their experienced eye-brows at the risk, they were simply told again to march. Accordingly, four hundred foot-soldiers set off from the camp at Stonyhurst and out into the damp darkness of the early morning drizzle. Across the 'miry ground' of Preston moor Major Smithson was already ahead of them, driving in the enemy's pickets with two hundred horse, clearing the way for the foot to deploy behind them.[1] Soon the thump-thump of musket fire was spreading across the moor, whilst around the streets and enclosures of Preston village the drums beat with alacrity and alarm. The Battle of Preston, upon the outcome of which hung the fate of a king, had begun.

The engagement on the moor intensified during the morning as Cromwell brought his main force to bear in the wake of the forlorn. Opposing him was Sir Marmaduke Langdale with around three thousand foot and five hundred horse fighting in the name of the captive King Charles I; for the civil war so recently concluded had reignited. The royalists held their line, exploiting the hedgerows and enclosures to the north-east of Preston. Across the moor they offered Cromwell's men a 'stiff and steady resistance', and neither musket-fire nor push-of-pike could dislodge them.[2] In the enclosed ground the parliamentarian cavalry were constrained, denied the strength of their knee-to-knee charge, and Langdale had reason to hope for success. He had only to hold and wait for relief, for his force was merely a part of a far greater army and the middle part at that. Perhaps half a day's march to the north was Sir George Munro, an experienced veteran with a force of foot and horse mainly comprising men brought over from the Scots army in Ireland. To the south, extending along the road from Preston to Wigan was an even greater force, a Scottish army under James, Duke of Hamilton, the premier peer of Scotland.

---

1 Letter from Cromwell to Speaker Lenthall, 20 August 1648, Carlyle, T. *Oliver Cromwell's Letters and Speeches*, 2nd Edition, (Glasgow, 1846), p. 217.
2 Letter from Cromwell to Speaker Lenthall, 20 August 1648, Carlyle, p. 218.

If Langdale held and allowed all this strength to concentrate, the army of Oliver Cromwell would be hard pressed indeed.

But the parliamentarian army, comprising both New Model and old North Association regiments, had a golden chance to break the enemy's force by exploiting the length of its column and splitting it at the centre. Under-supplied from the outset, consuming resources at a fast pace and advancing to its objectives at a slow one, the Scots-Royalist army was obliged to ease the pressure by extending over a wide area. Munro had quarrelled with Hamilton's lieutenant-general, James Livingston Earl of Callendar, resulting in a further separation as the rear-guard became effectively independent of the main army. With John Lambert shadowing their flank as he awaited reinforcement from Cromwell, the Scots lost their chance to break through to the royalists in Yorkshire and the road to London beyond. Their strategic direction became unclear, and their intelligence faltered.

As the battle on the moor unfolded therefore, an urgent concentration of strength was required to defeat the disciplined and determined assault which was being launched upon Langdale and the English royalists. But the scale of that attack was not yet fully appreciated. It was considered impossible that Cromwell himself could have transferred his strength from south Wales so rapidly as to now appear on the army's flank. The threat to Langdale was dismissed as a delaying action, and Baillie was directed to continue the army's march southward towards Wigan. Far from concentrating, the Scots-Royalists were continuing to extend. The Scottish infantry crossed the Ribble south of Preston over the bridge, the successor to which carries a busy crossing to this day. Two brigades were left to hold the bridge, but only a commanded party was sent to Langdale's aid along with supplies of ammunition. Nevertheless, the intensity of the protracted fighting on the moor betrayed the seriousness of the situation as the day wore on, and Hamilton himself crossed back to Preston to seek a clearer understanding. Munro remained out of contact to the north, and anyway Cromwell's right flank had by now extended around Langdale's left and cut between them.

Marmaduke Langdale and his men held their ground stubbornly, fuming at the failure of the Scots to provide adequate support. For four long hours they held off the weight of the attack, which outnumbered them heavily. Cromwell observed the 'shogging' of the royalist line towards Ribble bridge as Langdale sought to prevent his being cut off from the Scots beyond it.[3] It was an expression he would use again in a few short years to describe a different action. The main attack was funnelled up a lane, 'very deep and ill', which led off the moor and into Preston.[4] Foot and horse charged and charged again along the lane and the weight began to tell. The gravest threat to Langdale's position was on his right, where a steep-sided track was screened by woodland and followed the line of the river towards the bridge. As Cromwell's left finally secured the route, the risk of Langdale's force being isolated and destroyed increased exponentially. Exhausted, unsupported, desperate, the royalist line finally collapsed.

---

3   Letter from Cromwell to Speaker Lenthall, 20 August 1648, Carlyle, p. 218.
4   Letter from Cromwell to Speaker Lenthall, 20 August 1648, Carlyle, p. 217.

PROLOGUE

The situation now deteriorated rapidly. Cromwell's forces mixed with fleeing royalists, the horse at last able to come into their own as they slashed their way through into Preston and carried the battle into the streets. The Earl of Callendar barely managed to escape across the Ribble bridge towards Baillie's infantry at Walton-le-Dale, but that route was soon closed as the parliamentarians turned their strength to overwhelming the two brigades blocking the road to the crossing.[5] The defence was doomed, morale fatally undermined by the chaos in front of them and the desire to find safety with their comrades further back, but for the moment at least it held. Marmaduke Langdale rode hard through the wreckage of his army as Cromwell's deadly pursuit carried into the streets of Preston. Somehow he stumbled upon the Duke of Hamilton and other senior Scots officers; with the Ribble swollen from the rain and the fords virtually impassable, the command party was in serious danger of imminent capture.

Discovering a valour and decisiveness which had so far eluded him, Hamilton spurred his lifeguards into action and drove back the two troops of enemy horse pursuing them as they withdrew into Preston. But the Scots had bought themselves but little time, as Sir James Turner recalled: 'so soon as we turned from them, they again turned upon us.'[6] Hamilton's men charged successfully again, showing a determination born of desperation. Close to the river now but in constant danger of being cut off from what was left of their army, Hamilton and his companions were forced to charge the enemy for a third time. "Once more for King Charles!" the Duke cried. One of his troopers bridled, the thin veil of his royalism washed away by the rains of misery falling over Preston battlefield. Hamilton struck the trooper with the flat of his sword, and the charge surged forwards. This time the parliamentarian horse accepted their defeat and gave up the chase. Plunging their horses into the river, Hamilton and the others now battled nature as well as the enemy. Drenched and defeated, they finally reached the far bank where William Baillie was waiting with the surviving Scottish infantry.

As commander of the foot, Baillie had deployed the Duke's forces on the higher ground beyond the Darwen, a Ribble tributary which provided some small additional defence to their position. The enclosures around Walton-le-Dale further increased the defensibility of the line. The Earl of Callendar had reached Baillie ahead of Hamilton, directing six hundred musketeers down to hold the south bank of the Ribble. It was a hopeless task, as the ground on Cromwell's side was considerably higher and afforded the attackers considerable advantage. Under heavy fire, the Scots losses mounted. Lieutenant-colonel Claude Hamilton had his arm shattered by a ball and fell to await captivity. The parliamentarians came on at point of pike and in the ensuing push bodily drove the defenders backwards. Resistance collapsed. Cromwell's forces spilled over the bridge and on to the Darwen, securing the crossing there before finally halting their attack on finding Baillie advantageously placed above them. From the Unicorn Inn on the

---

5   Carlyle, *Letters and* Speeches, p. 213.
6   Turner, J. *Memoirs of His own Life and Times*, (Edinburgh: Bannatyne Club), p. 63.

'ESSENTIAL AGONY'

2. The bridge across the Ribble at Preston, scene of intense fighting. The original bridge has been replaced and the area is now built-up, but the higher ground which aided the Cromwellian attackers can still be discerned.

Darwen bridge, Cromwell scratched a letter to the Committee of Lancashire: 'the Enemy is broken.'[7]

In truth, however, parliament had only truly broken the English royalists under Langdale; the main Scottish army remained largely intact and considerable in strength. Most of the Scots infantry had not been engaged, and the Earl of Middleton's large cavalry force was sure to reinforce them soon as it returned from the south. Although isolated now, Munro was still hovering off to the north and could still pose a threat. And Cromwell's men were just as tired, just as rain-soaked and weary as their enemy; their powder was as susceptible to the damp as was the Scots'; the roads were just as muddy for Cromwell as they were for Hamilton. Cromwell posted his army defensively, ready to prevent the Scots from attempting to break back across the Ribble.

But on the ridge above the Scottish army was far from confident. The shock of Cromwell's concentration on their flank and rear, the confusion of coordinating a response across great distances based on uncertain intelligence, and the trauma of the breaking of Langdale's command: each had fallen on the Scots as a heavy blow. With the bridges in enemy hands Munro was cut off and out of contact. With the English royalists with the army routed, most of the survivors even now being rounded up as prisoners, Hamilton's army

---

7   Letter from Cromwell to the Committee of Lancashire, 17 August 1648; Carlyle, p. 212.

now assumed the appearance of an invader and its road homeward had been cut. Despite the relative strength of their position at Walton-le-Dale and the expected arrival of Middleton's horse, the decision was taken to retreat. The regimental colonels gathered about the Duke, and from their saddles the senior commanders held council. The Earl of Callendar dominated the conversation, advocating a withdrawal under the cover of darkness.[8] Few of the colonels had the status to speak against the lieutenant-general, especially as Hamilton showed every sign of accepting the advice. Baillie protested: night operations were complex and left the army vulnerable. The enemy was extremely close at hand, and should the withdrawal be detected the risk was immense. Worst of all, there was no possibility of safely and quietly extracting the baggage and ammunition.

As the rain continued through the night, the long Scots column trudged off the ridge onto the mud-churned road and headed deeper into the darkness. Orders were given in muted tones as the 'drumless march' began. Rain ran from the brows of their bonnets, all tones of grey coats turned black by their saturations. Plaids were drawn tight across the body by those who still bore them, grown heavy with water. Shoes and hose were indistinguishable under their covers of glistening mud. Match-cord was hidden under armpits, stuffed into bags or coiled under bonnets in an attempt to keep it dry; men carried what powder they could however they could. A team of unfortunates was assembled to stay behind and detonate the supplies of powder which were abandoned on the hill, with orders to light the fuse in three hours' time when the main body would be clear of both the blast and the enemy's response once they realised the army was moving. Perhaps understandably, the men tasked with blowing the dump slipped off into the night without performing their dangerous duty.

Cromwell's men realised too late what was happening and the main Scots army had almost slipped from his grasp. 'We were so wearied with the dispute that we did not so well attend the Enemy's going off as might have been,' he confessed.[9] After securing the Scots baggage and powder and sensing their disorder, he drove the parliamentarian army in pursuit: 3,000 foot and 2,500 horse chasing over 7,000 Scottish infantry. Cromwell's cavalry took the lead of course, passing three miles before reaching the rear-guard of the Scots army. This was now formed of Middleton's horse, around 4,000 saddle-sore riders who had rushed back towards Preston only to find the battle lost and the infantry had gone by a different road southwards. Doubling back Middleton managed to link up with the army in time to screen them from Cromwell's pursuit. The resulting encounters failed to either slow Cromwell or stop the Scots, and so the focus of battle flowed ever further from Preston and on towards Wigan. At Chorley Scots horseman drove lancers through the body, thigh and head of Colonel Francis Thornhaugh, the price he paid for 'pressing too boldly'.[10] In loose skirmish the Scottish lancer could be a viciously effective opponent. For their part, Cromwell's

---

8 Turner, *Life and Times*, p. 65.
9 Letter from Cromwell to Speaker Lenthall, 20 August 1648; Carlyle, p. 218-19.
10 Letter from Cromwell to Speaker Lenthall, 20 August 1648; Carlyle, p. 219.

horse captured amongst others Colonel Sir John Hurry – who had fought for the Covenanters in the Bishops' Wars, Parliament at Edgehill, and the King at Marston Moor – after he received what Turner called 'a dangerous shot to the left side of his head.'[11]

The success of the night march and the return of the cavalry seem to have encouraged the Scots command to recover something of their nerve. The army was drawn up on Wigan moor whilst it was assessed as a potential battlefield. But it was soon ascertained that the site was unsuitable, with a comparatively small space on which to deploy surrounded by enclosures. Although the latter had successfully slowed the Cromwellian attack at Preston, the Scots now lacked the reserves of ammunition to adopt a strategy which depended on a protracted firefight.[12] The army had also been further weakened by desertion during the night, as soldiers became increasingly conscious that they were marching further from home without getting closer to victory. Hamilton decided to continue the withdrawal, taking the army ever closer he thought to what remained of the royalist uprising in Wales. At Warrington the Scots could find shelter and supplies, with a river to protect them and a bridge to funnel Cromwell into a narrow assault. But with the enemy pressing hard and the prospects looking bleak, both morale and discipline were falling apart. Wigan, a potentially sympathetic town, was plundered.

Now as the retreat entered its second night the weakening discipline was compounded by increasing fear. Everything was on its head: the smaller army was chasing the larger; the retreating army getting further from home. James Turner's regiment formed the rearguard of foot, with Middleton beyond with a part of the cavalry to screen the march on Warrington. At last the rain had given way and the moon shone brightly as the mud-stained infantry moved through the unhappy streets of Wigan. Shouted warnings and clattering hooves gave notice that the horse about, hard-pressed by Cromwell's vanguard, and Turner feared that Middleton's troops had been overthrown. Accordingly he drew up his pike across the market place, presenting their bristling points forwards to bar the road south. Behind them rose the square tower of All Saints' Church, from the pulpit of which the Presbyterian minister James Bradshaw had spurred on those laying siege to the Royalists at Lathom House four years before. The colonel sent orders for the rest of the column to continue its march whilst his own men held the square.

The pikemen stood 'shoulder to shoulder' and braced behind shafts three times as long as a man was tall, but their nerves were strained and the prospect of imminent action did little to steady them.[13] A troop of horse appeared from the darkness of the street, moonlight casting black and unnerving shadows, the mounts tossing and snorting. Recognising them as part of Middleton's command, Turner spurred over and instructed them to halt until the road was reopened. Wheeling about, he rode back calling upon his men to open their ranks. But instead of obeying the pikemen went quite 'demented', and

---

11 Turner, *Life and Times*, p. 65.
12 Turner, *Life and Times*, p. 65.
13 Turner, *Life and Times*, p. 66.

seeing the officer bearing down on them two of them rushed 'full tilt' toward him. Turner grabbed the first point that thrust toward his belly with his left hand, but with the other tore into the inside of his right thigh. Twisting free as his own men cried out that the enemy was upon them, the furious officer forgot 'all rules of modesty, prudence and discretion' and demanded the troopers ride down the infantry. But the horsemen were just as unnerved, trapped now between the enemy behind and the bristling pike ahead. Turner rode around their rear and cried that Cromwell was upon them, inducing into the cavalry such a fury of a charge that the pikemen threw down their weapons and leapt through the nearest doorways. The rearguard lost all order in the face of this desperate mass of horseflesh, and Sir William Lockhart of Lee was thrown from his horse in the ensuing chaos.[14]

Turned found his drummers and at their beating some form of order was at last restored. Middleton himself then arrived with the last of the horse, and after hearing of his troopers' disorder he rode on ahead to recover their discipline. Despite the two-inch wound in his thigh, Turner continued to lead his men as they withdrew into the dawning day. When he finally linked up with General Baillie, the latter urged him to rest in an adjacent cottage. But in the midst of the unravelling campaign there was no rest to be had, and the exhausted officer was obliged to leave the course of his march to his horse as he slept in the saddle. Oliver Cromwell had meanwhile halted his 'very dirty and weary' army in a field beyond Wigan, having driven them through twelve wet miles down roads already churned up by the Scots.[15] The general received a letter from none other than the Duke of Hamilton, requesting fair treatment for the latter's relation Claude, captured at the Ribble bridge fight.

Cromwell entered Wigan the following morning, 19 August, and remarked that the citizens had been plundered 'almost to their skins' despite their own malignancy.[16] He pressed on, hard at heel of the Scots as they sought the perceived sanctuary of Warrington. As the pursuers approached the village of Winwick, their road south passed through a defile flanked to the west by a bluff above the Newton Brook. Reaching to the brook from the east was a burn running through the marshy bed between a man-made bank on its north side and a high hedge-topped bank on its south. Here, at Red Bank, Cromwell's vanguard suffered a bloody nose. It was, as Captain Hodgeson said, 'snaffled' by the Scots.

To prevent the total collapse of the Scottish army, it was essential to hold back the relentless pursuit. Whilst Hamilton rode on to begin preparing the new defensive position at Warrington, William Baillie was left at Red Bank with perhaps 4,000 infantry. Closing the road with his massed pike, and lining the hedges overlooking the burns with musketeers and a few frame guns, Baillie held a formidable position. Here he would need to stop Cromwell, grinding him to a standstill until darkness provided the cover for the Scots to retire the last few miles to the Mersey.

---

14 Turner, *Life and Times*, p. 66.
15 Letter from Cromwell to Speaker Lenthall, 20 August 1648; Carlyle, p. 219.
16 Letter from Cromwell to Speaker Lenthall, 20 August 1648; Carlyle, p. 219.

'ESSENTIAL AGONY'

3. The Red Bank at Winwick, from the Scottish side of the ravine.

Alerted by his troopers that the Scots had turned to face him, Cromwell immediately appreciated the urgency. He needed to maintain the pressure if the enemy were going to crack. As soon as there were enough foot present to mount an attack the Parliamentarians launched their assault. The focus of the action was the road itself, where pikes came repeatedly to the push. But on this narrow front the Scots managed to hold despite their weariness and Cromwell's men were obliged to attack uphill on a roadway slick with mud. Although short of ammunition, the Scots musket maintained their fire whenever their opponents tried to push them off. A Major Cholmley fell before this effective defence, and he was unlikely to be the only one: Cromwell admitted he had been forced 'to give ground'. The high steep sides and boggy bottom of the Red Bank valley removed any realistic prospect of success across this sector, and the distance between the two sides neutralised the effectiveness of musketry. The battle would have to be focused on the roadway itself and its narrow defile at Winwick Pass.

By mid-afternoon the guns had fallen silent and the two forces, neither of whom could get a clear view of the other in such an awkward landscape, waited warily for the next attempt at a resolution. Baillie was happy to let the clock tick, praying that his men could find the reserves of energy to safely disengage and continue the retreat once night fell. But he also knew that Cromwell's strength was growing as more regiments arrived on the field ready to renew the action; better fed, better supplied, and in better spirits. At last Pride's Regiment was brought forward to renew the 'sharp dispute'.[17]

Strong as it first appeared, Baillie's position possessed that fatal flaw which has undermined so many static postures of defence: it was formidable only from the front. Cromwell had not been idle as he concentrated his infantry. The Parliamentarian cavalry had begun working their way around the eastern flank of the Scottish line, threatening to cut them off from Warrington and fall upon their rear. Now as the battle was re-engaged from the north, horsemen appeared behind the defenders and the situation began to unravel just as it had done for Langdale at Preston two days earlier. At first there was uncertainty: perhaps these are Scots horse come to relieve the pressure on the infantry? If so, then rather than engage the building threat to the right they disappeared as quickly as they had appeared. With Pride's men 'charging very home upon them' from the front and the flank about to fold, the Scots had little option but to abandon their position on the banks.[18]

This was the moment Cromwell had been waiting for since Preston. The Scots were out in the open, attempting to withdraw across the broad wheat field which separated Red Bank from Winwick village about a mile behind. At first their discipline held, 'a little spark in a blue bonnet' being singled out for praise as the officer who held the Scots together until he 'was killed on the spot.'[19] An effective fighting retreat along the road to Winwick might just have been manageable had the cavalry not already fatally compromised Baillie's position. Instead the line collapsed under the impossible pressure, men now abandoning cohesion in the desperate hope of reaching safety. Troopers rode them down, pistols puffing and swords slashing as they maximised the opportunity for destruction. Baillie and a small force managed to fight their way through and on along the road to Warrington, but most were forced to make a final fight of it around the village green.

St Oswald's Church, sat on a small mound which dominates the village, made a fitting scene for a last stand, but all serious hope of resistance was over. Exhausted, defeated, the survivors threw down their arms. Perhaps a half of Baillie's infantry were rounded up, the church and its walled yard providing their temporary prison, whilst Cromwell rode across a landscape now littered with the bodies of a thousand men. The vast majority had fallen in the rout rather than in the main engagement. Most of his own casualties, and he does not tell us how many, were back at the pass. Baillie's men had held Cromwell back 'for many hours', but the cost had been catastrophically high. It is hard to see how they could have done more.

The fortunate few who evaded the pursuit were able at last to reach the protection of Warrington. Here the bridge across the Mersey was defended by what Cromwell called 'a strong barricado and a work upon it, formerly made very defensive'.[20] It was ten miles to the next crossing, so there would be no flanking manoeuvre to relieve the pressure on the frontal assault. Despite

---

17 Heath's *Chronicle*, quoted in Carlyle, p. 215.
18 Letter from Cromwell to Speaker Lenthall, 20 August 1648; Carlyle, p. 219.
19 Heath's *Chronicle*, quoted in Carlyle, p. 215.
20 Letter from Cromwell to Speaker Lenthall, 20 August 1648; Carlyle, p. 219.

'ESSENTIAL AGONY'

4. The parish church at Winwick, sited on a prominent knoll. Here the remaining Scottish soldiers were forced to surrender, having fought hard and long to buy time for Hamilton to prepare Warrington.

their successes thus far, therefore, the Parliamentarian army seemed only to move from one difficult operation into another. If the Scots made a fight of it, the battle of Warrington would be their third gruelling fight in four days of constant engagement.

But it was not to be. When William Baillie reached Warrington bridge with the shattered remnants of the Scottish infantry, the cavalry were already gone. Against his own judgement, Hamilton had been persuaded once more by Callendar that the retreat should continue in order to preserve the horse. The foot soldiers at Winwick had been sacrificed, the survivors abandoned. Baillie found only the wounded Turner, his dutiful steed having carried him successfully to the Mersey, and an order left behind by Hamilton instructing Baillie 'to make as good conditions for himself and those under him as he could.'[21] It was now Baillie's turn to lose his cool, declaiming the dishonourable nature of such an order and begging to be saved from its execution by someone putting a ball in his head. His anger can well be understood, the sense of betrayal tasting bitter after the futile efforts of his brave soldiery at Winwick. Baillie had known defeat before, at Alford and Kilsyth at the hands of the Royalists' Scottish champion Montrose. Now he was fighting for the same king as his former adversary, ordered to surrender to the same Cromwell who had fought alongside him at Marston Moor.

Turner bade farewell to Baillie, preferring to take his chances on the road if the latter was obliged to yield. A little way along the road he met with Middleton and, presumably, the rearguard of the cavalry. Behind them the infantry manned the barricade and made a show of preparing to defend in order to strengthen their faltering hand in the coming negotiations. Cromwell was relieved when he received Baillie's note, and after promising them 'civil usage' he accepted the surrender of all the remaining Scottish infantry with all their arms and ammunition.[22] Since Preston the Scots had lost their allies, their baggage and supplies, and now their entire infantry force with the exception of Munro's unengaged command which was retiring through Cumberland towards the border. Over 8,000 men had been taken prisoner, a huge burden on the Parliamentarians and, in the context of scattered Royalist risings across the three kingdoms, a potentially dangerous body to keep together. If the Scots made a move back towards Preston – and only Munro was really in a position to do so – then the four thousand prisoners held there were to be slain by Cromwell's order.[23]

Defeat had turned to disaster, but the Duke of Hamilton still had up to 3,000 horse under his command and most of them had not been heavily engaged except in rearguard skirmishing. By contrast, Cromwell was lamenting that his cavalry were 'so harassed and haggled out' that they could barely walk in pursuit, let alone attempt a trot.[24] Fortunately for Parliament local forces were proactively pressuring the remaining Scots and rounding up the stragglers or deserters from the main column. Unless Hamilton

---

21 Turner, *Life and Times*, p. 67.
22 Letter from Cromwell to Speaker Lenthall, 20 August 1648; Carlyle, p. 220.
23 Letter from Cromwell to Speaker Lenthall, 20 August 1648; Carlyle, p. 220.
24 Letter from Cromwell to Speaker Lenthall, 20 August 1648; Carlyle, p. 220.

found new sense of purpose for his forces, it was only a matter of time before they disintegrated. Cromwell was soon reporting that his opponent was striking out for Nantwich, likely with the intention of swinging up towards the Royalists at Pontefract or the Scottish border beyond it. He wrote to the committee at York on 23 August warning them of Hamilton's coming and requiring them to bar his way. Lambert was in pursuit.

In the end however, it was Hamilton's own men who brought the campaign to its sorry conclusion. Exhausted, surrounded, hopelessly outnumbered and deep within enemy territory, the troopers had simply had enough. They would go no further with their unhappy duke. On Friday 25 August the last vestiges of the Scots-Royalist army surrendered. Callendar and Hamilton held their last disagreement, each blaming the other, and then Scotland's premier peer resigned himself to the coming captivity. Unlike his colleagues, Hamilton also held an English title: he would be tried as a rebel in arms. The so-called Second Civil War would stutter on for a while longer yet, but its back had been broken and the outcome was now certain. Without the intervention of a major field army the scattered Royalist forces which yet remained were doomed to be bottled up and defeated in detail.

At first glance, it appears that nothing had been changed by the bloody battles of the Preston campaign. King Charles I remained in captivity; the English parliament remained triumphant. But in fact the war of 1648 had brought the outstanding issues of the great civil war into far sharper focus, and laid the foundations for further battles to come. The king's last hopes of recovering power has been irrevocably dashed, and the moderate voices amongst his enemies were being drowned out. England's Parliament was struggling to satisfy the independent will of the army which had fought its cause. Men who had fought alongside one another in some of the greatest battles of recent memory had been driven into opposition. After Hamilton's brief coup, Scotland had lost the stability of government which had made it so effective in arms for the past decade and was divided into armed camps. The English parliament now saw Scotland – once its most significant friend – as a potential threat. The young Prince of Wales, hovering at sea with one eye on England and one on Ireland, now sensed growing possibilities in Scotland. The collapse of Hamilton's army in no way simplified the political tangles which knotted the three kingdoms.

But there was one lesson of the Preston campaign which was not lost upon its most significant student. Oliver Cromwell had learned it on those wet and muddy battlefields between 17 and 19 August, when he had beaten his enemy by appearing on their flank when they least expected him, splitting the foe and defeating them in detail. Cromwell learned that, with the experienced leaders and regiments he had at his disposal, he could beat his opponents whatever their number. He learned he could defeat the Scots.

'ESSENTIAL AGONY'

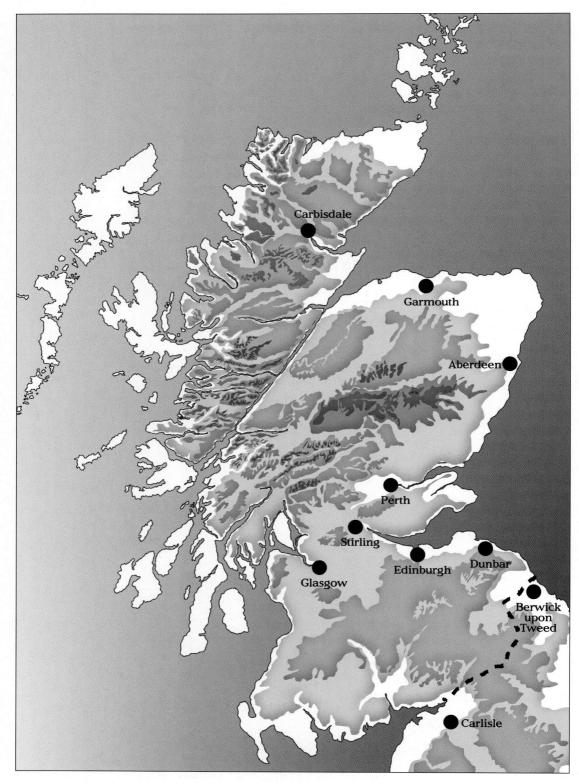

Map 1. Scotland.

1

A Bitter Engagement

King Charles I was executed on a specially constructed scaffold outside the banqueting house of his own palace at Whitehall in London, on 30 January 1649. As he stepped out of a first floor window onto the freshly erected timbers, wearing two shirts so as not to be seen to shiver from the cold, the king left behind him Rubens' magnificent painted tribute to the divine right of kings. Fortified by the image of his royal father ascending into heaven, Charles faced his death with incomparable dignity and gravitas. It was one of the most significant deaths in British history. To the king and his most ardent followers, this was martyrdom. To his enemies, a lawful execution and the end of a decade of civil devastating conflict. With the stroke of an axe, the king of England, Scotland and Ireland had been killed by his own subjects.

The wars between Charles I and his people had begun with the widespread resistance in Scotland to the king's religious reforms, leading to the creation of the National Covenant in February 1638. The document became the focus of a nationwide movement which, although accepting the king's authority, asserted the independence of the Scottish kirk. Charles was both deeply committed to his own form of Anglican Protestantism, with himself as its head, and assertively conscious of the rights and dignities of the modern monarchy. He was benign by instinct, thoughtful and highly intelligent, but also aloof, jealous of infringement, and more often naïve than wise in his political dealings. Charles I was a paradox, simultaneously both brilliant and disastrous. His Stuart stubbornness meant that he found defeat difficult to accept, whilst his innate belief in the essential nature of kingship precluded meaningful compromise. Such a king could not accept the rejection of his authority by his Scottish subjects, and he rightly saw in the National Covenant something which even many of those who had initially signed it had not fully understood: a challenge striking at the roots of the monarchy.

The king's response was to attempt to overawe the Covenanters, who still paid lip-service to the king's authority whilst seizing control of Scotland from him and suppressing his supporters. A grandiose military strategy was drawn up for a campaign in the summer of 1639, involving a Royalist rising in the north-east of Scotland, the transfer of Irish forces into the western Highlands, an amphibious landing in the Firth of Forth by the Marquis of Hamilton, and an English royal army advancing from the south under the king's personal command. Such a plan required determined leadership, coordination across huge distances, and a huge outlay of military and financial resources. The 1639 campaign – the First Bishops' War – lacked all of these essentials. The Covenanters rapidly subdued the northern threat and faced down the challenge from the south without coming to blows. Hamilton dithered in the Forth and achieved nothing. Charles negotiated and the armies stood down, but the causes of the crises had not been resolved.

War resumed the following year, and a pre-emptive strike by the Covenanters seized Newcastle in the north-east of England and again forced the king to seek terms. Charles lacked the financial stability to wage war effectively, constrained by his reliance on royal prerogative to raise funds and the traditional support of the nobility to levy and command his forces. In early 1640 the king had accepted the need to call a parliament in England, the first for eleven years, in order to authorise the taxation required to subdue the rebellious Covenanters, but the session lasted only three weeks on account of its preference for discussing domestic grievances. Humiliated once again by the Scots, who were led in the field by the immensely able Alexander Leslie, the king was forced to recall parliament again at the end of the year in order to raise the funds required to satisfy the demands of the Covenanters. The king was now appealing from a position of weakness and his parliamentary critics were eager to exploit it. Many members felt more common cause with the Scots than with the king. Ironically, Charles' willingness to engage in both military operations and the subsequent negotiations personally made the damage to his authority all the greater.

The situation continued to deteriorate for the king. The Covenanters had proven that a show of force could secure concessions, and that English domestic divisions, religious discord and constitutional disagreements were sufficient to distract the most powerful of the three kingdoms from intervening meaningfully in the others. In 1641 Catholic revolt broke out in Ireland, far bloodier than events in Scotland had been, and the rebels' professions of loyalty to the king further exacerbated the latter's problems. Both English and Scottish forces were despatched to Ireland, but within a year civil war had erupted in England too. Hopes of a swift outcome soon evaporated and the war spread throughout the country. The king proved more adept in this crisis than in those before, rallying considerable support and securing notable successes. Unable to bring him to heel alone, the English parliament sought a military alliance with the Covenanters in Scotland. The latter, having already secured from Charles most of what they had demanded, were under no obligation to intervene in England. But the crusade of extending Presbyterianism into England, and the fear of a triumphant monarch turning his attentions back to Scotland should he defeat parliament, proved sufficiently motivating. The Solemn League and Covenant was signed in the late summer of 1643, and a large Scottish army entered England the following January to open a new front against the king, paid for by the English parliament.

Scottish intervention turned the tide in the north of England. On 22 July 1644, the Parliamentarian and Covenanter armies united to inflict a devastating defeat on Prince Rupert of the Rhine, the nephew of the king and his most formidable commander. The battle was hard-fought and the outcome far from certain, but the close cooperation of the parliamentarian and Scottish cavalry commanders on the left eventually secured the isolation of the royalist foot and paved the way for a stunning victory. Those commanders were Oliver Cromwell and David Leslie. In the wake of the battle the royalist stronghold of York was compelled to surrender, and the Scots marched on to Newcastle. The king had lost the north of England.

With the royalist cause under intense pressure, the king released the Marquis of Montrose to create a major diversion back in Scotland. Leading a mainly Highland army supported by a core of Irish warriors under Alasdair MacColla, Montrose secured a string of victories over the Covenanters as the latter desperately tried to contain him without seriously weakening their armies in either Ulster or England. But the campaigns in Scotland were becoming bitter and bloody, hardening attitudes and alienating potential support. In September 1645 David Leslie was detached with an experienced force from the Scots army in England in order to deal with Montrose decisively, whose forces were attempting now to break out towards the king following news of his defeat at the Battle of Naseby. At Philiphaugh in the Scottish Borders, Montrose's small army was routed and their champion took to his heels. Although the war staggered on, the royalists were beaten.

Finally accepting that his cause had been broken military, King Charles sought other means to recover his position. Slipping away from his besieged capital at Oxford, he surrendered his person to the army of David Leslie which was engaged in the final protracted siege of Newark in Nottinghamshire. The king's hope was that cracks in the alliance of his enemies could be exploited to his advantage, or that at the very least the Scots would grant more generous terms than a vindictive parliament. After all Charles was a Stuart, a Scot. Nor was he without cause for believing the alliance amongst his enemies was weakening. Parliament had fallen behind in its payments to the Scots army which was serving its cause so effectively, whilst its representatives in London dragged their feet over the religious settlement. Robert Baillie was one of the Scots commissioners there, and he reported with growing concern that Scottish views were little regarded in England and that the politicians were only doing lip-service to the terms of the Solemn League. The Independents, whose rejection of hierarchy would take the form of worship outside the control of the church, were growing in power particularly within parliament's New Modelled Army. The Covenanters observed their rise with increasing anxiety.

The concerning reality for the Scots was that the balance of power had shifted in their alliance. When the Solemn League and Covenant had been signed, the Scots army was probably the most potent in all the three kingdoms and perhaps the best led. After its victories of 1639 and 1640 it certainly had an unrivalled reputation. Both the king and his enemies had courted the Covenanters, creating something of a seller's market. To win the civil war in England, the parliamentarians needed the Scots; but once the king's cause had been unravelled that need dramatically diminished and the costs associated with sustaining their army seemed ever less worthwhile. Moreover parliament's military capacity had transformed, and it now had a highly motivated veteran army of its own, which in turn was developing its own ideas as to the settlement of the nation. With the crisis seemingly passed, there was little appetite for Scottish influence over English domestic affairs. Oliver Cromwell, rising star of both the army and the Independents, was talking openly of future war with Scotland as early as 1644.[1]

In this context the appearance of the king at Southwell strengthened the hand of the Covenanters considerably. Strict measures were enforced to restrict access and communication with the king, and he was soon moved a safe distance to Scots-controlled Newcastle. Negotiations began, and the king had become a pawn. It took nine months for the terms to be agreed, but in January 1647 the Scottish army transferred the care of King Charles I to the parliament of England in return for an immense financial settlement. The Earl of Leven marched his army back into Scotland and the greater part of it disbanded. It seemed the civil war was over.

Of course it was not. Although the English parliament had possession of the king they had no real plan as to how to deal with him, and despite his hopeless position Charles was fortified by his self-belief and was not to be cowed in negotiations. The army, mainly composed of men who would otherwise have no political voice even under a triumphant parliament, had no intention of disbanding and leaving the king's fate to the politicians. In June the king's person was seized by the army, revealing cracks which Charles once again hoped to exploit. Parliament and the army presented different terms to their king, the debates dragging fruitlessly forward. Radical elements emerged out of the army which its own commanders were hard pressed to contain, let alone parliament. On 11 November the king made his move, fleeing from captivity at Hampton Court and seeking the coast. But he misjudged the sympathies of the governor of the Isle of Wight and found he had simply exchanged one jailor for another. He was however out of the grip of the army.

The ashes of the civil war were still hot, and King Charles now felt his position could only be served by reigniting the conflict. The rise of the Independents and radicals gave some measure of common cause to both royalists, English Presbyterians, and Scots Covenanters. This was the basis of the Engagement, the deal by which the king agreed to a three-year trial of Presbyterianism in England in exchange for military support towards his restoration to power. Ironically then, for both King and Covenanter, the best hopes of success seemed to rest with those they had first drawn swords against a decade before. It was a sign of the extent to which the world had been turned upside down, and yet the National Covenant – for most of its signatories at least – had never been anti-monarchy, and most of their domestic demands had been secured after the Bishop's Wars. So if the king's concession to trialling Presbyterianism in England could be trusted, then perhaps the new alliance was less surprising than its first appearance. A radicalised army of Independents, bent on overturning what was left of

---

1 'Cromwell… who has spoken contemptuously of the Scots' intention of coming to England to establish their Church-government, in which Cromwell said he would draw his swrod against them.' Baillie, *Letters and Journals*, Vol. II, p. 245.

the religious, political and social framework of England, was a sufficiently frightening prospect for all who seemed at risk of being marginalised by their triumph.

The king's immediate problem of course was that, from his prison at Carisbrooke, was in no real position to influence events once they were underway; nor could his cause rally around his person. Instead the so-called Second Civil War was to open as a series of uncoordinated and mutually unsupported operations. This did however create the opportunity to disperse and dilute parliament's military capacity. In early 1648, Pembroke Castle declared for the king and soon all of South Wales was royalist. In the north of England, the immensely powerful Pontefract Castle and the impressive coastal fortress of Scarborough Castle were both secured for the Royalists, and Sir Marmaduke Langdale seized Berwick-upon-Tweed to open the road south for the Scots. Carlisle was taken on the opposite end of the border, as the Scottish Engagers assembled a powerful field army. Kent and Essex rose for Charles, and after parliament attempted to replace its veteran admiral William Batten from his command on account of his Presbyterianism, the fleet defected. This opened the Channel for the young Prince of Wales and any overseas support he might now muster in support of his captive father. There were attempted uprisings in Surrey and the south-west too. It was a serious challenge.

Parliament was blessed with veteran commanders and experienced troops. Its soldiers were highly motivated: having made themselves a political power in their own right, they simply had too much to lose. They had also beaten royalists like Langdale before, whilst possessing the advantages of the apparatus of state to support their response. Oliver Cromwell rushed to Wales; Sir Thomas Fairfax to the south-east; John Lambert headed north to contain Langdale and shadow the Scots; local defence forces were mobilised. The royalists lacked resources and coordination; ships crews which had declared for the impoverished royal cause started to repent when they found they had become volunteers. Everything rested on the Scots, the only significant field army available to the Engagers with access to serious state resources and a wide area of free recruitment (in theory at least). But their intervention was crippled by indecision and delay. The delay was fatal: Langdale alone was too weak to destroy Lambert, who was too canny to risk his command but too assertive to allow the northern royalists any comfort; Cromwell had the time to complete his operations in Wales and link up with Lambert, resupplying in the Midlands as his went. Naively unaware that they had missed his best opportunity, the Duke of Hamilton simply did not believe it could be Cromwell on his flank at Preston. The piecemeal destruction of the Engager army between Preston and Warrington doomed all the royalist garrisons across England; in Scotland, it triggered yet another civil war.

And so our attention at last transfers to the theatre of war which will occupy our minds for most of the coming pages. James, 1st Duke of Hamilton, was the premier peer of Scotland and as such had been tasked with enforcing the royal will during the early crisis of the Covenanter revolution. His efforts to tread a middle line failed, and he prevaricated as leader of the king's amphibious operations in the Forth during the First

'ESSENTIAL AGONY'

5. The first two Dukes of Hamilton: James on the left, and his brother William, Earl of Lanark. Both are deserving of more sympathy than is traditionally afforded them. Both died too young.

Bishops' War. No friend of James Graham, the great Montrose, who emerged as the king's most dynamic military champion in 1644-5, Hamilton briefly fell out of favour at court during the civil war. But his disassociation with the bloody civil war back home in Scotland meant that, although treated with suspicion by the Covenanters, he avoided the implacable hatred which attached itself to Montrose. Despite creditably leading an expeditionary force on the continent in 1631-32, Hamilton was a courtier not a soldier; pulling off the Engagement was perhaps his greatest coup, and had it succeeded militarily then the service done to the king would have been unparalleled.

Hamilton had successfully built a moderate Presbyterian majority in Scotland which, as the king's person seemed to be coming under increasing danger into the second half of 1647, was able to assert control of the government. Archibald Campbell, Marquess of Argyll, who as one of the country's most powerful magnates had effectively run Covenanter Scotland for the past nine years, had been side-lined. The Engagement with the king was agreed in December, and it seemed the wheel had turned full circle. But Hamilton's next step would commit Scottish soldiers to take up arms against men they had formerly fought beside and to take common cause with those they had opposed. The Solemn League and Covenant remained in force, the alliance with the English Parliament still live, and many simply could not turn against it. Whilst few in Scotland could have contemplated a country without a king, fewer were ready to rally to the aid of a king whose policies they had so implacably opposed. From the pulpits, ministers maintained their opposition and Hamilton was powerless to prevent it. Recruitment for the levies was slow and, far worse, some of the ablest Covenanter commanders refused to serve.

Alexander Leslie, Earl of Leven, who had twice led Scottish armies into Newcastle and earned an unrivalled reputation, was amongst them. Without Leven, perhaps the greatest general Scotland had ever produced, the rather more limited Hamilton took command of the army himself. His second in command was to be James Livingston, Earl of Callendar; a veteran of the continental wars, Callendar had served under Alexander Leslie but was no friend of Argyll. He was also prickly, and Hamilton would find him a difficult and disruptive subordinate as has already been shown. On 11 May 1648 the Duke commissioned David Leslie, vanquisher of Montrose at Philiphaugh, as his Lieutenant-General of Horse, but by 10 June that post was formally declared 'vacant' after Leslie 'refused to accept'.[2] It was therefore offered to John, Earl of Middleton, who had fought under Montrose in 1639 when the latter was still a Covenanter and then against him in 1645. In between, Middleton had fought for the English parliament, rising steadily through the ranks since joining them at Edgehill. He was a capable, credible pair of hands and will have understood the scale of what Hamilton was putting them up against. William Baillie of Letham, another continental veteran, was appointed Lieutenant-General of Foot. He had proven his loyalty to the Covenant by facing Montrose twice, at Alford and Kilsyth, proving himself both courageous and unsuccessful.

Two days after Baillie's commission was recorded in the parliamentary record, the Engagers went into battle for the first time.[3] The earls of Callendar and Middleton led a force to Mauchline in Ayrshire, where a large assembly was preparing formal opposition to the Engagement, including a number of ministers. A sharp engagement ensued but the Engagers had the advantage; several dozen were killed on each side. It was hardly a decisive encounter, but it was a clear sign that those who opposed Hamilton's policy – known as the Kirk Party – were not only numerous but also prepared to take up arms. There were deserters from the army amongst them too. The civil war in Scotland had so far been defined by the fight between king and Covenant; now, with the royalist purists long defeated, the Engagement had split the Covenanters into factions. By the following January the Scottish parliament would be speaking of 'the honest and conscientious people that met at Mauchline Moor for their own defence' whilst condemning Callendar and Middleton for dispersing them.[4] The south-west of Scotland would continue to be the richest recruiting ground for covenanting sentiment throughout the century; a colour hangs on the church wall which is claimed to have been carried in 1648 and then again at Bothwell Brig thirty-one years later.

The Duke of Hamilton led the Engager army across the Border into Cumberland a little under a month after the skirmish on Mauchline Muir. Astonishingly, his march to Preston (barely 90 miles) took almost six weeks. Even allowing the rain the pace was appalling slow and a gift to his enemies. The campaign ended in disaster, the northern Royalists and the

---

2 *The Records of the Parliaments of Scotland to 1707*, K.M. Brown et al eds, St Andrews (2007-2019), 1648/3/239.
3 *RPS*, 1648/3/240.
4 *RPS*, 1649/1/30.

Scottish Engagers being defeated in the running fight between Preston and Warrington. Huge numbers of Scottish prisoners were taken by Cromwell's forces, and to remove their hungry mouths from parliament's responsibility instructions were given to transport over a thousand to Virginia and New England into indentured service. The Venetian ambassador accepted more for pressed service against the Turks.[5] After his surrender, William Baillie retired into obscurity. Middleton was also taken prisoner but broke his parole and returned to Scotland. The Earl of Callendar escaped into exile, linking up with the Prince of Wales.

The Duke of Hamilton was eventually put on trial under his English title, Earl of Cambridge. In court he appealed that as a Scotsman and a prisoner of war who had voluntarily surrendered, he could not be tried for treason under English law. There was detailed legal debate on each of these points, including over whether the Union of the Crowns in 1603 meant that Scots could no longer be considered foreign aliens. Even the case of Mary, Queen of Scots was referenced, and the extent to which Hamilton's father could be classed as a naturalised Englishman examined. As to the articles of Hamilton's surrender, the court concluded that such terms made with the army could save a prisoner from the sword but not the magistrate.[6] On 9 March 1649, James Hamilton was led to his execution at Westminster with an air of resignation. On the scaffold, with modest dignity and without show, he professed his love for the king, his equal affection for the kingdoms of both Scotland and England, and he forgave his enemies. Fairly, he claimed never to have wished for anything but peace and to have endeavoured never to stand as an 'ill instrument' between the king and the people. "I wish the kingdom's happiness," he said, "I wish its peace; and truly, Sir, I wish that this blood of mine may be the last that is drawn." His head was severed with a single clean stroke; two servants caught it in a crimson scarf.[7]

Much had happened between Hamilton's defeat and his execution, but it had happened without him. Despite the disaster of the Preston campaign the Engagers were far from being finished in Scotland. Sir George Munro was still in the field with the rear-guard of Hamilton's army, cut off from the rest when the fighting began at Preston and now retiring relatively unscathed. He withdrew through northern England with a vengeful destructiveness, heading towards Berwick in the north-east which he reached on 8 September. Hamilton had left his younger brother William, Earl of Lanark, in command of the Engager forces at home during the invasion of England. As news from England spread, Lanark marched his forces through East Lothian to link up with Munro to create a potent combined force. Dr George Wishart paints a promising picture of Lanark's infantry: 'for the most Part, old trained

---

5   Murdoch, A. *Scotland and America c1600-1800*, Macmillan (2009), p14.
6   Steele, W. *Duke Hamilton Earl of Cambridge his case, spoken to, and argued on the behalf of the Commonwealth, before the High Court of Justice*, London (1649).
7   Anon, *The several speeches of Duke Hamilton Earl of Cambridge, Henry Earl of Holland, and Arthur Lord Capel upon the scaffold immediately before their execution*, Cole, Tyton and Playford, London (1649).

Soldiers, 6000, with good Officers, all of them hearty, well arm'd, and every Way well provided.'[8] They were supported by '5000 excellent light horse'.

But the opponents of the Engagement seized their chance whilst Lanark was in the borderlands. Supporters of the Kirk Party marched on Edinburgh from the west, led by the Earl of Eglinton. The march became known as the Whiggamore Raid after the nickname given to the raw rustic levies, described by Wishart as 'a Parcel of unarm'd and cowardly Fellows.'[9] It would later be shortened to "whigs". Unpromising though this force initially appeared, it was strengthened in its confidence by the support of the ministers who preached in its support up and down the country. Edinburgh was taken and, when both the Earl of Leven and David Leslie came out for them, the coup appeared complete. Arms were distributed and the rabble, bolstered by those veterans who had refused Hamilton's call, became an army. The Committee of Estates was driven from the capital, and just as Lanark's focus should have been countering the coming of Cromwell, he was obliged to turn his attention to his rear. Scotland was in a state of civil war.

At Musselburgh, where the so-called Roman Bridge crosses the Esk on the historic battlefield of Pinkie Cleugh, Lanark's vanguard attacked the Kirk Party's forward pickets. The latter were broken by the Engager attack,

6. The "Roman" Bridge over the Esk at Musselburgh, where Lanark's forces drove in Leslie's out-guards. The bridge is in fact sixteenth century, but is built on the site of the ancient Roman crossing point beneath Inveresk fort.

---

8   Wishart, G. *A Complete History of the Civil Wars in Scotland under the Conduct of the Illustrious James Marquis of Montrose, in two parts*, 2nd Edition, Edinburgh (1724), p156.
9   Wishart, p156.

routing towards Edinburgh and indicating a clear disparity in the quality of the rival forces. Lanark's success was achieved 'without having so much as one Man kill'd or wounded.'[10] George Munro was more a man of action than his commander, despite being fifteen years his senior, and pressed Lanark for an immediate recovery of Edinburgh whilst the enemy was in disorder. But Leven had secured the mighty castle for the enemy and Leslie had more than 6,000 foot within the walls of the city. An attack could prove ugly if the Whiggamores chose to fight it out. Meanwhile the Marquess of Argyll, head of the Kirk Party, had occupied the city of Stirling with around a thousand men and was attempting to pressure the castle into abandoning the Engagement. Stirling, controlling the bridge over the Forth which opened the roads to the north, was of immense strategic significance; its castle was second only to Edinburgh in importance. Despite protestations from many of his officers, Lanark bypassed Edinburgh and marched on Stirling.

At first glance this decision appears counterintuitive, as it left Edinburgh Castle and the seat of government in hostile hands. On reflection however it must have made sense to Lanark strategically as well as politically. Cromwell was advancing on Berwick, and if he was to be resisted then the burgeoning civil war in Scotland had to be resolved not only swiftly but with as little animosity and bloodshed as possible. Fighting Leslie and Leven in the streets of Edinburgh meant giving battle on uncertain terms with his back to Cromwell and nowhere to fall back to in the case of defeat. With the west hostile to the Engagers, Lanark could not afford for Argyll to also cut off the north by controlling Stirling and turning it into an armed camp in reserve supporting Leslie's base at Edinburgh. As chief of clan Campbell, Argyll had considerable military resources of his own and if left unchallenged he could mobilise considerable strength from his Highlanders. In contrast to this scenario, a successful attack on his position at Stirling held the benefits of ensuring the castle's continued loyalty, dispersing Argyll's latest levies, opening the roads north and threatening Leslie's rear. Leslie's troops, already believed by many in the Engager army to be of dubious courage, might lose heart after the rout of Argyll and seek terms. In such circumstances a reconciliation was not impossible, and the Engagers would be treating from a position of strength. Like his older brother, Lanark was reluctant to solve internal problems through force alone.[11]

Munro led the vanguard of the Engager army to Stirling on 12 September, with 220 dragoons (mounted infantry) and 820 horse under his command. Stirling was defended by a line of walls along its open eastern and southern sides, not unlike Edinburgh, whilst the river Forth protected the northern approach by funnelling any attacker across the famous bridge before they could fight through to the narrow closes and yards beyond under fire from the castle. Finding the gates closed and barricaded, Munro swing round into the Deer Park to the east and past the ornamental garden at the King's Knot. He located a small sally port in the town walls close beneath the castle and

---

10   Wishart, p156.
11   Wishart is less forgiving of Lanark's reasoning, professing he had already determined to give up his army and reconcile with Argyll.

A BITTER ENGAGEMENT

7. Stirling's town walls were formidable, but clearly inadequately watched by Argyll's force in 1648.

managed to break it down: 'his Soldiers followed him one by one very slowly, being hindered by the Narrowness of the Passage.'[12] Argyll was at dinner, completely unaware of the imminent threat. Caught completely by surprise and panicked by the sudden appearance of the enemy inside their own lines, the Kirk Party garrison was all but destroyed. The strong point at Mar's Wark was swiftly overrun, Munro himself kicking down a front door as Argyll fled from the rear 'like a Hart from the Pursuit of the Hunter.'[13] Those at the barricade found themselves cut off from their comrades, and as musket and pistol fire echoed through the streets all resistance collapsed.[14] Hundreds perished as they fled towards the river; Argyll himself barely managing to slip across Stirling Bridge before Munro came up to secure it.

It seemed however that the Battle of Stirling had barely begun, and that a far bloodier sequel to Munro's stunning assault still lay ahead. Argyll linked up with David Leslie's main army on the Edinburgh road, whilst Lanark arrived in Stirling with the main Engager force and reunited with Munro. They now possessed all the advantages of the castle, town and bridge, with most of the country at their back to resupply and reinforce them. Leslie had

---

12 Wishart, p158.
13 Wishart, p158.
14 The adjacent Holy Rude church bears the scars of intense musket fire, and some of this may have been caused in 1648. The relative speed and efficiency of Munro's attack however suggests that most relates to the events of 1651. Warwick, L. *The Second Battle of Stirling? Or When is a Battlefield not a Battlefield?* (currently unpublished).

'ESSENTIAL AGONY'

8. Mar's Wark in Stirling, a fine renaissance residence capable of doubling-up as a defensive strong-point between the town and the castle above. It stands adjacent to the Church of the Holy Rude.

Cromwell in his rear, but the latter was already in communication with the Kirk Party and limiting his threats to their common enemy. If Lanark and Leslie came to blows with all their strength then it might prove to be a bloody affair, and even if the Engagers were triumphant then they would have to face Cromwell. Now that it had come to it, there was little appetite for such a contest, and Lanark avoided a full confrontation for the second time during this short campaign. A temporary truce was agreed which then turned into protracted negotiations. It must have been an anxious time for the citizens of Stirling, perhaps only around 1,500 in number, who not only feared being caught up in a battle but also dreaded the burden of so many soldiers in their immediate vicinity for an extended period, threatening shortages, violence, and disease.

On 27 September a treaty was concluded in which Lanark accepted the necessity of a peaceful solution and the failure of the Engagement either to rescue the king's fortunes or unite Scotland in his cause. Munro would take his men back to Ireland and Lanark's would disband. Argyll and the Kirk Party resumed the government of the kingdom. To committed royalists such as Dr Wishart, Lanark's capitulation whilst at the head of a powerful army was incomprehensible and reprehensible: his hero Montrose would never had betrayed the cause so. But even he accepts that Lanark was 'a wise and smart Man,' and a more dispassionate analysis reveals a genuine hope for a compromise settlement which limited the damage to the kingdom.[15] It was

---

15 Wishart, p157.

perhaps naïve, as attitudes were polarising across the three kingdoms, but it was understandable and well intentioned.

During the negotiations Oliver Cromwell had been firing appeals and threats into Scotland whilst trying to induce the surrender of Berwick. This town, protected by immense bastioned walls from the previous century, responded with what the general called 'a dilatory answer'.[16] Cromwell was in fact trying quite hard to seek a swift resolution to the crisis, and when some of Colonel Wren's Horse crossed the Tweed to plunder the inhabitants he not only punished them but also wrote to Edinburgh explaining that he had done so.[17] Cromwell's position was in fact not so strong as he wished the Scots to believe: his forces had been long in the field, covering large distances in often poor weather, and the campaigning season was coming to a close. His troops were not provisioned for a protracted expedition into Scotland should it be required, and his inability to seriously threaten Berwick likely indicates the fact that he was travelling light without the equipment needed for a siege. Cromwell's best hope lay in an accommodation with the Kirk Party, and he emphasised to them that his main aims were to remove the threat of the Engager Army and to recover Carlisle and Berwick for England. Argyll agreed to the latter and instructions were sent, although the governor of Berwick refused to yield until the Kirk Party's order had been seconded by the Earl of Lanark.

The Engagers were clearly not yet a spent force militarily, and Cromwell needed to deploy more pressure. Major-General Lambert was sent into East Lothian with six regiments of horse and another of dragoons, heading up the approximate line of the modern A1 to threaten Edinburgh. An infantry force moved up in support and secured the gorge at Cockburnspath, where the road plunged dangerously into a defensible ravine. According to a strong local tradition, it was at this time that Cromwell destroyed the venerable priory at Coldingham. A garrison there supposedly held out for two days until cannon mounted upon Coldingham Law were able to bring down the south wall and render the priory indefensible. The story is repeated on interpretation panels at the ruined priory as well as elsewhere, although it seems to originate in an old history of the church rather than the records of 1648. Cromwell, who had no reason not to report it, says nothing about encountering any such opposition as to require such an operation. It is also unlikely that he possessed the artillery required to achieve it. The uncertain truth of the tale is suggested in some modern retellings which, whilst perpetuating the narrative, confess that it might have taken place in 1650. In fact it might not have taken place at all.[18]

The will to fight had evaporated and Scotland would offer Cromwell no resistance. With the Treaty of Stirling concluded the civil war in Scotland

---

16 Letter from Cromwell to the Earl of Loudoun, 18 September 1648, printed in Carlyle, p323.
17 Carlyle, p235-6.
18 Cromwell probably marched close by as the main road carried his army onto Coldingham Moor, but the road bypasses the settlement itself. A cannonball found in the vicinity is of a large size and may well be much earlier in date; the priory was fought over repeatedly during the sixteenth century, for example. There is no necessity for the collapse of the neglected priory's south wall to be ascribed to military action.

'ESSENTIAL AGONY'

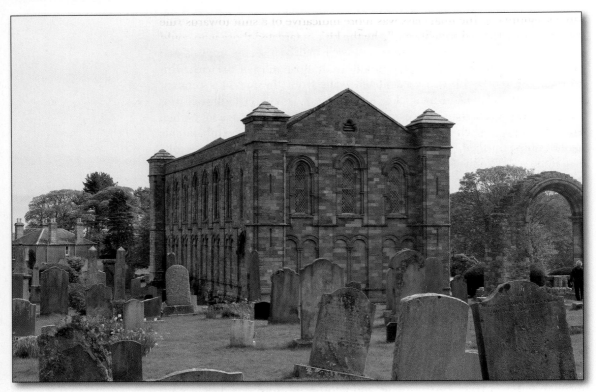

9. Coldingham Priory, which by tradition is said to have been blasted into submission during Cromwell's foray into Scotland in 1648.

was brought to an end and, accepting defeat, Lanark approved the surrender of Berwick. Satisfied now that they had been ordered to stand down by the same party from which they had received their original orders, the garrison marched out on Saturday 30 September. Carlisle was also returned and Colonel Bright was dispatched to receive it. Both the Engager and Kirk Party armies agreed to disband, leaving only a token force to ensure the terms of the Stirling accord were carried out, of which Leven was to have the command.

Cromwell meanwhile occupied Seton Palace near Prestonpans, and on Wednesday 4 October the Marquess of Argyll escorted him into Edinburgh and hosted him at Moray House on the Royal Mile.[19] There, under guard of English soldiers, the Kirk Party unwrapped the Engagement and abandoned their king. Cromwell was satisfied, accepting that Hamilton had led his army into England against the true wishes of the Scottish nation and that a friendly government had been reinstated. As reassurance, he demanded that 'any who have been active in, or consenting to, the said Engagement against England, or have lately been in arms in Stirling,' must be excluded from all public offices.[20] This measure, which had the benefit for the Kirk Party of securing their own dominance, resulting in the Act of Classes on 23 January 1649. This act identified four classes of citizens to be barred from officers, the first three of which covered those who had served in the armies of Montrose, Hamilton or Lanark or the Engager government and those had accepted the

---

19 The property is now part of the University of Edinburgh's education department.
20 Letter from Cromwell to the Estates of Scotland, 5 October 1648. Carlyle, p241.

latter's legitimacy. The final class was more indicative of a shift towards rule only by those deemed suitably godly by the kirk: it targeted those who could be accused of 'uncleanliness, bribery, swearing, drunkenness or deceiving or are otherwise openly profane and grossly scandalous in their conversation, or who neglect the worship of God in their families.'[21] This was a victor's settlement; there was no attempt to reconcile the divisions in Scottish society.

The Kirk Party began raising a small loyal army to guarantee its security, requesting the support of a mounted English force until this was achieved. Cromwell departed from Scotland well satisfied with his bloodless pacification, leaving behind under Argyll a chastened but friendly legitimate government which considered itself the continuation of the Covenanter movement which had led the country successfully for the previous decade. In fact the Covenant had lurched to a more extremist position: the Engagers represented a broader political church, having accommodated both royalists and Covenanters under the cause of the king. They had been neutralised but not eradicated. Lanark went into exile.

The Second Civil War had some small life within it yet, and the Yorkshire Royalists would hold out for a while longer in Pontefract. The Prince of Wales remained a threat overseas, although for the time being he had returned to exile. Ireland was still in a state of total war, as Protestant royalists struggled to decide whether to find common cause with either the Protestant parliamentarians or the Catholic rebels. The greatest loser of the conflict was of course the king himself. The failure of the Engagement had brought more division rather than unity, strengthened his enemies rather than weakening them, and had proven to his more radical opponents that whilst he lived there was no real chance of a settled peace. And so King Charles I was put on trial for his life; he was executed on 30 January 1639. The office of king was formally abolished a few days later, and the parliamentary revolution in England was complete. But in the extremity of their solution to the Second Civil War, the victors had sown the seeds for the Third.

---

21 *RPS*, 1649/1/43.

2

Kings and Covenants

A little before noon on 5 February 1649, a solemn procession stepped onto the hard-frozen square before Edinburgh's Parliament House.[1] Crossing the square into the shadow of the High Kirk of St Giles, the members of the Scottish parliament advanced in a column of twos between two ranks of the Trained Bands of Edinburgh. Sixteen years before these same soldiers had turned out in their finest white satin doublets for Charles I's ceremonial entry into his Scottish capital. On reaching the Cross, topped by the unicorn emblem of Scotland, they formed around it with the shire members to the right and the burgh members to the left.[2] In the centre stood the noblemen of the kingdom, foremost amongst them John Campbell, Marquess of Argyll. The drum-shaped body of the Cross was draped in ceremonial hangings, the fabric stiff in the cold air. At midday three trumpets blasted; John Campbell, Earl of Loudoun and Lord High Chancellor, approached the stout wooden door where he was ceremonially challenged by Sir James Stewart the provost of Edinburgh to confirm his lawful purpose. With the doorway cleared, Loudoun entered the Mercat Cross, reappearing moments later on the parapet above. He was accompanied by Archibald Johnston, Lord Wariston, the King's Advocate and one of the authors of the National Covenant, and Sir William Scott of Clerkington, parliamentary clerk and author of the proclamation now being handed to Loudoun. The heralds of the kingdom, decked in their richly embroidered tabards, brought colour to an occasion palled with an unnatural sobriety. Loudoun's voice echoed above the gathered crowd upon the High Street:

> We, the estates of parliament of the kingdom of Scotland, do therefore most unanimously and cheerfully, in recognisance and acknowledgement of his just right, title and succession to the crown of these kingdoms, hereby proclaim and

---

1   The hall had been completed only ten years before, and although the exterior is now cloaked by a splendid later façade but it is possible to visit the stunning interior. The west wall can be identified amongst the later architecture from the vantage point of George VI Bridge.
2   The Mercat Cross which stands today is a Victorian replica of the earlier cross, although it incorporates some original stonework. It stands slightly closer to St Giles that it did in 1649, the former location being marked by ornamental cobblestones.

KINGS AND COVENANTS

10. The Mercat Cross, Edinburgh. It was the interface between government and the people, where all proclamations of note were issued directly into the commercial heart of the capital, in the shadow of the High Kirk of St Giles.

declare to all the world that the said lord and prince Charles is by the providence of God and by the lawful right of undoubted succession and descent king of Great Britain, France and Ireland.[3]

The bells of the city rang out and from the castle's rocky summit boomed the thunder of a gun salute. Scotland had a new king, Charles II.

The Scots' response to the execution of Charles I was hardly surprising, but it was immensely significant. For most people monarchy was simply the natural order, a state of government which was so essential as to preclude any serious expectation of an alternative. Attitudes to kingship were slightly different on either side of the Border, and Scotland's history provided ample evidence of a robust approach to dealing with royalty when personalities or policies proved unpopular. The king was expected to be accessible, challengeable, and personally engaged with the nobility of the country. The latter were not above seeking to control, constrain or even remove an unpopular monarch, but the office of king still provided an essential central authority. Even the occasional occurrences of royal assassinations had not led to the abolition of the monarchy. This is not to say that the king of Scots was not treated with respect and obedience, but rather that it was a qualified power based on the king's successful management of a nobility who considered him to be the first amongst equals rather than a divine other. In England however, especially since Henry VIII had united the authority of the king with the sanctity of religious supremacy, the aura surrounding the royal person had evolved differently.

On the Union of the Crowns in 1603, unsurprisingly enough, the more elevated status of English kingship had appealed to King James far more than the turbulent environment in which he had grown up in Scotland, battling to assert himself over a nobility riven by ancient rivalries after a long and uncertain minority. His mother, Queen Mary, had been overthrown by overmighty Protestant nobles opposed to her faith, and the Stuarts had long memories. His son Charles, although spending his youngest years in the somewhat uninspiring chambers of Dunfermline Palace, grew up free from the trials of his father's youth and inherited his kingdoms without challenge. His reserved nature suited him to the formality and ceremonial dignities of modern French-style monarchy, the king becoming the centre of a spectacular court which was a cultural stimulus and the source of patronage and opportunity as well as government power. The challenge for Charles I had been how to accommodate consultative parliaments into this model of personal rule, resulting in eleven years without his calling one.[4] In the Scottish context the king's absence from the kingdom removed the direct relationship on which successful Scottish reigns had tended to be built, and when he did visit Scotland in 1633 for his much-delayed northern coronation his formality came across as distant and aloof. For the king's part, he found his Scottish nobles brash and over-familiar, and the independence of the kirk

---

3   *RPS*, 1649/1/71.
4   For a detailed exploration of these issues, see Wedgewood, C. The King's Peace 1637-1641, (London: Folio Society, 2001).

presented a barrier to the uniformity and centralisation which his policies sought. But the National Covenant had never been intended, except in the most cynical interpretation, to remove the king permanently.

In Scotland therefore, the death of King Charles I was immediately followed by the proclamation of the Prince of Wales as his successor. It was simply the natural and expected order of stable government. This explains how men like Loudoun, Argyll, and Johnston of Wariston could be found on the Mercat Cross on that cold February morning in 1649, after more than a decade of opposition to royal policy and the late king's armies. Even so, the proclamation of Charles II included important caveats: before the king was able to govern he would be required to 'give satisfaction to this kingdom' as regard to his religious policy, committing to rule 'according to the National Covenant and the Solemn League and Covenant.'[5] Thus the new king would begin his reign with an acceptance of the concessions which had been demanded of his father. Importantly, the reference to the Solemn League reasserted the alliance with England, and the associated commitment to extend Presbyterian forms of worship into its church. The new king could however take considerable comfort from other parts of the proclamation: his rights and claims were 'undoubted' in their legitimacy; the people of Scotland were 'bound humbly and faithfully to obey, maintain and defend' his rule; and, most importantly, Charles was proclaimed king of 'Great Britain, France and Ireland.' The French claim was of course an empty tradition, but the fact that the Scottish parliament had proclaimed the king's rights to reign in England and Ireland was immensely significant. Two days after they did so the English parliament voted to abolish the monarchy.

The establishment of the new republic, or Commonwealth as it became known, was the climax not only of the wars against Charles I but also of the power struggle amongst his opponents in England. It represented the triumph of the Independents and, ironically since the conflict had been fought to oppose the supposed tyranny of the king, of the army over the parliament. In an age of only very limited suffrage, by the time the king was in captivity the army which had brought him down argued that it was more representative of the people than the parliament which commanded them. The Self-Denying Ordinance of 1645 had been an important step towards the division of the two, separating military command from political office, although as one the measure's leading advocates Oliver Cromwell was a significant exemption. The act removed from the army many of the moderate commanders who were more inclined to a more conservative accommodation with the royalists. The "new modelling" of the army centralised its command and as well as greatly increasing efficiency it also further facilitated its politicisation. The parliamentarian cause had begun as a broad church, but with its success a pandora's box had been opened. The Independents gained the upper hand and marginalised the Presbyterians within the army, and in late 1647 the famous Putney Debates saw the army debating the future constitution of the land rather than the parliament. Cromwell and others were deeply concerned

---

5 *RPS*, 1649/1/71.

by some of the more radical proposals – including almost universal male suffrage. The king watched optimistically, hoping these divisions amongst his opponents would open the opportunity for a meaningful restoration of his power.

It was in this context that the king, in the possession of the army since his seizure by Cornet Joyce, made his escape to the south coast and gambled on the Engagement to rescue his position. The renewal of war and the efficiency of the army's victories strengthened its position further; hope for a moderate settlement with Charles I evaporated quickly after the defeat of the Engagers. In late November 1647 the army presented its proposals to parliament, but they were voted down. The army marched on London. On Wednesday 6 December, Colonel Thomas Pride led the regiment which had formed so well at Preston to Westminster; as members of parliament arrived for their session Pride's officers checked their names against an approved list. Members were turned back or arrested, others staying away as word spread on wings of fear. Fewer than half were permitted access, and Pride's Purge reduced the parliament to a mere Rump. It was an efficient and bloodless coup, and it sealed the king's fate. Cromwell was lying before Pontefract Castle as these dramatic events unfolded, although he left the siege to Lambert and reached London on the evening of the purge. Clearly complicit – why else would he chose that day to quit Pontefract whilst his task was incomplete – Cromwell's absence from the act also gave him a plausible deniability in the case of failure. The Scots commissioners in London reported anxiously that the balance of power had shifted decisively: 'we have few or no friends.'[6]

The Scottish commissioners in London had been directed to use 'all means for preventing the king's death,' but on their failure their orders were extended to registering a 'formal dissent and protestation in the name of this kingdom.'[7] They were then authorised to make their way home as soon as it was politically expedient. In Edinburgh the parliament approved the financing and distribution of experienced 'and well-affected' military officers around the country, to be ready to respond should it prove necessary to assemble the levies once again. But the source of their nerves not so much the new republic to the south, but the risk of the royalists dragging them into a new conflict. The levies were ordered on 28 February to assemble in arms, remaining in their shires, in response to 'attempts to involve this kingdom in new troubles' from overseas.[8] This emphasises the conflicting messages of the Scottish government's position: Charles II had been proclaimed and they were in correspondence with his court in exile, whilst still seeing Engagers and royalists as their principal enemy.

In England, the problems between army and parliament had not gone away either. The limits of rival authorities were being tested in small ways as well as large, as exemplified by Bulstrode Whitelocke's wish that military

---

6 Letter from the Commissioners in London to the Committee of Estates, 4 January 1649; *RPS*, A1649/1/1.
7 *RPS*, 1649/1/76.
8 *RPS*, 1649/1/225.

men like Cromwell 'would not so irregularly meddle' in civilian affairs.[9] Radical elements like the Levellers continued to threaten the stability of the fledgling republic. To ensure discipline was not further eroded, the army command forbade its men from directly petitioning parliament. Pay arrears exacerbated political frustration, and sporadic mutinies broke out. They were efficiently suppressed but an idle army, unwilling to disband, remained a serious problem. There was at least some good news: Pontefract Castle finally surrendered in March, ending the civil war in England. Lambert was voted a reward of £300 a year in gratitude.

Both England and Scotland were led by anxious governments afraid of threats from both within and without, with war weary populations and exhausted economies. The Scottish parliament acknowledged the scarcity of victual within this kingdom and the present dearth and famine,' by outlawing the export of foodstuffs and the confiscation of any such cargos as might be discovered.[10] This was one of the reasons why the levies were instructed to stay in the shires and not to assemble as an army, so that the burden of supply was diluted across the country. As it turned out, the Kirk Party were right to be on their guard, as in February a royalist uprising in the Highlands saw the seizure of Inverness. David Leslie rushed north with a flying column and the Highlanders withdrew. With the town recovered and the revolt failing to gather wider momentum, its leaders accepted terms. Leslie was authorised to erect new fortifications in Sutherland to contain any further mischief. March brought the news of Hamilton's execution in London, and a few weeks later George Gordon, Marquess of Huntly, was beheaded at the Cross in Edinburgh.[11] Huntly had led opposition to the Covenanters in the north-east of Scotland from the outset.[12] His execution, following a long period in hiding, was a further demonstration of the Kirk Party's determination to suppress overt royalism within Scotland.

At the same time the Scots were negotiating with their new king, negotiating the basis on which he could be admitted into his rule. The terms were reported in London: Charles must take the Covenant, recruit no mercenaries, and bring fewer than a hundred people with him out of exile, none of whom could be those who had 'assisted his father in the war, particularly Montrose.'[13] James Graham, Marquess of Montrose, had emerged from the civil war as the paragon of Scottish royalism. His string of victories in 1644-5 had, however, done little to recover the king's position in England and had caused such disruption and fear in Scotland as to consolidate sympathy

---

9   On this occasion, Cromwell had given a permit entitling two citizens to a part of Windsor forest. Whitelocke, B. Memorials of the English Affairs, from the Beginning of the Reign of Charles the First to the Happy Restoration of King Charles the Second, Volume 3, Oxford University Press (Oxford), 1853, p3.
10 *RPS*, 1649/1/45.
11 Whitelocke, p3.
12 Huntly had been a determined but isolated royalist, but he would not support Montrose's uprising in 1644-5 on account of how Montrose had treated him during the Bishops' War when the latter was still a Covenanter.
13 Whitelocke, p3.

'ESSENTIAL AGONY'

11. King Charles II in 1650 by Wenceslaus Hollar, presenting an unpretentious image which might well suggest his suitability for becoming a new type of covenanted king. Too pragmatic to show it whilst he needed the Covenanters, his character was quite unsuited to that vision. (National Galleries of Scotland).

with the Covenant.[14] A brilliant, dedicated but polarising personality, on hearing of Charles I's execution Montrose 'fell down in the midst of those about him, and all the Members of his Body became stiff as if he had been quite dead.'[15] His commitment to the royal cause was unquestioned and he stood ready to be the new king's champion. But Montrose was also a serious blockage to an accommodation with the Scots. Faced with the Covenanters' demands but little real evidence of their support, the king was keeping his options open.

King Charles II was born at St James' Palace on 29 May 1630, England's third Stuart monarch and Scotland's eleventh. Unlike his father, who had spent his first three and a half years in Dunfermline, he was born and raised exclusively in England. When the Scots first marshalled an army against the king, Prince Charles was a healthy young lad of nine; when he accompanied his father into battle against parliament at Edgehill he was twelve. In 1645 the prince was made commander of the royalist armies in the south-west of England, a nominal authority but also a significant learning experience if not a positive one. Charles was obliged to assert himself over quarrelsome subordinates, holding together a cause in serious decline. In September of that year he wrote to his chief opponent, Sir Thomas Fairfax, seeking safe passage for Lords Hopton and Culpepper to travel to the king to discuss 'earnest endeavours to stop this issue of blood' before the royalist cause collapsed completely.[16] Peace proved elusive as we have seen, but the king's wisdom in delegating a separate theatre of war to his teenage son ensured that the latter was not obliged to surrender with his father the following year. Prince Charles sailed from Pendennis Castle with a large entourage, first to Scilly then to Jersey, and finally on to his mother in France. During the Engagement of 1648 the Prince had sailed from his new base in The Hague in the hope of influencing events but he was obliged to return into exile. He was still only eighteen.

In regard to Scotland, the young king was being pulled in two directions: Montrose's party, the true royalists, had perhaps the greatest claim to the king's affection on account of their commitment and suffering. In Montrose himself they had the most dynamic and engaging leadership, but domestically they had the weakest hand. The Engagers were led by Lanark, who in March 1649 had succeeded his late brother to become 2nd Duke of Hamilton. As George

---

14 Particularly so in the Lowlands, as Montrose's forces were primarily comprised of Highland and Irish troops.
15 Wishart, p165.
16 Letter from Prince Charles to Sir Thomas Fairfax, 15 September 1645; Bryant, A (ed). *The Letters, Speeches and Declarations of King Charles II*, Cassell (London), 1935, p4-5.

Wishart recalled, 'the King loved Montrose, and fear'd Lanark, and therefore since it was not possible to reconcile them in Principle, he endeavour'd to prevent the ill Consequences of their differing of Opinion, and to reconcile them.'[17] Montrose was for swift and direct action, the new Duke of Hamilton was for a negotiated settlement with the Covenanters. When the latter opened discussions, it seemed Hamilton's wish to avoid further bloodshed might yet be achieved; but the king was not yet ready to concede so much as was asked whilst there were other options on the table. It seemed to Charles that his greatest opportunity lay not in Scotland at all, but in Ireland.

The situation in Ireland was complex and fluid, and bloody but largely inconclusive fighting had been raging since 1641. As the Catholic uprising had ignited during the narrow window between the conclusion of the Bishops' Wars and the opening of the English civil war, opposition to the Irish Confederates was divided between Scottish Covenanters (usually referred to as the New Scots, to distinguish the expeditionary force from the established Ulster-Scots population), as well as royalists and parliamentarians. It was a complicated four-way war in which nobody seemed able to gain a permanent advantage. The confident Scots army under Robert Monro was unexpectedly defeated by Owen Roe O'Neill at Benburb in June 1646, as a result of which it was driven onto the defensive. Monro had already been weakened by sending forces to oppose Montrose in Scotland before his defeat, then in 1648 he sent a large detachment under his nephew George Munro to support the Engagement. By then, accepting that the king's cause was lost, most Protestant royalist forces in Ireland opted to surrender to parliament rather than to the Catholics. James Butler, Duke of Ormond, surrendered his office as Lord Lieutenant and handed over Dublin. Robert Monro and most of what remained of the Scots army in Ulster were bottled up at Carrickfergus by George Monck; in September 1648 he was betrayed and the town had fallen. Monro was taken prisoner and sent to the Tower of London. For a while it seemed as if the lines of allegiance were simplifying in Ireland, pitting the Confederate Irish against the English parliamentarians, but then Murrough O'Brien, Earl of Inchiquin, declared for the king again.

On 3 October 1648, the Royalist cause in Ireland was further revived by the return of Ormond. By January he had succeeded in creating an alliance with the Confederate Irish which posed a serious challenge to the parliamentarian forces under Michael Jones at Dublin. Prince Rupert, that epitome of the dashing cavalier, arrived in Kinsale with a small royalist fleet in order to harry Jones' supply lines to England. These developments survived the news of the king's execution, and Charles II wrote from The Hague approving Ormond's treaty: 'I will make all the haste I can to come to you into Ireland.'[18] It was a case of my enemy's enemy is my friend, the royalist cause uniting Catholic and Protestant elements against the forces of parliament. There were qualms on both sides; a hard-line Catholic faction rejected the terms, leaving the Owen Roe O'Neill standing aloof in the north. The victor of Benburb, with an experienced army behind him, was thus to

---

17 Wishart, p168.
18 Letter from Charles II to Ormond, 27 February 1649; Bryant, p11.

play no part in Ormond's campaigns. In fact, he even agreed a temporary ceasefire with Monck in Ulster. Nevertheless, Ormond and Inchiquin were moving onto the offensive by the early summer of 1649 and threatening Dublin.

Parliament needed to respond robustly to prevent Ireland being overrun and turned into a secure royalist powerbase from which Irish troops could threaten England. An expeditionary force began assembling, which would have the additional benefit of providing activity for the army. Lots were drawn to determine which regiments would be sent over: 'papers with Ireland writ in them were put into a hat, and being all shuffled together, were drawn out by a child.'[19] Cromwell accepted the command and set about ensuring his army was sufficiently resourced for the seriousness of the operation: artillery and ammunition were shipped ahead; large sums of money were raised through the sale of royal estates and through loans from the city of London; and 1,660 barrels of beer were forwarded to Bristol.[20] Supplies of corn were sent to Michael Jones in Dublin, who was facing Ormond's approach with limited forces and inadequate defences. Meanwhile Cromwell departed London 'in very noble equipage, with coach and six horses,' and eighty lifeguards. A day of humiliation was ordered to seek God's blessing.

In the event, the decisive battle in Ireland came before Cromwell had even set sail. On 2 August Jones marched out to intercept Ormond at the Battle of Rathmines: 'there never was any day in Ireland like this, to the confusion of the Irish.'[21] Ormond was routed, leaving Dublin secure and the royalist cause in retreat once more. 'This is an astonishing mercy,' wrote Cromwell.[22] The army landed on 15 August and seized the strategic initiative. With his field forces broken, Ormond fell back on a strategy of placing strong garrisons in heavily fortified towns; Cromwell was forced into a grinding campaign of siege and storm. Drogheda fell first, then Wexford. These bloody episodes continue to divide opinion and to stain Cromwell's reputation today. Militarily however, they were efficient and effective. Whilst the main army prepared to head into winter quarters, a detachment sent into Ulster successfully engaged George Munro at Lisnagarvey (Lisburn) in December. Munro's demoralised army disintegrated on contact, ending the Scots' involvement in Ireland after eight years of war.

In London the positive news from Ireland was mixed with rumours from Scotland regarding the burning of witches, raising of levies, and rejoicing triggered by false reports of Cromwell's failures. The king meanwhile had reached only as far as Jersey, which had proclaimed him shortly after the death of his father, but he lacked any real prospects of breaking through to Ireland. Even had he been able to the options there were reducing rapidly: Owen Roe O'Neill had finally agreed to support Ormond at the end of October but died within weeks. Cromwell in turn lost his formidable subordinate Michael Jones, exhausted by years of war, before the end of the year. Together Jones

---

19 Whitelocke, p19.
20 Whitelocke, p63.
21 Whitelocke, p85.
22 Letter from Cromwell to Richard Mayor, 13 August 1649; Carlyle, p288.

and Cromwell had knocked the stuffing out of Ormond's royalist revival, inflicting materiel losses which could not be replaced and cutting off the hope of overseas support. As the armies finally withdrew into winter quarters at the end of the year, Cromwell clearly held the initiative.

King Charles, although still moved by Ormond's entreaties for him to come to Ireland in person, was beginning to realise that Scotland would soon have to come into play. He invited the Covenanters to send commissioners to Breda, writing to the Marquess of Argyll with the promise of gratitude: 'it is now in your power to oblige me to a very great degree, and it shall be my care to remember.'[23] At the same time, Charles encouraged Montrose to raise support for a military expedition to Scotland: 'proceed in your business with your usual courage and alacrity.'[24] Argyll and Montrose were implacable enemies, but Charles needed to bring the country together.

In his dealings with two seemingly irreconcilable Scottish factions, the king is often presented as acting duplicitously; but his approach was based more on a misjudgement of Scottish attitudes than out of purely callous self-interest. If he was to pin his hopes on Scotland then Charles must come to terms with his father's former enemies there, but he remained reluctant to accede to their stringent terms. He therefore hoped that Montrose, who struck fear into the Covenanters, was a powerful bargaining counter which he could deploy to secure a better deal. If the Covenanters, dominated by the Kirk Party, remained stubborn, then it was just possible that Montrose could gather enough support to put them out of government: 'Montrose had many Letters from the Scottish Nobility, inviting him to head them, promising him all manner of Assistance.'[25] But Charles II had fatally underestimated the extent to which his champion was hated by many of his countrymen.

The year 1650 began therefore with uncertainty. Whilst Cromwell and his subordinates were making good progress in Ireland, the war was far from complete and there was much blood still to shed. Montrose was busily encouraging support for the king in the courts of northern Europe, in preparation for a military expedition. The Covenanters were preparing, if necessary, to resist Montrose with all their strength even whilst treating with the king he represented. The English parliament reported successes in Ireland enthusiastically, but viewed rumours of Scottish mobilisation with anxiety as those levies might yet be directed at them. Reiving was renewed in the Borders, and letters from Carlisle reported that the 'insolent' parties were 'harboured by the Scots'; whilst news from Berwick was that the Scots were already purging their regiments of 'sectaries and insufficient men, that is, such as never before were in service.'[26] Both the king and Montrose were reportedly heading to Scotland, whilst in places as far apart as Blandford and Durham there had been attempts to proclaim Charles as king in England. These were all worrying signs and as early as 12 January MPs were discussing

---

23 Letter from Charles II to Argyll, 2 January 1650; Byrant, p13.
24 Letter from Charles II to Montrose, 12 January 1540; Bryant, p14.
25 Wishart, p177.
26 Whitelocke, p137.

the need 'to send an army into Scotland to divert the war from England,' and Lord General Sir Thomas Fairfax was approached on the matter. He however was found by the members to be 'more a friend to the Scots than they wished'. As a result, they began agitating from Cromwell's re-assignment from Ireland.[27] The General Assembly of the Kirk of Scotland published a proclamation instructing its congregations to deny support to any royalist rising unless they sanctioned it themselves. The situation was dangerously combustible. Mutual suspicion was moving Scotland and England towards a war which neither really wanted.

Oliver Cromwell had no immediate wish to give up his Irish command, suggesting that he had received only 'private intimations' regarding his recall, as opposed to a formal summons. By the time the latter came, he said, he was already in the field with his army and it would have been inappropriate to obey a letter which had been written many weeks previously whilst his army was in quarters. Cromwell asked for clarification, exploiting the delay to push his new campaign to a successful conclusion.[28] He took Kilkenny on 27 March, the capital of the Confederacy and a blow which he described as 'so much in their bowels.'[29] The Catholic and Protestant elements within the royalist alliance were increasingly hostile, and on 26 April many Protestant royalists agreed to lay down their arms. The next day, Cromwell summoned the fortified town of Clonmel to surrender or face assault.

Elsewhere however events had also been moving swiftly: on 23 March the Marquess of Montrose had finally returned to his homeland. George Hay, 3rd Earl of Kinnoull, had already landed in Orkney the previous September with a force of a hundred Danish soldiers and a further eighty officers to held train and lead the hoped-for recruits. Kinnoull was to raise the Orcadians ahead of Montrose's appearance with a larger force of continental soldiers around which the army would be built. These were a disappointment, described by Wishart as 'not above the Number of Six or Seven hundred at the most… most of them Holsteyners or Hamburgers.' The Queen of Sweden had at least provided an additional armoury of 'fifteen hundred Arms, complete for Horse, Back, Breast, Head-piece, Carabines, Pistols and Swords.'[30] Kinnoull fell sick and passed away even before Montrose's arrival, an inauspicious start to the new royalist uprising. The Orcadian recruits were not so warlike as their Viking descent might have promised, but almost a thousand were brought out nonetheless.

With Montrose was Sir John Hurry, who we last met being shot down and captured in the Preston campaign, described as 'a Man who had engaged in all Quarrels, but never prosper'd in any.'[31] Hurry had led the Covenanter army against Montrose at Auldearn five years before, an army which included many men from the area in which the royalists now hoped to recruit.[32] On 9 April

---

27 Whitelocke, p139.
28 Letter from Cromwell to Speaker Lenthall, 2 April 1650; Carlyle, p352-3.
29 Letter from Cromwell to Richard Mayor, 2 April 1650, Carlyle, p353.
30 Wishart, p180.
31 Wishart, p182.
32 Reid speculates that locally the memory of Auldearn was a powerful disincentive to join Montrose. Reid, p13.

their vanguard landed in Caithness to secure the road south for Montrose and the main body which followed via Thurso a few days later. The advance was slow and deliberate, as Montrose was determined neither to sow undue fear nor move so quickly as to prevent allies from joining him. In leaving small garrisons behind him to maintain his territorial gains Montrose was obliged to further weaken his modest force. Meanwhile, David Leslie was assembling the Covenanter army at Brechin in Angus, whilst a small force under Archibald Strachan moved north from Inverness in order to deny Montrose free movement southwards. Strachan was a humble Musselburgh-born soldier who had gone south to fight for the parliamentarian cause in England, before joining the Scottish army towards the end of the First Civil War. During the Engagement he had taken up arms against Hamilton's expedition, and in his politics he had a great deal of sympathy with the motivations of the Cromwellian army. In 1649 he had helped disperse the short-lived Pluscardine uprising and his efficiency in doing so will have been fresh in local minds. Now he was marching towards the fortified encampment of the Covenanters' most feared bogeyman with just five troops of horse and a small party of musketeers detached from Campbell of Lawers' Regiment.

On 27 April 1650 the Battle of Carbidsdale brought to an end the brief and inglorious conclusion of one of Scotland's most extraordinary military careers. Strachan was confident that veteran cavalry had a considerable edge over raw levies even when heavily outnumbered, but he was further supported by four hundred Highlanders who joined him on his march. These he sent on a flanking march whilst he laid his trap for Montrose on the banks of the Kyle of Sutherland. The royalist force barely mustered fifty cavalry troopers, which advanced from camp under Major John Lisle ahead of the main body of infantry. Strachan had left a single troop visible in the open whilst deploying the other four behind the Culrain Burn and a screen of musketeers. Montrose's rapid forward movement left his infantry 'out of Breath and Order,' leaving Lisle's cavalry completed isolated.[33] Strachan's men 'made good their Charge' and attacked, killing Lisle and seizing Sir John Hurry. The surviving royalist horse fled over their own foot, whilst the main body of the Covenanter forces stormed into the open through smoke of a musket volley. The green and terrified Orcadians 'threw down their Arms and call'd for Quarter,' others fleeing towards the illusory safety of the deep water to their left. the mercenaries 'bestowed a Volley or two amongst the Horse' before attempting to withdraw into woods behind them. There they faced the unexpected appearance of the Highlanders on the hills above them; they surrendered only after a bitter contest.

Montrose's standard bearer, carrying a sombre banner bearing the image of Charles I's severed head and the words 'Judge and Revenge my Cause, O Lord,' was slain after refusing to yield. His commander meanwhile was driven to flight, casting off first the cloak which bore the Star of the Garter, then his sword, and soon his horse.[34] Montrose discarded his clothes and put on Highland dress – presumably a plaid – and took to the hills. He made

---

33 The description of the battle is taken mainly from Wishart, p184.
34 Membership of the Order of the Garter had been granted to Montrose by his new king.

it only as far as Ardvreck Castle, where MacLeod of Assynt had him cast into the cellar before conveying him into the care of David Leslie. The latter, arriving in the north to deal with the final mopping up operations whilst Strachan went south with news of his success, 'fretted not a little' to see the emergence of a potential rival.[35] Montrose was executed with great dignity on 21 May 1650, beneath the Mercat Cross of Edinburgh at which the Scottish parliament had proclaimed the king the previous year. Argyll, distracted by the birth of a daughter that same day, and notwithstanding the loathing he felt towards Montrose, considered it 'a tragik end'.[36] The head of Montrose was placed above the Tolbooth in the heart of Edinburgh, whilst his arms and legs were displayed in Glasgow, Perth, Stirling and Aberdeen.

This was the distant but significant backdrop to the negotiations at Breda, in which the king endeavoured to soften the demands of the Kirk Party at least so far as to bring the former Engagers back into the national fold. He was also reluctant to impose Presbyterianism on England, but as a central pillar of the Solemn League and Covenant the Kirk Party was insistent.[37] As the cause unravelled in Ireland, and with Montrose defeated in Scotland, only the Covenanters possessed the resources, manpower and infrastructure to pose a serious challenge to the forces of the new English republic. On 1 May the king finally gave way on all points and prepared to travel to Scotland. In England meanwhile, Whitelock heard rumours that 'the Scots commissioners went beyond their instructions in promising their king assistance against England... and that their army is marching southward.'[38]

12. Oliver Cromwell (1599-1658) by Pierre Lombart. A confident image of a triumphant commander. It is tempting to see a reference to Dunbar in the background image of pikemen and cavalry troopers in a coastal location.

In Ireland meanwhile, Cromwell launched a frontal assault on Clonmel on 17 May. The Irish commander had however barricaded the streets beyond the breached walls to funnel any attackers into carefully prepared killing zones. Cromwell's men stormed straight into the trap, suffering heavy casualties as they were driven back in disorder. For hours the English army threw itself into the assault with appalling losses on both sides. When they finally disengaged, the royalists had used up most of their powder but had inflicted almost 3,000 casualties on their enemy: 'there was never so hot a storm of so long a continuance, and so gallantly defended, neither in England nor Ireland.'[39] Cromwell had suffered a rare but significant defeat, and when the mayor of Clonmel sought terms Cromwell was so quick to accept that he failed to ensure that the enemy's

---

35 Wishart, p186.
36 Letter from Argyll to the Earl of Lothian, 22 May 1650; in Laing, p262.
37 *RPS*, 1650/3/12. See Appendix I for the terms issued by the Scottish parliament.
38 Whitelocke, p197.
39 Whitelocke, p196.

main force was included in the surrender. They had already slipped out under cover of darkness. It may well be that the pressure for a decisive result in Ireland, freeing him for service against Scotland, had forced Cromwell into rash action, although his successful storming of other such towns may also have encouraged a regrettable overconfidence. Whatever the cause, Clonmel had proven that a stubborn defence was capable of beating Cromwell's army, and there were lessons from this which might yet influence the course of affairs. Although the general himself will have felt some disappointment and frustration, the town had still fallen and the war was for the winning. By finally agreeing to return to England, Cromwell was also able to control the narrative.

Cromwell arrived to a rapturous reception: a crowd of MPs and army officers rode out to meet him on Hounslow Heath to the west of London, and when he reached Hyde Park there was a gun salute and a volley from the musketeers of Barkstead's Regiment. A train of distinguished persons paid visits to his lodgings at Whitehall, whilst in Scotland it was put about that the real cause of the recall must have been the severity of Cromwell's defeat. But despite all the rumours reaching London, there had still been no national levy in Scotland, Engagers and royalists continued to be denied office and purged from the small army which had mobilised against Montrose, and there had be no overtly hostile act towards England. Nevertheless, the imminent return of a king presented to parliament a *casus belli* in and of itself. It was resolved at Westminster that the Scots assuredly planned an invasion, that the Solemn League and Covenant no longer bound the English because the Engagers had rendered it void, and that these beliefs, along with the memory of the Preston campaign, 'were sufficient grounds for the parliament to provide for the security of themselves and countrymen; the which could not be so effectually done as by carrying the war, which they designed upon us, unto their own doors.'[40]

The proposed invasion was not universally supported: the Lord General refused to lead the army which was assembling for that purpose. The council of state instructed a committee, which included Cromwell, Lambert and (helpfully for the historian) Bulstrode Whitelocke, to meet with Fairfax and examine his reasons. He was frank with them: 'I think it doubtful whether we have a just cause.'[41] Cromwell pointed to the invasion of England by the Engagers, but Fairfax retorted that the Scottish parliament 'disowned that engagement, and punished some of the promoters of it.' Whitelocke argued it would be better for a war to be fought in Scotland than in England, but again Fairfax was unmoved: 'what warrant have we to fall upon them unless we can be assured of their purpose to fall upon us?' Thomas Harrison, who would command the home army once the war with Scotland was underway, suggested there could be no other reason for Scotland to be raising men in arms, apparently without considering any anxiety that England's obvious preparations for war might have caused north of the Border. 'Human probabilities are not sufficient grounds to make war upon a neighbour nation,'

---

40 Whitelocke, p206.
41 Whitelockee, p208.

replied Fairfax, 'especially our brethren of Scotland, to whom we are engaged in a solemn league and covenant.' Cromwell pressed the Lord General for his acceptance that the Scots had broken that agreement, meaning that the English were therefore no longer bound by it. He replied that he could only answer for his own conscience. No evidence of a planned Scottish invasion was presented, only the fact that the Scots had invited in the king. Fairfax did not deny that war might well be likely, and in the event of a Scottish invasion he would have taken his place to resist it; but he would not lead an unprovoked invasion. Harrison retorted that it would be 'the most righteous and the most glorious cause that ever any of this nation appeared in.' The Lord General was unimpressed: 'I must desire to be excused.'[42]

Sir Thomas Fairfax resigned his commission. Oliver Cromwell was appointed 'captain-general and commander-in-chief of all the forces raised and to be raised by the authority of parliament within the commonwealth of England.' The Scottish parliament also wrote to Fairfax, enquiring with panicky politeness whether the forces assembling in England were meant purely for defensive purposes. They protested the seizure of Scottish trading vessels too, writing simultaneously to Sir Arthur Haselrigge at Newcastle to remind him of 'the large treaty' between the two nations. Most importantly, the Scots parliament wrote to its English counterpart, on 21 June 1650, stressing that the terms of their covenant bound each country to give the other three months' notice if they intended to break the treaty and declare war. Their letter demanded confirmation that the English would honour the three-month notice period if they did indeed intend hostilities, appealing 'to particular treaties and to the many ties, bonds and declarations passed between these kingdoms, but also to the law of God.'[43] Explicit mention was made of the fact that the Scots had punished the Engagers, denying the events of 1648 could be a cause for war two years later. Towards the end of their letter, however, the tone of the Scottish message hardened: 'the covenanted God of these kingdoms do still live and reign, and will bring shame and ruin upon whatsoever party in either of these nations that without a necessary cause and clear calling shall offend and invade the other'.

Two days after this letter was written, King Charles II landed in Scotland.

---

42 Whitelockee, p211.
43 *RPS*, A1650/5/97

3
The Storm Gathers

The cannon of Edinburgh Castle thundered in salute, competing with the ringing bells of the capital's churches. Bonfires were lit in celebration. For as much as the king's coming was the key cause of the coming conflict, he also appeared to be just what Scotland needed. Charles was young, just shy of his twentieth birthday on his landing, but the naivety of youth was tempered by a pragmatism born from spending half his life witnessing the turmoil of the civil wars. His experience in the south-west had prepared him for a role as mediator between his own commanders as well as leader in his own right. Most importantly, Charles' rights had been proclaimed in Edinburgh by even his father's most active critics in Scotland, and his legitimacy gave to him and him alone the potential to unite the nation. He proclaimed his desire for 'the burying all bitterness and animosities' and, leaving aside any who had colluded in his father's death, 'an act of oblivion and indemnity.'[1] His open features, dark eyes and flowing curls matched his personal pleasantness and easy charm to give an impression of accessible but natural dignity. Constrained by his relative poverty, he came to Scotland with an endearing modesty and lack of pomp which contrasted well with the aloof coolness of his martyred father. The manner of the latter's death had also proven that the royal person was no longer considered inviolate: by returning to Britain the young king was sharing the extreme risks of the coming campaign and had everything to lose. As the Kirk Party was quick to discern, his pragmatism in finally acceding to their terms was a sign of the weakness of his bargaining position but not of his character. Charles II would be a difficult king to control.

The actual arrival of the king was without ceremony. He signed the covenants at the last possible moment before being rowed towards the small village of Garmouth near Elgin. The king had to be carried ashore on the back of the boatman, Milnes, reputedly rewarding his helper by honouring his daughter with a kiss. Sir Robert Innes then hosted the king to dinner before he moved on to Bog of Gight (Gordon Castle), seat of the Marquess of Huntly. Innes would later be commissioned to raise a regiment of horse in

---
1 Letter of Charles II to the Prince of Orange, 11 April 1650; Bryant, p16.

'ESSENTIAL AGONY'

this area for the king. Charles slept at the Gordon stronghold, no doubt deeply after the trauma of more than three weeks at sea, dodging parliamentarian warships, during which he had been extremely vulnerable and utterly unable to control his fortunes.

The Kirk Party were determined that, having compromised enough themselves in letting the king land, he must look to them alone for support and advice. Within days of Charles' arrival, Argyll was acting to isolate the king from any other sources of counsel by having himself appointed as master of the royal household.[2] Trusted commissioners were despatched northwards to surround the king, who was permitted to keep only a small delegation of English exiles with him. He was expected to 'cordially and speedily condescend' to the directions of those Church and Parliament 'authorised'.[3] Charles was denied the services of experienced officers who had served during the Engagement, particularly William Hamilton, the second duke. With the English unmoved by the Kirk Party's efforts to distance themselves from the Engagers of 1648-9, the reasons for keeping them out of the coming war were purely domestic and, ultimately, self-defeating.

Charles' arrival had coincided with belated moves to mobilise Scotland's manpower for a war which Scotland had tried hard not to provoke. David Leslie sent a list of urgent points to the parliament in Edinburgh: with the professional's eye, Leslie proposed recruits were first used to raise existing units to full strength. Care was to be taken to blend experienced men, and there should be plenty amongst the levies after a decade of conflict, with the raw troops being levied for the first time. This was partly undermined by Leslie's overt support for a purge of 'disaffected and profane persons' from the army, although this would disproportionately affect the officer class. The lieutenant-general concluded his letter with a promise to 'hazard life and fortune for the common cause and against the invasion of whatsoever.'[4]

The initial levy ordered by the Scottish parliament on 25 June 1650 called for a repeat of the numbers required by the orders of 6 August the previous year combined with a proportion of those of 28 February. As the crisis drew closer an even bigger levy was ordered on 3 July which called out 'all fencible persons between 60 and 16.'[5] This levy was 'over and above' the call of 25 June, increasing the strain on the shire committees tasked with raising and equipping the forces, assigning their officers, and endeavouring to fulfil Leslie's instructions to fill existing regiments

13. David Leslie (c1600-1682), by Michael van der Gucht. This is a confident image of a dynamic officer, illustrating Leslie at the peak of his powers after Montrose's defeat and Leven's retirement from field command. His hair appears to have been a sandy or chestnut colour.

---

2 *RPS*, M1650/5/39.
3 Letter from the Earl of Loudoun to Charles II; Gardiner, p131.
4 *RPS*, A1650/5/108.
5 *RPS*, A1650/5/116.

before creating new ones. The doubling of the levy ran the risk of increasing confusion without increasing the army, resulting in large numbers of smaller units. The central and north-western Highlands were not called out, perhaps due to government's suspicion as to their loyalty to the Covenant, but this had the advantage of leaving a potential reserve of manpower in the rear when the army moved south. The exception of course were the Argyll lands, but also the areas around Inverness and the Moray Firth, and up into Caithness beyond. But although the main strength of the army came from the Lowlands, the area of recruitment covered all the many faces of Scotland: this was a national army.[6]

The committee for purging the army continued its work ensuring only appropriate officers were appointed, a move which undermined one of the crucial elements in the success of Scotland's armies in the previous decade, the appointment and distribution of officers based on experience. Men of suitable politics might now be better placed than soldiers who knew their trade, although Reid also argues that the purges provided a mechanism to remove those who were utterly unsuitable once the army was assembled.[7] Needless to say the numbers required by the levies were rarely achieved by the committees. If Cromwell is to be trusted in his assessment of the Scots army at Dunbar then Leslie had 16,000 infantry and 6,000 horse by the beginning of September, which means he must have originally mustered an even higher number for the preceding campaign. If anything, Cromwell is likely to be over-estimating; a conclusive figure remains elusive.

The Scottish infantry, like their opponents, were formed into regiments containing both pikemen and musketeers. The pike not only provided essential defensive cover for musketeers, who were particularly vulnerable to cavalry attack, but were also used for attacking enemy infantry and physically driving them backwards with their walls of massed pike-heads. The musket was however becoming the dominant weapon on the battlefield, its firepower creating greater effect in return for less physicality. The ideal ratio for battle was considered to be one pikeman for every two musketeers, and both types of foot-soldier should, in theory at least, be armed with swords as their secondary weapon.[8] A swinging musket-butt was often a necessary substitute for the sword in hand-to-hand combat. The cavalry were to be 'armed with pistols and lances, broad swords and steel caps,' suiting them to fast strikes and close-quarters fighting.[9] At least some of the Scots horse were presumably equipped more heavily, identically to their opponents, using the 1,500 complete sets which had been 'taken untouch'd' from Montrose's failed expedition.[10]

As regiments disbanded at the conclusion of earlier campaigns, arms had been inventoried and placed in storage either in formal magazines or else in

---

6 See Gerrard et al, Lost *Lives*, p.113 for a useful illustration visualising this.
7 Reid, *Dunbar*, p.28.
8 The post-Dunbar levy at the end of 1650 specified the infantry should be arranged, 'two part muskets and third part picks and all with swords.' *RPS*, A1650/11/16. The March 1648 levy had specified the same.
9 *RPS*, A1650/5/116.
10 Wishart, p.180.

improvised ones. Ahead of the June 1650 levy, 349 muskets, 360 collars of bandoliers, 210 pikes, and 139 swords were collected from John Cranston's cellar in Edinburgh and transported to Stirling Castle. They had been placed there in August 1644 and inventoried in January 1649.[11] Similar stockpiles were no doubt being centralised around the country as the army began to assemble. An order survives from 1647 which specifies how arms were to be transported: 1,200 muskets required forty chests, which were to travel on twenty carts; 1,500 pikes required 15 carts; sixty horses were needed to move powder, lead ball and matchcord. Food supplies were drawn in to central stockpiles too, driving up prices and triggering complaints to parliament from the civilian population. On 5 July, Archibald Johnston drafted the order for all levied forces to march from their local muster points to the appointed regimental rendezvouses, and all units north of the Tay were to move southwards. They were to march with 'drums, colours, standards and trumpets.'[12] The landscape of Scotland was alive with activity, as horses, waggons and men filled the roads and marketplaces, a major concentration of manpower and materiel which, although a regular feature of the past decade, assumed a greater sense of scale and urgency in the face for the first time of a major foreign invasion.

Scottish foot regiments were expected to muster eight companies of 126 men according to the 25 June levy, making their total just over 1,000 men. Leslie himself suggests 108 men as the company complement, making a regiment's strength 864. The June levy also laid down the organisation for cavalry regiments: 'every regiment of horse shall consist of six troops and no less, every troop having 75.'[13] The total regimental strength of at least 450 troopers may not have been regularly achieved. The reality is, especially in the wake of a hurried levy in a time of imminent crisis, regimental strengths across the Scottish army will have varied considerably just as they did in most campaigning forces, and in action units would expect to be brigaded together to form tactical units.

If assessing numbers for the Scottish army is difficult, evaluating its levels of experience is next to impossible. The majority of regiments involved the Dunbar campaign were not in fact newly raised, but that does not mean that the older regiments can be considered as any more experienced as Leslie's sound insistence on mixing raw recruits with seasoned soldiers makes it very hard to assess with any confidence. Scotland had been at war continuously since 1639, often fighting on several fronts simultaneously with theatres of operations across all three Stuart kingdoms. Even before the civil wars in Britain there had been large numbers of Scots fighting overseas in Europe. The resultant pressures on the available manpower had therefore been considerable; the Preston campaign had been particularly damaging in terms of numerical loss.

But there is nothing in the records of the 1649-50 levies which indicates any greater concern over the quality of the levies than was customary, and

---

11 *RPS*, A1650/5/95.
12 *RPS*, A1650/5/124
13 *RPS*, M1650/5/37.

any delays in gathering the required numbers are suggestive more of a general war weariness than a shortage of available men. The levy system also meant that, after repeated disbandment of regiments and even whole armies during the lulls in the conflict, soldiers with experience from previous levies will have turned up again in 1650; there was no method of recording such men any differently to the green faces which came in with them. One of the bodies excavated in Durham, a survivor of the Battle of Dunbar who perished in captivity, was over 46 years old and showed signs of healed injuries in his upper body which might suggest he was a veteran of previous campaigns.[14] There were also an unknown number of professional European soldiers available, including the German officers who travelled to Scotland 'expecting employment' in the coming war.[15] So while protracted conflict means increased drains on manpower, it also means a larger pool of men with at least basic military experience. In short, the Scots army which Leslie assembled should not be dismissed simply as large but raw; it was probably smaller but more capable than is customarily assumed.

The army could certainly boast high levels of experience in its senior commanders. The most important, both called Leslie, had refused to join the Engagers in 1648 and had therefore survived with both their military reputations and political credentials intact. At the top of the chain was Alexander Leslie, Earl of Leven, who had masterminded the creation of the Covenanter armies which had performed so effectively between 1639 and 1647. Leven had been a career soldier, making his name in the Swedish army, reaching the rank of field marshal. Courageous, disciplined, level-headed, Leven carried immense military prestige. He was also sixty-eight years old, and after around forty-five years of intense military service Leven's 'age and infirmity' meant that he was no longer able to direct major field operations.[16] Nevertheless, Leven retained the rank of Lord General and considerable influence.

Actual field command was delegated to the lieutenant-general of the Scottish army, David Leslie. Unlike Leven, whose social heritage was fairly modest, Leslie's grandfathers were the 5th Earl of Rothes and the 1st Earl of Orkney. At around fifty, Leslie's career had already lasted twenty busy years. He had fought for the Swedes, the Russians and then the Swedes again, before returning to Scotland after the outbreak of the Bishops' Wars. Leven was keen to employ experienced professionals in his army, and Leslie was promoted to major-general in the Army of the Solemn League and Covenant which marched into England to support its parliament. At Marston Moor in July 1644, Leslie fought alongside Oliver Cromwell and led a critical cavalry

---

14 Gerrard et al, *New Lives*, p.138.
15 Whitelocke, p174. The Thirty Years War had finally drawn to a close, and there were large numbers of career soldiers across Europe looking for opportunities. Many will have fought alongside Scots in continental wars. Three of the bodies excavated from the mass grave at Durham can be been shown to be of European rather than British origin, perhaps Sweden, Poland or Southern Germany. These are the areas with which eastern Scotland had strong bilateral trading and migratory connections, as well as being the primary theatres for Scotland's military diaspora; Gerrard et al, *Lost Lives*, p.94.
16 Act of approbation in favour of Alexander Leslie, earl of Leven, 11 May 1648; *RPS*, 1648/3/174.

charge which recovered the army's position and tipped the balance against the royalists. His crowning success however was the triumph over Montrose at Philiphaugh the following year, effectively destroying the royalist threat in Scotland at the time.

Leslie was uncompromising in victory: the merciless killings which followed Philiphaugh and his hard-line approach to suppressing resistance in the Highlanders thereafter are indicative of a ruthlessness in his commitment to the cause. There are also indications that his grip on the discipline of his forces was looser than Leven's had been. The Covenanters bestowed rewards on Leslie in recognition of his service, and in 1649 he had purchased Newark Castle on the Fife coast to reflect his status.[17] Leslie had not only refused to support the Engagement, but had actively worked against it as soon as Hamilton's army marched into England. He was ambitious – we have already heard from Wishart how he had viewed Strachan with jealous eyes after Carbisdale – and supported the Kirk Party's purges. King Charles cannot have expected Leslie to be an enthusiastic natural supporter, but he could at least appreciate his capabilities. In one of the most prescient letters of the war, Charles wrote to Argyll on 19 July 1650: 'there is one thing I shall desire you to do; it is, not to let the Committee send any positive orders to David Leslie, either to fight or not to fight, but to leave it to his judgement what to do.'[18]

The highest ranking of Leslie's immediate subordinates were also experienced men. Lieutenant-General Sir James Lumsden, a fifty-two years old Fifer, had served with distinction in the Swedish army before leaving the German wars at the same time as David Leslie. Whilst the latter was leading the cavalry charge at Marston Moor, Lumsden was rallying the faltering infantry. The Earl of Loudoun wrote to King Charles of Lumsden's 'affection to the cause and to your Majesties service,' whilst recommending that 'he is a person of so much valour and experience in war, that your Majesty would give him all encouragement'.[19] Sir James Holborne of Menstrie was appointed major-general, having previously fought for the English parliament under the Earl of Essex and Sir William Waller. Holborne knew Oliver Cromwell personally, and had escorted him into Edinburgh in 1648 after the defeat of the Engagers. His politics were close to those of Robert Montgomerie, also a major-general and another veteran of Marston Moor. Montgomerie had raised forces in the west of Scotland to oppose the Engagement, and his father the Earl of Eglington had been a leader of the Whiggamore Raid. Cromwell trusted Montgomerie sufficiently to order the release of two thousand prisoners from Preston into his care, with confidence that they would not be used against England again.[20] Such men might not have been the king's first choice politically, and it becomes clear from their careers why they were not keen to reconcile with the former Engagers, but they did at

---

17 The name is a corruption of New Work, rather than having any connection to the town of Newark in England which Leslie had besieged at the end of the First Civil War.
18 Letter from Charles II to Argyll, 19 July 1650; Bryant, *Letters,* p.17.
19 Letter from Loudoun to Charles II, 10 August 1650; Gardiner, *Letters,* p.134.
20 Letter from Cromwell to Speaker Lenthall, 8 October 1648; Carlyle, *Cromwell,* p.242.

least hold serious military experience. More to the point, they understood their enemy.

The wording of the Scottish summer levy accepted that since Charles II had signed the Covenant the country was obliged to protect him and defend his cause. The Kirk Party remained determined to keep the king away from the army which was assembling in his name, fearful that his presence might galvanise royalist sympathies. The king occupied his family's palace at Falkland, where access to his person was granted only according to an approved list. As befitted the royal dignity as well as the king's security requirements, a Lifeguard of Horse was appointed for the king on 3 July with the determined anti-Engager Alexander Montgomerie, Earl of Eglington at its head. It was formed from a troop which had fought at Carbisdale, considered therefore to be sufficiently immune to royal charm.

A Lifeguard of Foot was also appointed, and this was formed from 'the Irish companies'.[21] In August 1649 survivors from the Scots army in Ulster who had made it back to Scotland were consolidated into six companies of foot. These were experienced men, possibly a mixture of Scots and Ulster-Scots, and too potentially useful to disperse. Lord Lorne, heir to the Marquess of Argyll, was made colonel; James Wallace of Auchans, a veteran of the Ulster campaigns and the war against Montrose, was made lieutenant-colonel.[22] At least some of the King's Lifeguard may have been wearing red coats if they had retained uniform that had been issued to them in Ireland, where part of the Scots force had been supplied by England. Perhaps a lack of uniformity is implied by Lorne's later appeal that his men 'may all have coats of one colour.'[23] The king presented his Lifeguards with a spectacular set of colours, combining royal emblems with Covenanter mottos; a visual symbol of the confusion of the times.

David Leslie understood the capacity of the enemy he was facing and the potential weaknesses in his own position as he mobilised, maintained and motivated an army containing soldiers who brought with them varying degrees of enthusiasm. He therefore advocated a defensive strategy which would minimise the risk to his army during the opening phases of the campaign. As Cromwell would surely strike for Edinburgh – there was no attempt by the English to disguise their intentions – the capital needed to be prepared for a serious defence. Even before the general levy was issued the inadequacies of the city's defences were ordered to be rectified. Edinburgh itself had the Flodden Wall but this had failed to keep out the well-equipped English expeditions of the 1540s. A recent extension, the Telfer Wall, had not improved the defensibility of the city, and there were no earthen banks to protect the rubble walls from modern artillery. In fact Edinburgh's best defence lay in the narrowness and steepness of its streets, inviting potential horrors such as those Cromwell had witnessed at Clonmel. But the city was also a tinderbox of tall ungainly tenements packed with a large population,

---

21 *RPS*, A1650/5/117.
22 McGavin, W. (ed), *The Scots Worthies*, (Oxford: University Press, 1839), p.422.
23 Lyon, C. J. *A Personal History of King Charles II from His Landing in Scotland to his Escape from England*, (Edinburgh: Stevenson, 1851), p.40.

as well as the seats of law and government; no sensible plan would rely on a fight through the streets.

To the north of the city was Edinburgh's commercial lifeline, the port of Leith, and here the old French ramparts of the previous century formed the basis of a renewed fortification. It would be the coastal anchor of Leslie's deployments around Edinburgh and would prevent Cromwell landing supplies and artillery close to the capital as the Earl of Hertford had done in 1544. On 24 June the burgh council approved the allocation of 1,200 soldiers for the work at Leith, and two days later all servants in the city were ordered up to Castle Hill to help demolish the renaissance spur which projected out from the front of the castle.[24] Supplies of ale and beer ('aile and beir') were stockpiled for the garrison. The city's trained bands were on standby to assemble at Greyfriars kirkyard, spiritual home of the National Covenant, at the sound of the drum.[25] Sixteen new velvet coats were ordered for their officers, at a cost of £944 19s 8p.[26] Amidst all this activity came the pressures of simultaneously stockpiling resources for a potential siege, building up the military supplies for the coming campaign, and feeding the thousands of soldiers who were now assembling between Edinburgh and Leith. On top of this came the refugees; Lesley ordered the path ahead of the English army to cleared of goods and people. Edinburgh's council issued the following appeal:

> The present necessitous condition of the Army [requires the citizens] to contribute harden sheets, blankets, pots and pans and such like, and to send them this night to their several parish churches within this burgh where they shall be received off their hands.[27]

Hard times were coming. Cromwell was coming.

The English army had begun mustering for the invasion of Scotland almost two weeks before the Scottish levies were authorised. Having determined to make the expedition regardless of the Scots' intentions, and whilst the latter were still seeking reassurance, the army of the Commonwealth had seized the initiative. On Cromwell's arrival in York, once the symbol of northern royalism, he was feted by the mayor and aldermen; his star was in the ascendant and everyone wished to be close to its heat. Cromwell was fifty-two years old, just a few years older than David Lesley, but his military career had not begun until late 1642. Before that he had been an unspectacular Cambridge-educated gentleman who, after a period of depression and

---

24 The spur had been badly damaged after the Lang Siege in 1573 so was presumably no longer considered defensible. In which case it would have provided obstacles to the garrison's field of fire and potential cover for attackers. Evidence of its footprint have recently been uncovered during excavations on Castle Esplanade.
25 Wood, M. (ed), *Extracts from the Records of the Burgh of Edinburgh 1642-55*, (Edinburgh: Oliver and Boyd, 1938), p. 245.
26 Wood, *Records*, p. 251.
27 'The present necessitous conditoun of the Armie… to contribut harden sheits, blankets, potts and panis and such lyk, and to send them this night to their severall paroshe churches within this brugh quhair they sall be resaved af their handis.' Wood, *Records*, p. 251. 'Harden' refers to a cheap coarse cloth.

financial loss, found comfort by re-aligning his faith. As a rural member of parliament with modest means, there had been nothing in Cromwell's early career to foreshadow the brilliance of his later life. He was deeply principled but also, when the doors of power began to open during the turmoil of civil war, assertive and ambitious. Disciplined and severe when necessary, Oliver Cromwell also had a lighter side which endeared him to his soldiers almost as much as their confidence in his unfailing abilities. The experience of Cromwell was different to his friend than his enemies, and he continues to polarise both the public and historians. For better or worse, Cromwell was a force of nature.

Cromwell had risen high and fast in the parliamentarian armies of the civil war, eventually eclipsing noble commanders like the earls of Essex and Manchester. His authority was sufficient to ensure that he survived the Self-Denying Ordnance of 1645 by which he should have been obliged either to resign his military command or his seat in the Commons. Cromwell did neither, and when the regional armies were "new-modelled" he emerged as lieutenant-general of horse, second only to Sir Thomas Fairfax. Successfully steering a course between the radical elements of the army and the conservative forces in the victorious parliament, Cromwell retained his authority and saw it considerably reinforced after smashing Hamilton's army in 1648. The Preston campaign, messy as it was, allowed Cromwell to present himself – and his army, as he was ever keen to extol their achievements – as the saviours of the nation. Fairfax's victories over the ill-equipped royalists in the south-east were, by contrast, less dramatic. Fairfax had also demurred at the prosecution and execution of Charles I, and the civil breach this opened permitted Cromwell, after his string of victories in Ireland, to reach the very highest military command. And with the parliament purged to the army's satisfaction, Cromwell had the opportunity to dominate affairs if he retained its loyalty. Victory in Scotland would secure his place as one of the most powerful figures in the British Isles.

Of course, Oliver Cromwell was not the only man to have risen high, and he was therefore blessed with the support of men who, whilst ambitious themselves, were also able. Young Henry Ireton, something of a protégé of Cromwell's, was considered a safe enough pair of hands both to marry his daughter and succeed him in command of the army in Ireland. Cromwell had knocked out the main Irish powerbases, leaving Ireton to fight a brutal war of occupation as the country was ground into submission. This task would prevent Ireton's involvement in the Scottish campaigns, and would end in his death to the plague before the end of the following year. Cromwell must look to others for support in his Scottish campaign.

The most significant of Cromwell's lieutenants was John Lambert. At just thirty-one, Lambert was a Yorkshireman who had trained for a career in law before civil war had revealed his talent for fighting and command. Like so many senior officers on both sides of the Dunbar campaign, Lambert was a veteran of the dramatic events at Marston Moor in 1644, but it was his performance during Hamilton's invasion which had really revealed his talents. Simultaneously cautious and aggressive, Lambert's confident manoeuvres had deterred Langdale's royalists from striking whilst he was unsupported,

'ESSENTIAL AGONY'

14. George Monck (1608-1670) by David Loggan. Depicted here after the Restoration, at which he was raised to Duke of Albermarle, Monck joined the expedition to Scotland with an uncertain reputation. Cromwell had seen in him greater abilities than his record suggested to others.

and his harrying had denied Hamilton's army freedom of movement and applied a constant wearying pressure on its flanks. Cromwell and Lambert understood each other well, but Lambert was also aware of his great talents and developed a flamboyant vanity as a result.

Charles Fleetwood was of roughly the same age as Lambert and also trained in law, but he had risen to a relatively understated form of prominence towards the end of the civil war in England. Fleetwood had gone on to be a key player in the power games between the army and parliament, and in 1650 Cromwell appointed him as lieutenant-general of horse for the march into Scotland. Fleetwood's military credentials were less impressive than some of his companions' – he had done little in the way of independent command – but he was reliable and respected. A sign of Cromwell's trust in him was that Fleetwood would succeed Ireton in two significant respects in 1652: as Lord Deputy of Ireland, and as Cromwell's son-in-law after marrying his widowed daughter.

A rather more complex career was that of George Monck, a forty-one-year-old officer and something of an outsider to Cromwell's inner circle. His military experience had begun in his youth, when a scandal had driven him into armed service overseas. On returning to England, Monck had served in the royal army against the Scots at Newburn in 1640, witnessing the skill and capacity of the Covenanters under Leven. The king had given him a regiment under Ormond to resist the Irish uprising the following year, and he proved himself to be efficient, calm and unflappable. When civil war broke out in England however, Ormond became suspicious as to the depth of Monck's loyalty to the royalist cause and had him sent back to England, where he recovered his position by impressing King Charles I in person. But the recovery was to be short-lived; Monck was taken prisoner by the parliamentarians in January 1644 after Thomas Fairfax's victory at Nantwich.

George Monck had then languished in the Tower of London until a dramatic reversal of fortunes saw him return to Ireland in 1649, this time as a major-general in parliamentary service. The campaign went badly for him however. Monck was forced to agree a ceasefire with Owen Roe O'Neill in recognition of the weakness of his forces, and after a large number of his men deserted to the enemy he was obliged to surrender Dundalk to Inchiquin.[28] The ceasefire was disavowed and parliament summoned Monck to explain his actions, exonerating him of blame but leaving his reputation in parliamentarian circles even more clouded.[29] Fortunately Monck's friends were willing to lobby on his behalf, and Cromwell must have seen in him a

---

28 Whitelocke, p.72, p.77-78.
29 Whitelocke, p.83-84, 86.

THE STORM GATHERS

potential which had yet to make itself fully manifest. After a career of false starts, Monck's service in 1650 would be his making.

Beneath these men senior commanders were at least 16,354 soldiers, many of whom had experienced combat and campaigning before. They had also experienced success and had no reason not to expect to do so again. These men were motivated, believing they were advancing against a foreign enemy which their general had already beaten in 1648 and which was planning to bring war into their own lands if they were not intercepted beyond the Border; an enemy which threatened to overturn all that had been achieved in the civil wars. Some care must be taken not to oversimplify the Cromwell's army by assuming all were high-minded fellows motivated by religious and democratic principles; even godly soldiers are capable of grossly ungodly acts. Cromwell's disciplinary edicts on the eve of the invasion, formally read out to each troop and company, are a reminder of their capacity to commit outrages rather than proofs that they would not. Those who were caught were punished and much was made of the general's efficiency in doing so, but it was politically and military important not to alienate the civilian population from which Cromwell would need to seek both sympathy and supplies.

The red-coated infantry expected to fight in the same way as their Scottish counterparts, deployed in mixed brigades of pike and shot. They were supported by heavy cavalry, highly trained horsemen sufficiently disciplined to advance knee-to-knee, combining the firepower of their carbines and pistols with the unstoppable weight of their armoured charge. The horse were the pride of Cromwell's army. The sixty carriages reported by Captain John Hodgson of Bright's regiment were presumably the treasure wagons which Whitelocke records as departing to support the army. The army was to be well supplied with money at least, limiting the need to alienate the local population.[30] The baggage train was however to be limited, as Cromwell wanted to keep his army compact and mobile. It was a strategy which pressured for efficient results.

The general quit York for Durham, with the high-spired towers of its cathedral looking down from their roost above the looping river, and there met Arthur Haselrigge.[31] A staunch republican, Haselrigge had given up his military commission for a political one and had served as governor of Newcastle since late 1647. The post suited him well, and the former bishops' castle at Auckland was the centre of a secure and profitable power base. Cromwell and the governor had much to discuss, as Haselrigge would be the army's nearest support once it entered Scotland, essential for expediting supplies and reinforcements. On 10 July the two travelled on together to Newcastle, another stronghold for the king during the civil war but which had twice fallen to armies led by Leven. As at York, the memory of the Scots laying siege to the walls was probably more powerful with its citizens in 1650 than any residual royalism. Across England the Scots were conflated with the cavaliers, 'drunk with carousing the king's health,' rumours of royalist plots south of the border circulated, and Scotsmen found fighting alongside the

---

30 Slingsby, p.127; Whitelocke, p.214.
31 The slender spires would be removed later that decade.

Irish reminded the people of that royalism and popery were hand-in-hand. Most ludicrously, given the continuing strictness of the Kirk Party, it was said that Charles had been granted 'all his regal power', the Mercat Cross being draped in crimson velvet as this was proclaimed.[32] The soldiers, and the people, must feel none of Fairfax's qualms.

At Newcastle, the last great city before Edinburgh, the general and his officers were feasted. The vanguard of the infantry force was Sir John Bright's Regiment which was posted ahead near Morpeth, with Captain Hodgson quartered at Sir William Fenwick's place at Wallington.[33] Here the soldiers of this battle-hardened regiment, which had fought at Nantwich, Marston Moor, Preston and Winwick, heard that their colonel had 'deserted' them.[34] According to Hodgson, who was well-placed to know, Bright was 'very valiant and prudent, and had his officers and soldiers under good conduct,' but astonishingly he was willing to resign his commission on the eve of a major campaign because Cromwell had denied him a fortnight's leave. Cromwell's reaction can only be imagined, but for the time being he was distracted by planning the arrangements for supplying his expedition by sea.

The army moved up to Alnwick, into the shadow of the once-mighty stronghold of the Percy family which then stood empty and stripped. Here the men of Bright's regiment were approached by a group of officers intending to offer them a new colonel. Cromwell had decided to offer them an experienced and capable officer: George Monck. The outcry was instant. Bright's had fought against Monck at Nantwich, and even without their doubts as to his loyalty there was little in Monck's recent service to commend him as replacement to a popular and successful commander. "We'll have none of him," cried Bright's officers.[35] This was either a gross miscalculation on Cromwell's part, or a more cynical act of theatre designed to motivate Bright's in the wake of losing their colonel. Certainly when the staff officers returned the following day to propose Lambert instead, the men threw up their hats with joy. Either way, it was a demonstration of the strong bonds which connected the rank and file to their officers; a relationship few regiments in the Scots army would be able to replicate. It also served as a reminder that Cromwell's army retained that precocious and potentially dangerous self-confidence which had caused parliament such difficulty after its victory of Charles I.

Monck can hardly have been delighted at the response of Bright's to the thought of being led by him, although perhaps not as disheartening as the wholesale desertion of his men in Ulster had been. It was clear he would need to prove himself soon to win the trust and affection of the rank and file. The episode did nothing to diminish him in the eyes of Oliver Cromwell however, who remained determined to accommodate Monck's obvious ability. A new

---

32 Whitelocke, p. 219.
33 Hodgson gives us the owner but not the location, stating it is about four miles from Morpeth. Wallington is more like ten but that is a reasonable margin of error. The property which now stands, cared for by the National Trust, dates to 1688 and sits on top of the Fenwick tower house.
34 Slingsby, p. 127.
35 Slingsby, p. 139.

regiment was formed for him by drawing five companies out of Haselrigge's garrison in Newcastle and adding to them to another five from Fenwick's Regiment at Berwick. These men would want to make a name for their new unit and it was down to Monck to build its *esprit de corps*.

In steady stages the army moved northwards, tradition insisting Cromwell stopped at the Old Angel coaching inn at Felton on the way.[36] Each night the army dispersed around the locale and the progress was made in easy stages; there was clearly no fear of the imminent Scottish invasion which the army was marching to prevent. The skies grew darker and the rain began to fall on around 17 July. A rendezvous was planned for the whole army on a hillside near Dunstanburgh Castle, the dramatic medieval promontory fort with its striking double-towered gatehouse.[37] Already its ruinous walls were being plundered for their stone. A number of regiments arrived there to await the rest of the army, huddling against the gusting rain which frequently lashes this wild coast. By the time Cromwell travelled out the rainfall was so heavy that he cancelled the review. The army was ordered to concentrate at Chillingham Castle instead, a day's march inland. This was the home of William Grey, the first commander of parliament's Eastern Association Army in the early phases of the war against the late king. An undistinguished general, he had soon been replaced by the Earl of Manchester. It was the army which had forged Cromwell. Lord Grey seems to have been unimpressed with the republican settlement of 1649, but his opposition was passive and Cromwell was no doubt welcomed to the fireside.

On 19 July Cromwell held his delayed grand review and, perhaps enjoying a break in the weather, the men exhibited 'extraordinary cheerfulness and resolution.' The paraded before the general regiment by regiment and then formed into battalia, the formations which would be deployed for battle. This was a useful exercise therefore in ensuring all parts of the army knew their place in the lines when the enemy came out to meet them. Cromwell was pleased with his men and sent them on along the road to Berwick-upon-Tweed, England's northernmost bastion. Only Charles Fairfax's Regiment and Cromwell's own veteran unit made it as far as Berwick itself, the town being a compact settlement constrained by the immense Elizabethan defences which remain its principal feature today. Berwick sat on the north side of the Tweed, the Scottish side, and its markets customarily drew traders from both nations; the latest had been ominously quiet. Word held that all the men between Berwick and Edinburgh had gone, leaving only women behind with orders to hurriedly bake and brew for the army. Everything was sent to the capital; East Lothian was being stripped.

Meanwhile most of the English army remained on the south side of the Tweed occupying an arc of hamlets and villages in the vicinity of Tweedmouth. Eleven years before, Charles I had assembled his army in

---

36 The site of the inn, at 6 Main Street, is marked by a plaque.
37 The source says 'Distaburnes, over against the Ferne Islands,' which I am assuming to be Dunstanburgh as I have not found a closer alternative which fits the bill. The fact that the estates at Dunstanbrugh and Chillingham belonged to the same family makes the case stronger still. Cromwelliana, p. 84.

this same landscape to face the rising threat of the Scottish Covenanters. Cromwell's unhurried march had honed his army's coherence and sense of camaraderie, allowing word of their coming to play upon Scottish minds. To apply pressure a declaration had been sent into Scotland to justify the coming invasion and to play on the fractious politics in Edinburgh. It was a carefully prepared document, calling the Scots their brethren and acknowledging their discomfort at the execution of the late king. But Charles I's crimes and 'backsliding' were emphasised, and Hamilton's invasion was cited specifically as freeing England from any obligations relating to the Solemn League and Covenant which had helped to bring him down. But the cause of the current conflict ultimately boiled down to a single issue: the Scots themselves had brought England's army upon them 'by taking our grand Enemy into your bosoms.'[38] The problem was the King.

Cromwell understood his enemy. He had seen most of the senior Scottish commanders in battle already, fighting alongside them in common causes; he had seen Scottish armies in both victory and defeat. He also understood their politics, and the very precarious nature of Charles II's authority over men like Archibald Strachan, victor of Carbisdale. From his meetings in 1648, Cromwell knew something of the character and inclinations of the leading Covenanters, especially the Marquess of Argyll who had been so eager to accommodate him. If the politicians thought his invasion unlawful, his declaration would disabuse them. If the ministers preached that the common people should fear his soldiers, his army's discipline would prove them to be liars. If the army thought that God was on their side, he would teach them otherwise. And so Cromwell had planned his campaign as an efficient, targeted strike towards the Scots capital. If they tried to stand in his way by offering battle, he would break them in a decisive engagement. A defeat on their own territory would bring to terms those who were closer politically to himself than they were to their king.

He would also be travelling through a landscape he had carefully observed on his previous visit; he knew its roads, its resources and its risk points. Cromwell could feel confident.

---

38 Rushword, J. *A Declaration of the Army of England, Upon Their March Into Scotland*, (Newcastle: Husband and Field, 1650), p. 14.

4

Cromwell Comes

On Monday 22 July 1650, Oliver Cromwell addressed his troops to remind them why they were embarking on their expedition. He exhorted them 'not to doubt of the blessing of God upon their undertakings.'[1] Exactly where it was delivered cannot be known, but as the town itself could not accommodate the whole army perhaps the regiments were formed up in the fields within the thumb-shaped bend of the Tweed to the east of Tweedmouth village. From here, Berwick Bridge carried the main road over the river diagonally towards the north-east and into the town itself. Once a prosperous Scottish burgh, Berwick had been sacked by the English in 1296 and thereafter changed hands repeatedly until the future Richard III had secured it finally for England. By then its prosperity as a trading burgh had been crippled by war, and Berwick's role as a military staging post superseded all other issues. The Tudors had transformed it by replacing the formidable medieval walls with a circuit of immense modern artillery defences, with huge stone and earth bastions. It had been an extraordinary expensive effort, and the works had never yet been put to proper test nor ever would they. The Elizabethan walls contained a smaller area than the old walls, and the once formidable castle was rendered obsolete.[2] Berwick was an English salient on the traditionally Scottish side of the river, as it remains today, protecting the roadway which connected Edinburgh to London.

Since 1624 that road had been carried over the river by the fifteen-arched stone bridge which still spans the Tweed today. It was a remarkable achievement in its day, 355m long, costing £16,750, and taking thirteen years to construct. A little over five meters wide, it could accommodate the traffic of a vital trade route, or marching soldiers four abreast. After the cheers had died down, Cromwell's army advanced now towards it. A forlorn hope formed from Okey's Dragoons went first, mounted infantry with blue-painted bandoliers and modern firelock muskets. Behind them came a screen of cavalry, possibly the two companies of Okey's which had already

---

1 Whitelocke, p. 224.
2 The tantalising fragments that remain hint at its former importance. The Victorians destroyed most of the ruined castle when the built the railway station.

'ESSENTIAL AGONY'

15. Berwick Old Bridge, photographed from the north bank of the Tweed, was in fact relatively new when Cromwell's army marched across it in 1650.

been coverted into a horse regiment.[3] Behind this advanced screen came the vanguard comprised of the Lord General's Regiment of Horse, Cromwell's own Ironsides, and Thomas Pride's Regiment of Foot, those same soldiers who had purged parliament. Then followed the rest of the army, colours billowing at the head of every company and drums rattling. The baggage and artillery were interspersed between the foot regiments. What a glorious and terrible spectacle it must have been as they crossed the long stone bridge into the narrow confines of West Street before turning west onto the broader space of Mary Gate. Then the whole army was required to pass through the Scots Gate, where General Cope would arrive ninety-five years later with news of his defeat by the Highlanders at Prestonpans. Beyond the gate they passed the undefended suburbs and the ruins of the old castle to their left. As the soldiers left their homeland behind, cheers rose from the ranks. The invasion had begun.[4]

But after that much-anticipated beginning, what followed was something of an anti-climax. The army advanced only around four miles, passing Halidon Hill battlefield, before settling down again.[5] The short march may

---

3   Heavier equipped and designed purely for mounted action, whereas most of the regiment was trained for mobile infantry tactics. The whole regiment would be converted by the end of the year.
4   *Cromwelliana*, p. 85.
5   In 1333, Edward III inflicted massive casualties on a Scottish army attempting to recover Berwick.

16. Site of the camp at Mordington, Cromwell's first stop inside Scotland. Lord Mordington's lands around Berwick were confiscated as an exemption to Cromwell's Act of Grace in 1654, and the family found itself in financial difficulties thereafter.

have been to allow time for the supplies from Newcastle to make progress by sea, or else to accommodate the bottlenecks at Berwick which would have taken time for 17,000 men to clear. Hodgson and his company of Lambert's Foot were quartered in the grounds of Mordington Tower, where the general staff took up residence despite the fact that they found there only a couple of unimpressive servants. The house had been cleared out, with not even a cup left for the invaders.[6] The owner, Sir James Douglas, had found himself between a rock and a hard place in recent years: made a Lord of the Scottish Parliament by Charles I in 1641, a special commission had been sent by the Covenanters to force the reluctant lord to swear to the Covenant, which he was made to do in his own kirk in 1644. Worse still, as he also owned land on the south side of the Border, he had been pressured into making a financial contribution to the parliamentary forces in England too. Little wonder he was unwilling to host Cromwell.

Mordington Tower, which was later to be transformed into a charming Georgian mansion, was already connected to Dunbar by the grave in its ancient churchyard of Agnes Randolph, the famous Black Agnes who successfully defended Dunbar Castle against the English in 1338. Now its grounds, centred on the old church which no longer stands, were filled with Cromwellian soldiers cooking meat on their back-plates and making porridge in their helmets.[7] Another party had chanced upon a kirn (churn) filled with

---

6   Slingsby, p. 129; Cromwelliana, p. 85.
7   Cromwelliana, p. 85.

cream; the soldiers crowded around to scoop it out with their bowls and hats. Eventually what was left within the vessel was so hard to reach that one incautious soldier managed to get his head stuck within it. The reaction of his comrades can readily be imagined as he staggered about with the urn on his head, cream tricking down his coat. At the resulting commotion, the general officers came to the windows of the house. Fortunately, 'Oliver loved an innocent jest.'[8]

The men at Mordington appear, according to Hodgson at least, to have had the benefit of a tented encampment. Most of the tentage was due to rendezvous with the army at Dunbar along with most of its food supplies. It seems likely therefore that the army was again dispersed around local settlements, although in a heightened state of alert. The key was to control the ridge over which the main road ran, and so the English pickets will have stretched across to Lamberton in the east, where the small church was an important landmark on the Border. Today the line of the road from Berwick across to Lamberton and beyond can only be traced as a tree-lined field boundary, before being picked up by a minor road towards Ayton.[9] Forward pickets may well have advanced as far as that village too. Although no Scottish scouts had been sighted, and the open landscape ensured there could be no surprises, that night the distant horizon showed the signal beacons had been lit. The Scots were expecting them.

Cromwell was eager to land a knock-out blow, or else to allow the coalition of compromise to collapse in Edinburgh. All day Tuesday and Wednesday he waited, but apart from the capture and release of eight Scottish troopers nothing of moment took place. Accordingly, on Thursday 25 July, the English army advanced across Lamberton Moor towards Ayton, the first substantial Scottish settlement they had entered. Again the modern road deviates slightly from the original route which is now difficult to trace except as belts of woodland on the eastern side of the old churchyard.[10] The army crossed the Eye Water over the old bridge (downstream from its successor), passing the peel tower on the high ground to their right where the magnificent Ayton Castle now stands. It may be Ayton village which is meant my Whitelocke's reference to 'a great town of Scotland' – a more than generous description – of which 'only two poor women' remained from the population.[11]

The line of march was now more or less straight, and the route can be traced easily once it has crossed to the north side of the modern A1 carriageway. It runs as a tarmac service road, not accessible to vehicles, as far as Cairncross farm, beyond which it can be driven as a straight road to the Ale Water at Press Castle. Cromwell's army then followed up onto Coldingham Moor, where the exposed and barely drained landscape meant it was often

---

8   Slingsby, p. 129-30.
9   The route out of Berwick follows the A1 as far as New East Farm, then heads along the ridge as a boundary line. The alignment of buildings above Lamberton church reveal the original axis of the original road. For more information, begin with Graham, A. 'Archaeology on a Great Post Road', *Proceedings of the Society of the Antiquaries of Scotland*, 96 (Edinburgh: Society of the Antiquaries of Scotland, 1963), p. 318-47.
10 The modern road runs to the western side of the churchyard and over a later bridge.
11 Whitelocke, p. 224.

17. The old road from Ayton, heading up towards Coldingham Moor. With fewer trees and enclosures, this was an open landscape, with visibility extremely changeable according to the weather conditions.

a difficult stretch of road for travellers. It was bleak and uninspiring terrain, with 'neither sheep, beast nor horse' in view.[12] As mentioned previously, it is unlikely that Cromwell found either the time or the need to distract himself with a siege of the nearby priory. After the bleak crossing of the moorland, today passing through a forest of wind turbines, the road begins to wind as it descends towards Old Cambus and the little church of St Helen's by the coast to the right. The army was now entering the most dangerous stage of the day's 20 mile journey, approaching a natural defensive line which it was essential the soldiers crossed and secured.

The Pass of Pease, an extremely steep-sided wooded gorge, provided a major obstacle to traffic until a high bridge was constructed across it in the late eighteenth century. The gorge is shaped like an upturned two-pronged fork, cutting inland southwards from the beach at Pease Bay before splitting into two branches to carry the Pease Burn and the Herriot Water. The exact route of the seventeenth century road as it descended the into the deep ravine is long forgotten, but it is likely there were a number of zig-zag paths which made their way down one face and back up the other; different paths being cut as others become too eroded by traffic and by weather. The best crossing place was immediately beside the bay, fording the burn at its foot, but one single route could not take the whole army. There was at least a

---

12 The description comes from Sir William Brereton, who travelled this way in 1636. Brereton, W, T*ravels in Holland, The United Provinces, England, Scotland, and Ireland*, (Manchester: Chetham Society, 1844), p. 96.

'ESSENTIAL AGONY'

19. Cockburnspath Tower, now an isolated ruin beside an overgrown trackway. Probably already abandoned as a residence by 1650, the remains of substantial outbuildings can still be traced and it seems likely that a large picket was placed here on 25 July.

bridge across the Herriot Water, the western arm of the fork, once dominated by the gunloops of Cockburnspath Tower which stands above it. No attempt had been made by the Scots to defend the Pass or garrison the small castle, beyond which lay the market village of Cockburnspath.

Reconstructing the activity of Cromwell's army in this area on the late afternoon of 25 July is not straightforward as the landscape is complex and unsuitable for the passage of large armies. Standing in the gorge today it seems impossible that 17,500 men, of whom 3,500 were mounted on war horses, supported by their waggons and baggage, could have worked their way down across the ravine. The burn itself, although it will have been swollen with rain, was no real obstacle but the sides of the gorge certainly were. Local tradition alludes to Cromwellian soldiers occupying St Helen's at Old Cambus, which was being phased out of service at this time after the streamlining of local congregations, which could only really mean on the night of 25 July although this is unlikely to have been more than a rearguard picket.[13] Another tradition places soldiers at Cockburnspath Tower, which as a strong point and bridge crossing seems extremely plausible. The bridge which led to the castle gained itself a new name from this day on, Cromwell's Bridge, and although no trace of it can be discerned with confidence today its approximate position is indicated by the arrangement of the castle ruins along with the evidence of antiquarians. A later single-

---

13 Rankin, W. *St Helen's Church, Old Cambus*, (Scottish Church History Society, 1938).

19. "Sparrow Castle" in Cockburnspath, where Cromwell is likely to have spent the night of 25 July. The adjacent church, sited on a raised platform, would probably also have housed troops.

arched bridge, confusingly known as Old Tower Bridge, can still be found and crossed. Cockburnspath Tower's ruins are substantial and of interest, but there has been a significant masonry collapse in recent years which reveals their fragility.

Cromwell himself meanwhile is said to have stayed in the marvellously curious building which is known as Sparrow Castle.[14] Sited adjacent to the churchyard and accessed by a lane from the market square of Cockburnspath village, the core of the building dates back to the middle of the sixteenth century and was clearly the most substantial structure in the settlement. It appears to have been owned by the Nicholsons, which therefore matches positive evidence provided in the *Large Relation of the Fight at Leith*.[15] There is also a further tradition placing Cromwell in the nearby village of Oldhamstocks, although this would have required the army to have taken a further sweeping detour to the south at the end of an already long twenty-mile march. Although the village had once stood on an important roadway, the Cromwell Hall which once stood at its eastern end was a wayside inn but a connection to 1650 seems unlikely.[16] Sparrow

---

14 Less romantic commentaries call it Cockburnspath House.
15 Original Memoirs, p. 206.
16 The old inn has gone but the new house on its site carries on the name, and across the road there are Cromwell Cottages. It has been suggested to the author that the name is simply an innocent corruption of other words which have grown the association with the Dunbar campaign subsequently.

Castle is a far more plausible location for the general on the night of 25 July, which saw most of his men sleeping in the open in the fields between the village and the Tower Dean, with pickets securing the bridge and fords to the rear and perhaps reaching back as far as Old Cambus. It seems certain that Cromwell will also have sent ahead a forward picket to secure the crossing point of the next ravine, the equally steep-sided Dunglass Burn immediately to the west.

The crossing at Dunglass was easier than at Pease as there already existed a stone bridge. It still stands, with later modifications, but it is barely known about as it is some distance downstream from its several successors. All the later bridges stand side by side, close to the large estate which contains the important collegiate church. In 1650 then shattered remains of Dunglass Castle stood close behind it, rendered useless by a massive magazine explosion in 1640. On the high bluff above squats a substantial Tudor earthwork, dug by English soldiers almost a hundred years before Cromwell's army arrived in the vicinity. However, the original Dunglass Bridge is far closer to the shore than those which are more readily discerned today. It was a narrow crossing but an important one, and although the bottleneck it created for the English army would certainly have slowed the advance there were only eight miles to march that day. From Dunglass the road crossed open fertile countryside straight to the harbour town of Dunbar and the promise of tents and supplies.

Cromwell's forward scouts, perhaps the riders of Okey's Dragoons, approached the burgh of Dunbar through a landscape 'replenished with

20. Dunglass Old Bridge, carrying the road across a ravine. Considerably closer to the sea than its successors south of the modern A1, the bridge is overgrown and the stonework in poor shape. The photograph looks west along the line of march.

corn and grain of all sorts.'[17] The cereals, not yet ready for harvest, were nourished by the tangle of seaweeds left upon the shore by the tides, which the local farmers collected and up for their fields. The road ran parallel to the coast, and on its south side the ground sloped upwards in graceful folds. In the distance loomed the barren barrier of the Lammermuir Hills which, uncrossed by any significant roadway, fortify the whole southern perimeter of East Lothian. As they led the army to Dunbar the riders will have gazed up on the mass of Doon Hill to their left, lunging sharply upwards from an area of rising ground which overlooked the town. Its northern face, looking out towards the North Sea, was cloaked in gorse; at the summit, the low rings of an ancient hillfort sat at around 177m (580ft) above the level of Dunbar harbour. Beneath the hill were the farms of Meikle Pinkerton, sitting a top a steep-fronted hump of ground, and Little Pinkerton further to the west, also sitting on a rise. The road however kept to the lower ground, although the land lifted to either side of it as it bent its way towards the town.[18]

The road passed a small cottage, a lowly place of no significance which probably consisted only of a single dark smoky room beneath a low roof of turf or thatch, lit only by narrow windows with crude shutters.[19] One Cromwellian account describes it as a 'poor house',[20] but there does not seem to be any corroborating evidence to suggest that he meant a charitable establishment and the comment is likely just a comment on its humble appearance and lack of 'household stuffe.'[21] The house probably stood on the north side of the road, so to the right of the passing soldiers, close to where a pyramid-roofed gate lodge which still stands was later erected. Past the cottage the road forded the Brox Burn, a narrow stream which ran at the bottom of a steep-sided ravine stretching all the way back to the village of Spott in the shadow of Doon Hill.[22] It seems likely that given the status of the road which it carried, the ford was at least tolerably maintained and may have had a paved base. On the right were the thorn hedges and enclosures of Broxmouth House, belonging then to William Ker, Earl of Roxburghe, who had succeeded his maternal grandfather that January. Roxburghe had to change his name from Drummond to Ker in order to inherit the title and estates, including both Broxmouth and the principal seat at Floors Castle near Kelso. He was a member of the Committee of Estates, and had surely removed most of the portable wealth out of Broxmouth ahead of the invasion.

Passing Broxmouth to their right and, once the road had straightened out a little, the farm of Newtonlees to the left, Cromwell's column now marched

---

17 Gardiner, *Letters and Papers*, p. 130.
18 It is this fairly unremarkable feature of the landscape which is referred to by some of the combatants at the battle as a 'pass'.
19 Gardiner, *Letters and Papers*, p. 140; Pugh, *Swords Loaves and Fishes*, p. 71-72.
20 Carte, *Original Letters*, p. 382. Reese suggests the cottage was sited at the Brand's Mill ford but it seems clear that it was on the eastern side of the burn and a roadside location makes greater sense. Reid, Grainger, Firth appear to be in agreement with me on this, and the house can be identified on Fisher's plan.
21 Gardiner, *Letters and Papers*, p. 140.
22 The Brox Burn is generally referred to by that name only in its lower course, as it approaches Broxmouth, but as the Spott Burn in its upper section nearer the village of Spott. To make it clear that I am referring to the same burn throughout, I will use Brox Burn throughout.

'ESSENTIAL AGONY'

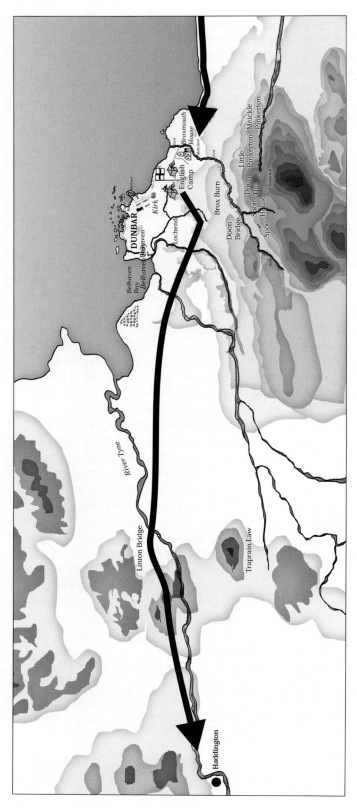

Map 2 Cromwell's army reaches Dunbar for the first time.

straight towards the prominent knoll atop which stood the parish church of Dunbar. The fabric of the former collegiate church of the Earls of Dunbar was of venerable pedigree but age had also given it an asymmetry despite its cruciform plan which undermined the overall charm. The most striking feature was its squat tower, enhanced by four corner turrets, which stood at the west end.[23] Attempts to remodel the church in the eighteenth century did little to improve the overall aesthetic, although a belfry was added to increase the impressiveness of the tower, and between 1819-21 the building was completely replaced. The new design does however evoke some elements of the original church: the corner turrets on the tower are the most obvious, whilst the triangular shaping on the side walls echoes the absent form of the lost transepts. The replacement church is loftier than its predecessor, but even the original church would have been an easily discernible landmark across the coastal plain thanks to its elevated position. A short distance over open ground beyond it, the road passed the tumbled remnants of the old *maison dieu* and became the town main thoroughfare.[24]

But as Cromwell's soldiers were marshalled off the road into the town's common grazing ground south of the church, it would not have been the church which occupied their interest. Rather, anxious eyes were scanning the heaving grey waters in search of their supply fleet. The wind had risen, bringing intermittent rain and brooding skies, and 'the soldiers have not had any tents' to give a modicum of comfort over the past few days.[25] But, as the newssheets had forewarned the previous day, Captain Cold and Captain Hunger were the enemies which awaiting Cromwell in Dunbar. The poor weather had prevented his supply ships from keeping to schedule. The army was already five days into the provisions of biscuit and cheese with which it marched, which was probably only intended to provide a week's worth of issue.[26] At Dunbar, as Cromwell himself admitted, there was only 'some small pittance' delivered by what little shipping had got through, and no tents.[27]

As the army prepared for a night on the damp grass beneath a brooding sky, parties will have advanced into Dunbar and secured the wider area beyond it. The town's broad high street, centred on the white-rendered hexagonal tower of its tolbooth, presented the same a strangely quiet spectacle the soldiers had experienced at Ayton but on a larger scale. There was no industrious bustle around the mercat cross at the head of the West Port; no fishermen hauling nets on the quayside. The warehouses and smokeries of

---

23 Fisher's battle plan shows the tower at the east end and without turrets, but then he was not an eyewitness and his intention was simply to show a church on a knoll.
24 The ruins of the hospital were cleared in the 18th century, although nothing appears to be known of their extent or appearance. There was once a fairly considerable range of monastic buildings in Dunbar, including a Carmelite convent and a friary of which at least the church tower was still standing on the edge of town when Cromwell arrived. It was later converted into a dovecot, and today it can still be found in carpark of a supermarket. All had of course closed during the Reformation.
25 *Cromwelliana*, p. 85.
26 Firth, C. *Cromwell's Army: a History of the English Soldier during the Civil Wars, the Commonwealth and the Protectorate*, (London: Greenhill, 1992), p. 222-3.
27 Letter from Cromwell to the Lord President of the Council of State, 30 July 1650; Carlyle, p. 366.

'ESSENTIAL AGONY'

21. Dunbar from the old harbour, showing the church on its raised mound to the east of the town and the looming presence of Doon Hill to the south.

the fish-packing industry were silent and dark, the valuable salts and coals gone. In an ordinary year, Dunbar would be just a few weeks away from being the epicentre of the massive herring drove which contributed so much to its economy: all manner of citizens would set up in partnerships to put small boats out for the bounty, literally thousands of craft filling the Firth, bringing more incomers to the town even than Cromwell.[28] But there was no commercially-minded welcome for the soldiers: 'we found not sheets in any house, and those beds that were left were most nasty and greazie,' one soldier complained. What bedding they could find was filled with 'lops and covenanters,' the army's slang for fleas and lice.[29] For those civilians who had remained behind it must have been an uncomfortable experience receiving the enemy, but the soldiers' privations were still mild and had not yet driven them to excesses.

We do not know for sure where Cromwell slept on the night of Friday 26 July, but it seems reasonable to assume he rested at Broxmouth House and that his army encamped roughly where it would do so again in a few weeks' time. Despite his frustration at the supply failure, Cromwell seems to have been in little doubt that he should press on immediately. Morale was still good amongst the rank and file, and given the limited provisions available there was little to be gained from waiting around in Dunbar and eating up

---

[28] Martine, J. *Reminiscences and Notices of Ten Parishes of the County of Haddington*, (Haddington: Sinclair, 1894), p. 120.
[29] Pugh, *Swords Loaves and Fishes*, p. 71.

what remained and simply watching for the ships. Accordingly, on Saturday 27 July the army moved out west. There were two roads available: through Dunbar itself, turning down the West Port and on to Belhaven along the coast; or the by-pass road which avoided the choke-point of the town as identified in John Adair's map. As this road was easily accessible from the presumed location of the camp it seems a the most likely, although it would have denied most of the soldiers a view of the dramatic ruins of Dunbar Castle, slighted in the previous century, perched on a rock promontory west of the narrow-mouthed harbour.

The two possible routeways met near Beltonford, where the soldiers splashed through the shallow burn of the Biel Water before heading straight across a flat open landscape towards Linton Bridge. This crossing point over the Tyne was an important and unavoidable bottleneck. A little downstream were picturesque falls of Linton Rocks, but immediately beside the high stone bridge the river was usually fordable. In 1547 the Duke of Somerset had crossed here with an army very close in size to that of Cromwell.[30] An eyewitness describes the cavalry and artillery crossing through the river whilst the infantry used the bridge.[31] Cromwell's army may have done exactly the same, eager to get the army across the obstacle quickly and efficiently, before turning sharply to the left and following the road as it climbed the rising ground towards Pencraig Brae. Perhaps the soldiers remarked on the ancient standing stone which they passed on their right, or observed the lines of ramparts which crowned the immense hulk of Traprain Law which dominate the view of the countryside to the south.[32]

Descending the western shoulder of the brae, the army reached the county town of Haddington. Roughly cruciform, the east end of the town was marked by a bridge over the Tyne which led to the ruins of the abbey. On the south side of the town, bounded on two sides by the turn of the river, stood St Mary's church. The siege of 1548 had left this grand church severely battered and only partly roofed, as indeed it remained until relatively recently. Some remnants of the earthen bastions which had so long defied the Franco-Scottish besiegers may have lingered on the edge of the town, which must have been rebuilt virtually from scratch in the aftermath of the siege. Haddington was only half a day's march from Dunbar but Cromwell decided to pause. It was the largest town in the county and it the most likely place to secure any supplies which had not been carried away by the Scots. It was also convenient base to await word of the Scots, the army now being sufficiently deep into the country as to provoke most enemies to engage.

The location of the camp is unknown but a site immediately west of the town, bounded by the road on the south and a wooded burn to the west was chosen by Sir John Cope's little army in 1745. There were springs here

---

30 Patten, 'Expedition to Scotland', in Pollard, A. (ed) *Tudor Tracts 1532-1588*, (New York: E P Dutton, 1903) p. 53ff.
31 The structure which stands today is the same as the crossed by Cromwell, but its carriageway has been widened.
32 Traprain Law had not yet been mutilated by quarrying. A rest stop on Pencraig Brae, beside the old A1 road, gives a chance to enjoy the views which had greeted Somerset, Cromwell and Sir John Cope in their turn across three centuries.

too, providing fresh water for the soldiers ahead of their final press towards the enemy. The same advantages of this location may have been apparent to Cromwell, although his numbers were so considerably larger that the camp likely covered both sides of the road and dominated the town. Early the following morning the drums beat with urgency. Cromwell's scouts had reported movement ahead, and it seemed the Scots 'meant to meet us at Gladsmoor,' a plateau of moorland between Haddington and Tranent which overlooked the coastal plan below.[33] It was Sunday, the Lord's Day, and Cromwell led his army west to seek the battle which would determine his campaign.

The Scots army, meanwhile, had been steadily growing around the capital as the national levies concentrated. There was much work for the soldiers, digging 'a running trench between the Abbey [Holyrood] and Leith.'[34] Leslie's defensive preparations were extensive. The left flank of the army rested on the strong rocky outcrop of Calton Hill, which then lay outside the city's defensive walls and is now topped by the famous memorials to Admiral Nelson and the fallen of the Napoleonic Wars. The entrenchments ran continuously until they reached Leith to the north, presumably aligned on the road between the capital and its port which is still known today as the Leith Walk. That line is almost a mile and a half in length, matching the estimated length of Leslie's line at Dunbar a few weeks later and so eminently defensible with the anticipated manpower the general would have available. Cromwell's slow pace through Northumberland and his conservative movements after crossing the Border gave Leslie much needed time to complete these works.

Anchoring the army's northern flank were the urgently renovated fortifications at Leith. The burgh council was laying out large sums for the work and as Cromwell lay at Mordington the Edinburgh merchant Adam Green was authorised to purchase 'all the spades and shovels he can get.'[35] What remained of the sixteenth century French fortress was a mere shadow of the strength it once possessed, despite the efforts to throw fresh earth onto its slumping ramparts and plug up the gaps. Previous works during the civil wars had already improved the defensibility of the port, and in the north-east corner there was a stone fort on the waterside which was repaired in the anxious summer of 1649.[36] The gun emplacements at Leith were able to cover the approaches to Leslie's trenches with flanking fire.

At the opposite end of Leslie's line was Edinburgh itself, crowned with its mighty castle. The entrenchments reached to the walled park at the royal palace of Holyroodhouse, overlooked by Calton Hill to the north on which Leslie emplaced some of his artillery, and Arthur's Seat to the south where an outpost was also installed. Behind these forward positions was the medieval city, protected on the north by the Nor Loch and girded on

---

33 Letter from Cromwell to the Lord President of the Council of State, 30 July 1650; Carlyle, p. 366.
34 Row, W. *Life of Mr Robert Blair, Minister of St Andrews*, (Edinburgh: Woodrow Society, 1848), p. 262.
35 Wood, *Records*, p. 230.
36 Wood, *Records*, p. 204. Part of the foundations of this work have been exposed between new apartment buildings off Tower Street.

all other sides by the Flodden and Telfer walls. The walls could no longer contain the growth of the city, and it was necessary for the council to order the demolition of properties; timber was sourced for scaffolding to reinforce the walls themselves and create firing platforms. As late as the 24 July the burgh council was issuing orders for gates in the stone walls to be blocked up at Heriot's Hospital and the West Port.[37] An earthwork was cast around the windmill which stood beyond the walls on the southside, protecting the approaches to both the Potterrow and Bristo ports.[38] At Potterrow itself, two small cannon were mounted and the porter's house was converted into a firing platform; the gardener's house at Heriot's Hospital prepared to mount a cannon. A report to the council required twelve cannon in total for the walls, although only six were available event as late as 3 August. The rest were requested from the castle, whilst the General of Artillery, James Wemyss, was also petitioned to supply 'the number of twenty shot at least to every piece,' as well as the necessary sponges and tools.

Edinburgh's council records give a sense of strenuous activity as the city prepared to resist the enemy, but the dates of the instructions are informative: it was all happening too late and too slowly. Orders for breaking down houses beyond the walls and for placing cannon on the defences were still being issued three weeks into August. The simple reality was that neither Edinburgh nor Leith were ready by the end of July to withstand a siege. They were only saved by the presence of the main field army, although that salvation came at the cost of having to bear the strains of supplying so many mouths. Bakers were forbidden to supply anyone else until the army's requirements were met. Commanded parties of musketeers visited properties beyond the walls to secure all private horses for the service of the train, with only ministers' horses exempted. Servants laboured at the fortifications whilst citizens manned the walls day and night 'without intermission.'[39] Others collected their valuables and left the city.

David Leslie, with the Earl of Leven at his side to advise, had few strategic options in the first week of the invasion. The regiments were still marching and even as late as 16 August the Earl of Loudoun was writing to hasten down the forces from the north.[40] It seems the king may have recommended gathering them as a reserve force at Stirling, but this was overruled, politely enough, but without any effort to explain the reasoning. That is understandable, as it was likely the fear of the king being able to husband a force of his own behind the lines whilst the Covenanters were distracted blunting Cromwell's thrust. A deeper defensive deployment would have reduced the burden of supply and, as hindsight suggests, might have reduced the impact of an initial defeat.[41] The desire to build as large an army as possible to overawe Cromwell was also an understandable one, however.

---

37 Wood, *Records*, p. 250.
38 Wood, *Records*, p. 249. It appears to have been at what is now George Square, part of the University of Edinburgh.
39 Wood, *Records*, p. 258.
40 Letter from Loudoun to Argyll, 16 August 1650; *Ancrum Correspondence*, p. 289.
41 Especially as, in the event, Leslie's number at Dunbar had brought him no advantage.

'ESSENTIAL AGONY'

22. Gladsmuir, where Cromwell's scouts suggested the Scots army might be willing to oppose him. An old prophecy of Thomas the Rhymer suggested a great battle would one day be fought here, but the English found the moor empty. This view looks west across the coastal plain towards Prestonpans.

The army of the Commonwealth moved rapidly west from Haddington in the hopes of reaching Gladsmuir before the Scots, giving Cromwell the chance to deploy his forces to advantage. The soldiers marched with that growing knot in their stomach as anticipation built for a decisive confrontation. But they were to be disappointed: the Scottish cavalry pickets which had triggered the excitement melted away immediately. Frustrated, Cromwell chose to press on towards the Scots capital and offer Leslie a direct challenge. Lambert was sent ahead with Colonel Edward Whalley and fourteen-hundred horse towards Musselburgh. The general himself followed at the head of the infantry. The elusive Scots horse reappeared before him, no doubt assessing the strength of the English column and reminding its soldiers that their presence was not in fact unopposed. But no sooner had they appeared they vanished again. The army halted at Musselburgh, where an old stone bridge carried the road to Edinburgh over the River Esk. Lambert's Regiment of Foot was billeted at Stoneyhill on the western side of the river, where its walls and ditches made for an appropriate forward bastion. The rest of the army camped tightly, on high alert. Like everywhere else, Musselburgh had been emptied of all but 'a very few women and children.'[42] The harbour here was too small to facilitate any substantial resupply, so the pressure for a decisive engagement remained.

On Monday 29 July, Oliver Cromwell led his forces west from Musselburgh. Lambert's reconnaissance the previous day had already identified that Leslie's army lay entrenched, and the task now was to survey the defences in detail and find a way to draw the Scots out from behind them. Following the main

---

42 Whitelocke, p. 225.

CROMWELL COMES

road brought Cromwell to Jock's Lodge, a where a change house named after a local shepherd stood to service travellers, and most of the army will therefore have filed off to the north to face the Scots trenches. The latter were anchored on Calton Hill, were fresh earthworks enhanced the strength of the natural outcrop. At its foot to the south, the walled enclosures in the King's Park around the renaissance palace of Holyroodhouse, which had not yet been renovated to the splendid symmetry of Charles II's future redesign. Overlooking this, an outpost at St Anthony's Chapel perched on the rocky crags on the forward slopes of Arthur's Seat. The latter would be able to fire on the flanks of any move against the park enclosures or Calton Hill, and so it was at this exposed end of the Scottish line that Cromwell decided to test them.

A detachment was sent to dislodge the St Anthony's picket, and puffs of musket smoke marked the opening shots of the campaign now that the two armies were at last in direct contact. The sounds of skirmishing were flattened by the rain which had now begun again, adding additional hazards to the task of scrambling towards the gothic chapel, leather shoes struggling for purchase on the jagged rocks above the small grey loch below. The pathway to the chapel snaked around beneath it, exposing the attackers to fire from above. The defenders made only a light fight of it however, exposed as they were on the extreme end of the line and with the fortifications of the city beyond them to fall back to. But when the English moved to mount two small cannon at the chapel, the threat they posed to the redoubt on Calton Hill was

23. The Palace of Holyroodhouse and Arthur's Seat beyond, with the ruin of St Anthony's Chapel on the lower crags. The view is taken from Calton Hill, site of another Scottish outpost.

too great to ignore. As the artillery crews struggled up the steep pathway, Leslie detached a force from Campbell of Lawers' Regiment to dislodge the Cromwellians in their turn. They were initially successful, sending the gun teams scrambling down whence they had come, but a further return threat obliged Campbell to withdraw the Scots outpost once again.

Meanwhile David Leslie was distracted by events on his opposite flank: four English warships were adding the deep thump of cannon-fire to the increasingly dark and rainy day.[43] A boom across the river mouth and the seaward bastions prevented the attack developing into anything more than a long-range bombardment, but it was a statement of English control of the seas. In fact, if Cromwell wanted the Scots to advance beyond their trenches then the warships were a disincentive: the Scots flank would be exposed to naval fire if they moved out, just as it had at Pinkie in 1547. Then came the most unexpected development of all: the arrival of the king.

Charles II appeared amongst his army most 'unexpectedlie,' making his first direct contact with the main body of his army.[44] To some of the soldiers, at this critical moment with the enemy finally in sight and the sounds of the guns building the tension in their bellies, the sight of the king amongst his people was stirring and inspiring. Certainly, he seems to have galvanized the army, and the royal visit may well have been the trigger for the coming burst of aggression. Part of this was the simple appeal of the king's presence; the rest was the political embarrassment that his positive reception had caused for the Kirk Party and their general. Any victory to be won must be there's not the king's; the *army* must be there's and not the king's. As the rain intensified, the young and charismatic monarch was bustled off to Lord Balmerino's house.[45] No doubt some hard questions were asked of his minders.

Meanwhile, Cromwell was facing an unexpected difficulty in his rear: 500 citizens had returned to Musselburgh after hiding out in the coal-pits which dotted the landscape around this part of the county. They barricaded the main street in the hope of trapping the expected fugitives from Cromwell's failed assault on Leslie's lines. Instead they found themselves facing a charge of heavy horse, as Major Hezekiah Haines of Fleetwood's Regiment stormed over the flimsy barricade, slaying thirty and wounding many more as the resistance quickly collapsed. Combined with reports that a party based out of Hume Castle in the Borders was menacing the road to Berwick, the hostility of the population to the rear had the potential to grow into a serious concern. For now, the rainfall was so heavy that Cromwell abandoned any further operations and withdrew slightly to a village named by Hodgson as 'Lichnagarie' (Lang-Niddery), by which he meant Niddrie near Craigmillar.[46] Thus ended a busy, dramatic and unsettling day, the inconclusive prelude to the coming crisis.

---

43 'Large Relation', in *Original Memoirs*, p. 210.
44 Wood, *Records*, p. 252.
45 Long since demolished, the site of the house lies in the tangle of back streets between Constitution Street and the Shore.
46 Not to be confused with Longniddry near Prestonpans. *Original Memoirs*, p. 132.

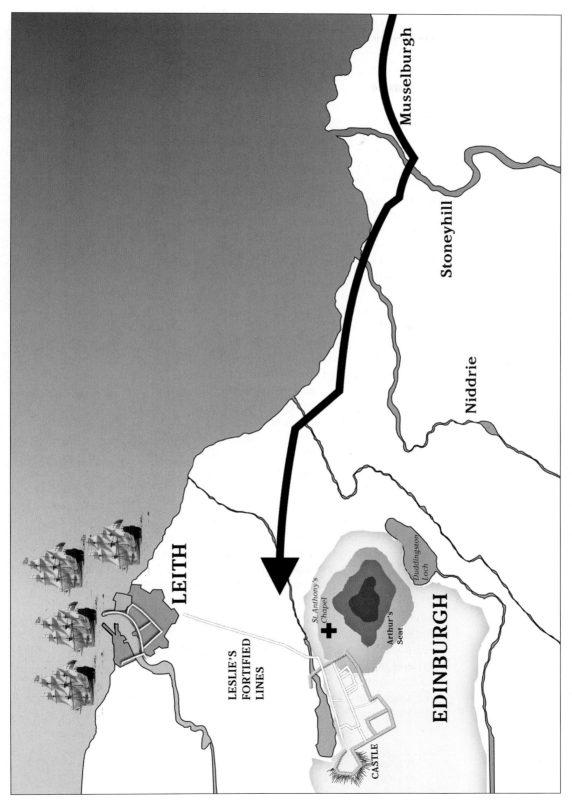

Map 3. Cromwell's initial advance towards Edinburgh from the east.

5

Retreat

The Cromwellian army spent the night of Monday 29 July in the open once again without canvas, and this time they were exposed to 'a most tempestuous night.'¹ So foul was the weather that the 'arms of the soldiers were almost spoiled and made at present unserviceable.' Powder and match were soaked, and now the men were cold and wet as well as hungry. The ground was slick with rain and would soon turn to mud as thousands of hooves and feet began to stir. Cromwell himself called it 'so sore a day and night of rain as I have seldom seen.'² In only one way was the weather a positive issue: it gave the general a reason to disengage from Leslie's defences. Launching a frontal assault could have been immensely costly, and even if the lines were breached there might well be further obstacles beyond. Clonmel will not have been far from Cromwell's mind. He simply could not afford to suffer high casualties with so small an army. Whitelocke's report certainly suggests it was only the rain which prevented the attempt.³ By 11am on Tuesday 30 July the English army was marching back to Musselburgh.

Cromwell was at pains to report that the army remained in good spirits despite these setbacks, but Hodgson remembers that the vanguard was so eager to reach Musselburgh that they drew too far ahead and split the army. Leslie seized the opportunity, returning to the more characteristically aggressive attitude which might be expected of a seasoned cavalryman. Two 'great bodies of horse' suddenly surged out of the Leith and Edinburgh. Near Niddrie, Captain Evanson of Whalley's Horse commanded a rearguard of just two hundred troopers; the Scottish charge overwhelmed them in moments. Cromwell's Regiment of Horse counter-attacked but were then driven back in turn as more Scottish cavalry arrived for the fray. Lambert turned his own regiment and another four troops of Whalley's into the action. The major-general charged characteristically at the head of his men, but it took three charges to finally blunt the Scots attack. Lambert's reward was a wound to the thigh and a lance-point in the upper arm, whilst his horse was shot in the head and neck as pistols burst at close range amidst what Cromwell

---
1   *Original Memoirs*, p. 132.
2   Letter from Cromwell to the Lord President of the Council of State, 30 July 1650; p. 366.
3   Whitelocke, p. 226.

called 'the grabble'.⁴ The Scots managed to get their hands on the wounded Lambert, but Hacker's Regiment was now engaged and Lieutenant Empson managed to cut his way through as the Scottish horse finally broke. Lambert was recovered, much mauled, to the great relief of Cromwell as his loss would have been serious indeed.

The Scots were pursued back to their lines, but although Cromwell was able to hail the performance of his troopers he confessed that it had been 'gallant and hot dispute.'⁵ Empson was promoted to captain for his bravery in rescuing Lambert. The Scots horse, although eventually beaten, had shown itself to be aggressive and competent, the lance proving its worth in disrupting Cromwell's ironsides during the free-flowing melee. Despite the gloss, this first serious engagement of the campaign was a salutary lesson: the stillness of the Scottish army was no indication of an unwillingness to fight. The army reached Musselburgh with no further incident, one more garrisoning Stoneyhill as a forward bastion. The army was, according to Cromwell, 'tired and wearied for want of sleep, and so dirty by reason of the wetness of the weather.'⁶ But this night would be no easier than the last.

Clearly the performance of the Scots cavalry had been sufficiently encouraging to Leslie, as he committed to an even bolder attempt in the darkness of the early morning.⁷ At around 3am on the morning of Wednesday 31 July, fifteen troops of Scottish horse advanced on Musselburgh with the owner of Stoneyhill house as their guide. They almost achieved surprise, being close enough to exchange words with the outguards of Fleetwood's Horse in an attempt to deceive them. But the suspicious pickets opened fire and the Scots launched their charge. This was a godly charge, 800-1500 troopers led by Major-General Robert Montgomerie and Colonel Strachan of Carbisdale fame, and it accordingly smashed through Fleetwood's hurriedly formed regiment. Triumphant, the Scots rode on through to Stoneyhill where, as they reached the warren park, they were checked by a massive musket volley.⁸ Hodgson describes the position at Stoneyhill as being protected by walls and ditches, and so the men of Lambert's Foot were protected from the cavalry as they split the night sky with their volley, firing their muskets within pistol range. Dozens of troopers were blown out of the saddle. Nevertheless, parts of the Scottish force penetrated into the town of Musselburgh itself.

With surprise and momentum gone, the Scots attack had stalled; when Lilburne's Regiment threw its weight forward, and with the whole English army now alerted, it was time to go. Worse, Cromwell's foot regiments had brought up their regimental guns, and a drake brought down three horses and tore off the leg of a Scots corporal, all with a single ball. As the Scots abandoned the attack and retreated, they found themselves pursued hard;

---

4 Carlyle, p. 367.
5 Carlyle, p. 367.
6 Carlyle, p. 367.
7 The English interpretation was that they tried again in order to redeem themselves for having been beaten.
8 Original Memoirs, p. 135-6. Later in the century, Slezer would draw a view of Musselburgh from Stoneyhill, and although it does not show the house as it is behind the sitter, it does show a foreground of rabbits atop a mound which may well be warren Hodgson refers to.

'ESSENTIAL AGONY'

24. The old centre of Musselburgh, centred on the Tolbooth. This may have been the area the townsfolk attempted to hold against the returning Cromwellians.

Montgomerie was believed to be slain in the confusion. Okey's Dragoons had mounted up and joined the action, able to intercept fleeing Scots on the road as they had seemingly been posted as an outlying picket closer to Edinburgh than Musselburgh. Around a hundred prisoners were taken, and Cromwell returned the Scots dead to Edinburgh in waggons to parade their losses. The general's despatches do not refer to his own losses, but Hodgson talks of eighteen or twenty wounded. Whitelocke records a higher figure of six killed and forty wounded. On neither side were the losses high, and again Cromwell could claim to have won the engagement – he called it 'a sweet beginning' – but it was another disrupted night which showed the Scots were controlling the flow of events. Hamilton, the owner of Stoneyhill and guide to the Scots attack, lay dead beside his home.

Following this burst of dramatic energy, aspects of which had given encouragement to both armies, Cromwell maintained his position at Musselburgh in the hope of receiving supplies there. He also wrote to the General Assembly of the Kirk of Scotland in scathing terms: 'your own guilt is too much for you to bear; bring not therefore upon yourselves the blood of innocent men.' There followed his famous appeal, aimed at separating the church from the king. 'I beseech you in the bowels of Christ,' he said, 'think it possible you may be mistaken.'[9] The letter was well-timed, as the Scots command was under increasing internal pressure.

Archibald Johnston of Wariston, author of the National Covenant, now headed a new committee of war to advise General Leslie, bringing politics into the military strategy just as King Charles had warned them not to. He

---

9   Letter from Cromwell to the General Assembly, 3 August 1650; Carlyle, p. 369-70.

Plate A

A1 Scots Officer, A2 English Officer.
(Illustration by Alan Turton © Helion & Company)
See Colour Plate Commentaries for further information.

Plate B

B1 Scottish Musketeer, B2 English Musketeer.
(Illustration by Alan Turton © Helion & Company)
See Colour Plate Commentaries for further information.

Plate C

C1 Scottish Pikeman, C2 English Pikeman.
(Illustration by Alan Turton © Helion & Company)
See Colour Plate Commentaries for further information.

D1 English Trooper, D2 Scots Lancer.
(Illustration by Alan Turton © Helion & Company)
See Colour Plate Commentaries for further information.

E1 & E2, Engager Foot Regiments, E3, Royalist Colour.
(Illustration by Dr Lesley Prince © Helion & Company)
See Colour Plate Commentaries for further information.

Plate F: English Army Colours

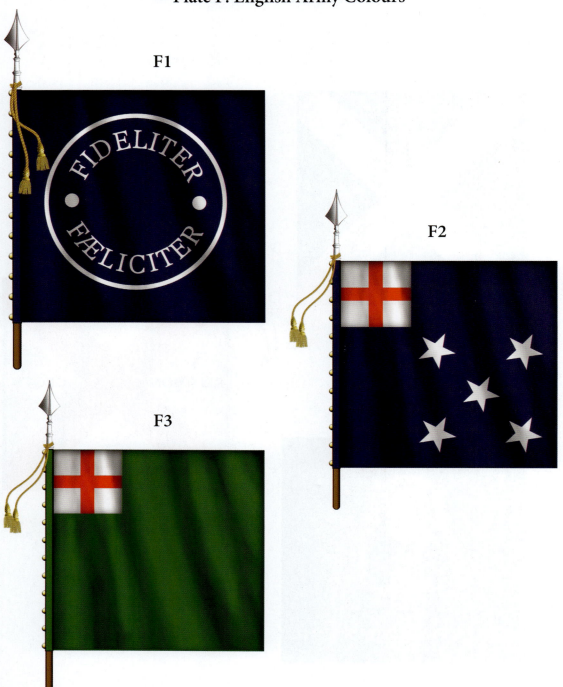

F1 Charles Fairfax's Regiment, Colonel's Colour, F2 Charles Fairfax's Regiment, 5th Captain's Colour, F3 Monck's Regiment, Lt-Colonel's Colour.
(Illustration by Dr Lesley Prince © Helion & Company)
See Colour Plate Commentaries for further information.

Plate G: Scots Army Colours

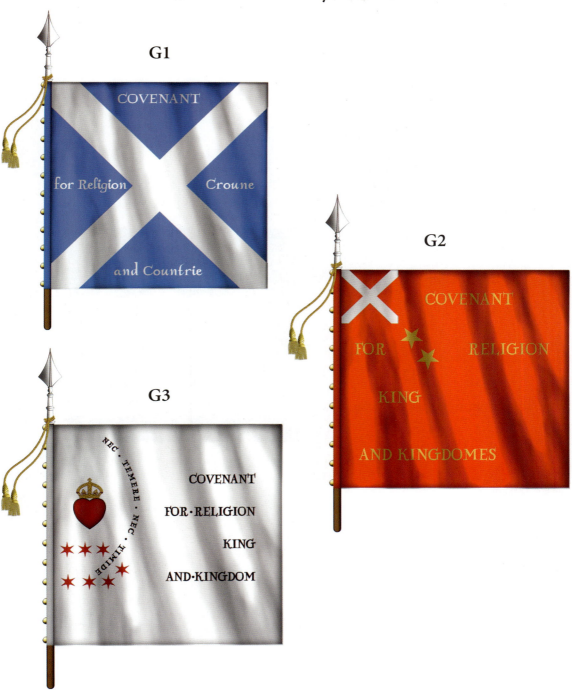

G1 Campbell of Lawers' Regiment, Captain's Colour, G2 Stewart's (Edinburgh) Regiment, Captain's Colour, G3 Douglas of Kirkness' Regiment, Colonel's Colour.
(Illustration by Dr Lesley Prince © Helion & Company)
See Colour Plate Commentaries for further information.

Plate H: Scots Army Colours

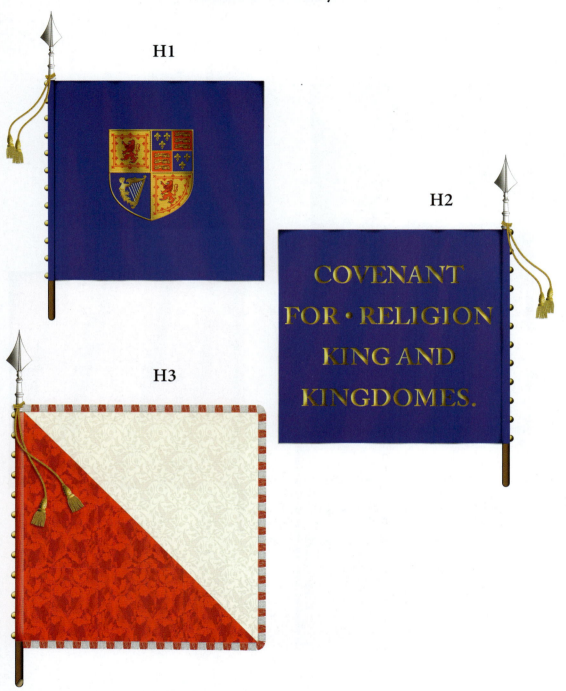

H1 Colonel's Colour, Charles II's Lifeguard Regiment, H2 Reverse side, Colonel's Colour, Charles II's Lifeguard Regiment, H3 Brown's Regiment of Horse, Cornet.
(Illustration by Dr Lesley Prince © Helion & Company)
See Colour Plate Commentaries for further information.

had his own tent in the lines.[10] Some argued for ever deeper purges and got their way, but even Wariston's own wife wrote to him that others feared the army was being inadvertently weakened. Leslie's defensive strategy was also controversial, with Wariston arguing it would 'undoe the poor land and people,' by starving the army and leaving the countryside to the enemy.[11] Leslie was no passive follower of political instruction however, and he argued 'bitterly' against those proposals with which he disagreed. The king meanwhile was returned to Fife, out of harm's way and safely distant from the army. But just as the cracks were starting to show, the pressure lessoned. At last informed by Haselrigge that the supply fleet had finally found a favourable wind, Cromwell decided to meet his supplies where he could refresh his troops unhindered. On Saturday 6 August 1650, the army of the Commonwealth of England returned to Dunbar.

The Scots were under no illusion that Cromwell's retreat would be lasting. They were sufficiently well informed to understand that he had withdrawn to link up with supplies, but the kirk nevertheless proclaimed its thanks to God for the temporary relief. The English meanwhile found Dunbar just as devoid of supplies as it was before, only now the soldiers were hungrier and wearier. Discipline was in danger of breaking down as a result of their 'great distress,' Captain Hodgson recalled. Soldiers turned over houses in search of provisions, intimidating civilians into revealing hiding places: 'it was sad to see the devastation that was made.'[12] Cromwell was obliged to court martial five soldiers for threatening a family, but he knew that such gestures would lose their effect if he were not soon able to improve his men's lot. Then at last the fleet appeared; ships' bellies laden with food and canvas. At that time Dunbar had only one of the two harbours it now possesses, the easternmost, and the narrow entrance beside the Lamer Island crag was difficult for bigger vessels. It was however a safe harbour, the best in the county, and over two days the grateful army was revitalised at Dunbar. The bustle of the disembarkation brought a sense of life back into the town, watched over by the slighted ruins of its once-mighty castle on its sheer-sided promontory.

The Earl of Loudoun wrote to the king of 10 August that the enemy had received more than a month's provisions. By contrast, the burgh fathers in Edinburgh were threatening to break down the doors of cellars suspected of containing private stockpiles of food as supplies in the city dwindled thanks to the army's high consumption.[13] Two thousand reaping hooks were ordered for the army via the Edinburgh council, as even prematurely harvested corn was more useful than crops trampled by armies. Ironically these shortages were starting to sow the seeds in Scotland of the very actions the English parliament had hoped to forestall by invading: Loudoun was contemplating ways 'to give the enemy work in England, rather than consume us with a lingering war.'[14] Such action had been expressly ruled out by Wariston barely

---

10   Wariston, *Diary*, p. 10.
11   Wariston, *Diary*, p. 8.
12   Original Memoirs, p. 137.
13   Wood, *Records*, p. 254.
14   Gardiner, *Letters*, p. 134.

'ESSENTIAL AGONY'

25. Dunbar Town House, one of the few surviving buildings which witnessed Cromwell's invasion. As burgh chambers, tolbooth and jail, it was the centre of the town's civic life and its tower a statement of its status and prosperity.

a week before, but if the campaign dragged on and threatened the harvest then the cost would be high indeed. The hint was also calculated to appeal to the king, who was personally eager to get into England and thus free of yokes he was under in Scotland. The Kirk Party was trying to secure his signature on a new declaration reaffirming his commitment to the Covenants, but he had demurred. The promise of opening a new front in England was likely a political one therefore, especially in light of the same author's comments to Argyll and Lothian just a few days later: 'charity begins at home, and many think our Armie should not move any where and leave such an enemy in our bosom.'[15]

On Saturday 10 August the English army marched out of Dunbar once again, covering the whole distance to Musselburgh in a single day. The challenge for Cromwell on his renewed march was that, having baulked once at attacking Leslie's lines, he had established them in the minds of his men as unsurmountable. The alternative to a frontal assault was a flanking manoeuvre, and since the proximity of Leslie's army to the coast made a naval landing impossible then the only option was to march the army around the south side of Edinburgh. Bringing Leslie out of his fortified position, which faced only one way of course, would even the odds considerably. Both sides expressed, to each other and themselves, their intention to fight as soon as the conditions were right. When the Scots heard that Cromwell was coming

---

15 Gardiner, *Letters*, p. 277.

once more they therefore resolved to face him and appointed a fast day to secure God's aid. Wariston, a pen-and-ink man rather than a soldier, prayed fervently that morning: 'I begged for courage and resolution to myself to do duty, to bide in my station, to be a good example and not an evil one in the day of battle, to honour and not dishonour His name by my carriage.'[16] The revolution he had given voice to over a decade before was facing an existential crisis, but his faith that he performed God's work was undiminished.

Cromwell moved his army on 13 August on a flanking march from Musselburgh, looping around to the south of Edinburgh. The inhabitants fled before him, and when some soldiers set fire to some gorse on the hills, perhaps to clear space for their encampment, the smoke was interpreted in Edinburgh as the burning of the outlying properties. The site of the encampment is traditionally said to have been Galachlaw, in the lee between Braid Hills and the Pentlands proper to the south. Apart from some light pickering between cavalry outposts however, Leslie's army did not move in response. Even from his new position in the south Cromwell was faced with having to assault the walls of Edinburgh, with the Water of Leith restricting his left flank and the guns of the castle able to support the defenders. The threat therefore was more to do with swinging around to the west and cutting the capital off from supplies and reinforcements, whilst giving Cromwell the opportunity to connect with his fleet again at Queensferry. Well informed as ever, the general hoped this increased threat would exert critical pressure on the fracture-lines inside Edinburgh.

In the wake of his appearance in Leith, the Kirk Party were doubling down on their king. They presented him with a declaration demanding that he reinforce his commitment to the covenants he had already signed but also formally abandon all those who had previously fought for the royal cause. He had to accept the faults of his parents and acknowledge his 'great sinfulness' in having encouraged Ormond to ally with the Irish Catholics. Most importantly, the king also had to agree to 'do nothing but by advice of the kirk and state.'[17] Charles refused, prompting Loudoun to write in terms unlikely to soothe the royal pride. The king, he said, was 'bound' and 'obliged' to accept the terms, and should 'cordially and speedily condescend to it.' If not, then the Covenanters would 'separate the preservation of religion from your interest.' The result, Loudoun warned Charles, would be that the king's 'enemies (who will grant anything which may destroy your Majesty) will win their ends.'[18]

Charles' obstinacy, testament to his strength of character even when his options were so limited, caused real concern amongst those who sought to manage their monarch. Loudoun also wrote to Argyll on 14 August, fearing that the refusal would 'provoke God to withdraw his Blessing from the King's Majesty, and from the army also.'[19] To ramp up the pressure, the committee of estates passed fresh restrictions on the composition of the king's household;

---

16 Wariston, *Diary*, p. 16.
17 Whitelocke, p. 234.
18 Letter from Loudoun to Charles II; Gardiner, *Letters*, p. 131-2.
19 Letter from Loudoun to Argyll; *Ancrum Correspondence*, p. 280.

Wariston exhorted his colleagues to stay firm; a remonstrance was drafted by some officers of the army echoing the voice of the government. It was now that the king suggested that the northern levies yet to join the army at Edinburgh assemble as a separate army at Stirling rather than marching on to Leslie. If Cromwell moved into the west, he could therefore be threatened from both sides, but more to the point there would be an army in Scotland which the king might be able to influence easier than that which was under the thumbs of the Kirk Party in the capital. The risk of a split was very real.

In the meantime, David Leslie was corresponding with Cromwell with the committee's authority, explaining that once the king had accepted the Kirk Party's latest demands then there was nothing to be feared from Charles II. The repeated and heartfelt rejection of the Engagement and all who had been involved in it ought to be demonstration enough that there was no need for war. Lesley asked that the declaration issued to the king be read to the English officers. Cromwell replied that he had no fight with the 'Honest People in Scotland,' but that any rejection of the Engagers and royalists was meaningless when they accepted 'he who is the head of them.'[20] Leslie went so far as to allow a conference on the beach near Portobello, at which the Scots were represented by Colonel Strachan and Gilbert 'Gibby' Ker who represented the most anti-royalist elements in the Scots army. Nevertheless, there was to be no peace whilst the Scots' position still seemed strong militarily and despite the increasing supply problem Leslie's army was formidable and well entrenched. The political crisis passed too: the king swallowed his pride and signed the declaration on 16 August. It was a humiliation which he would not forget.

By then, Cromwell was back in Musselburgh. His two-day probe to the south-west had lacked the portable supplies to press on further, but having revictualled and established a strong outpost once again at Stoneyhill, the English swung back to their Braid Hills campsite beneath the Pentlands. The Scots had been celebrating the king's concession by purging the army further, but also by reviewing the regiments. As Johnston of Wariston recorded, Loudoun accompanied Leslie on his reviews and encouraged the men, 'pressing resolution and order, and keeping in bodies and not breaking loose, either when [the] enemy runs or some other companies or companions of their own runs.'[21] The army was readying for action. So too was Cromwell: he entrenched his garrison at Stoneyhill and prepared it as a supply depot. One hundred and forty infantry from Monck's new regiment were posted here under Captain Richard Hughes, supported by another fortified outpost at Dalkeith under Captain Webb of Mauleverer's Regiment.[22] Francis Wilkinson's troop of Lilburne's Horse, forty men, with twenty dragoons in support, maintained communications between the fortified depots and the main army. Skirmishing between the lines was increasing.[23]

---

20 Letter from Cromwell to Leslie, 14 August 1650; Carlyle, p. 372.
21 Wariston, *Diary*, p. 20.
22 Hughes' company was one of those drafted from Fenwick's Regiment.
23 'True Relation of the Daily Proceedings', in *Original Memoirs*, p. 252.

Cromwell was intent on drawing Leslie out, and if his mere presence was not enough then perhaps the sight of the English fortifying themselves and controlling movement around the capital would. Sure enough, the Scots seemed to be stirring. Cavalry troops emerged and then withdrew again whenever they were approached. Cromwell's own pickets were fired upon by a Scots garrison based in Redhall Castle as they passed by, and he responded by posting two troops of dragoons in the tower house of Colinton Castle just a short distance upstream. Meanwhile Leslie drew his right wing out to Coltbridge near modern Murrayfield in order to be ready to oppose any move to close the road to Stirling. After an argument over who should be left in charge of the defensive lines, the Scottish command had decided at last to make a move. Initially the plan was to march out to Dalkeith and cut off Cromwell, but the new garrisons would have to be cleared first. Instead, in a more conservative counter to the English motions, the Scottish army moved out into a strong post on the south-facing slope of Corstorphine Hill.[24] Cromwell advanced with a forlorn towards Leslie but found the ground unsuitable for an engagement. It was at this point that a Scots trooper fired upon him with a carbine. Cromwell called out that if the would-be assassin had been in *his* army, then he would have been cashiered for firing at such long range. 'I did fight with you once,' returned the undaunted horseman, 'at Marston Moor.'

Leslie was now in the open, although still too well posted to attack directly, and the Water of Leith separate the two armies. Cromwell turned his attention on Redhall, perhaps to provoke Leslie or else to gain unhindered access to the river crossing downstream at Slateford. The strong little castle of Redhall, with walls at least 2'4" thick, occupied a strong position in a bend of the Water of Leith. The deep ravine protected it on three sides, the fourth was fronted by a semi-circular tower. Redhall was held by its owner Sir James Hamilton along with between sixty and eighty men.[25] They held their nerve as Cromwell softened the defences with his artillery. Traditionally it is said the batteries were placed on the high bluff across the river, but they would have been vulnerable whilst they had their backs to the Scots army. The bombardment was insufficient to induce the garrison, suggesting instead that it focussed on the frontal defences which were surely the strongest. It took 200 men of Monck's Regiment to eventually create a breach with petards, no doubt under heavy fire throughout. Short of ammunition, the garrison took their final chance to surrender, hanging out white sheets and receiving quarter. Cromwell's men finally took possession of Redhall 24 August.[26]

With the fords at both Colinton and Slateford secure, Cromwell at last advanced across the Water of Leith with his whole force on 27 August.

---

24 Wariston, *Diary*, p. 21.
25 All trace of the castle has gone, the ruins being cleared in the eighteenth century, but the location is well recorded and excavations in the late nineteenth century identified the forward turret's footings. The site of the castle has been, almost as if in testament to its historical significance, left clear of development. Its defensive advantages remain clear, and the adjacent walks along the riverside are rewarding. Whitelocke, p. 234.
26 See Douglas, Scotch Campaigns, p. 76. There is some uncertainty over the date, and the surrender may have been a few days later.

26. The site of Redhall Castle today, a quiet pocket of land surrounded on three sides by a steep gorge. It is hard to imagine the dramatic events which took place here in 1650.

This was his most determined attempt yet to force a battle, and as Leslie's army was out in the open there seemed a real chance the deadlock could be broken. The Scots move slightly to the west, commanding both the Stirling-Edinburgh road and the approaches to the coast; the vanguards of the two armies clashed as the main bodies drew up behind them. The English army likely positioned itself across the ridgeline before Over Gogar, an apparently strong post with an open field of fire. Opposite was Leslie's army, drawing up roughly along the line of the road west.[27] With its right flank at Ingliston the Scots army will have centred on Nether Gogar and the already disused medieval church, with the relatively recent structure of Gogar Castle close to the rear. A small loch, now drained, protected the left. In today's landscape, the sprawling commercial village of the Royal Bank of Scotland headquarters dominates the area over which the battle was set to be fought. In 1650 this land was crossed with a network of small streams which created a marshy mossland, centred on a cluster of turf-walled sheep enclosures around Gogarburn.

Cromwell's moment had come at last: the enemy was before him. Leslie's army was clearly the larger, and Captain Hodgson remembers that the Scots line outwinged them. Lambert's regiment was posted on the left of the English infantry line, protected by a cavalry wing beyond. The Scots advanced a force into the sheep pens in order to restrict the movement of Cromwell's scouts,

---

27 Still the modern A8 road, leading from the city out to Edinburgh Airport.

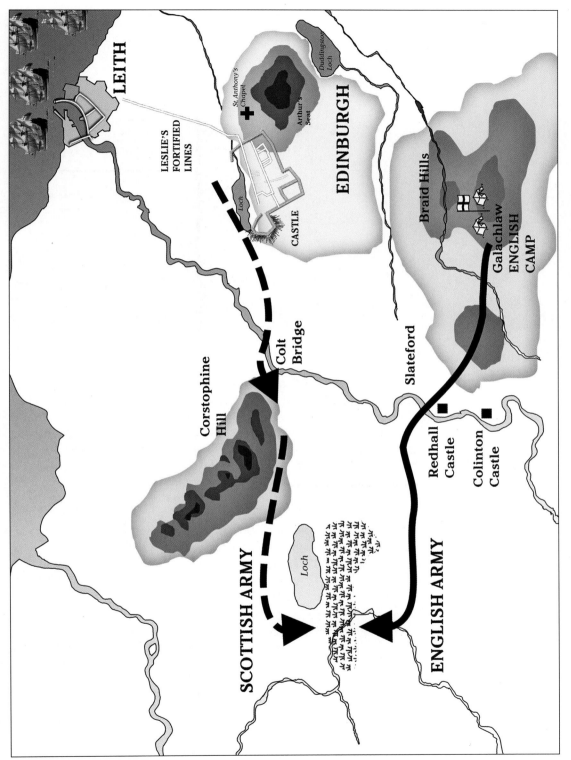

Map 4. Cromwell's attempt to outflank Edinburgh to the west, resulting in the action at Gogarburn.

'ESSENTIAL AGONY'

27. The fields of action at Gogarburn, viewed from the higher ground occupied by Cromwell's army. The Royal Bank of Scotland headquarters village lies in the depression to the right-of-centre, the boggy ground over which the cannons blazed. Leslie's position is today screened by the trees. His former position at Corstorphine Hill rises in the background to the right.

and in the boggy ground between the armies the puff and crack of sporadic musket fire presaged the coming violence. 'Oliver calls for a couple of guns,' recalled Hodgson, 'and batters their shelter about their ears.'[28] As the Scots abandoned the enclosures, the English army cheered. Many of the men had cast off their excess baggage in anticipation of the coming battle, and now they were rousing themselves for the advance. Then from the east to the west Cromwell's battle line erupted into a cacophony of thundering cannon. The air pulsed as the guns punched smoke and shot across the moss. The Scottish cannon responded, and beneath the grey sky the ground shook. The soldiers could feel the reverberations in their knees; to those facing their first battle the spectacle was awesome.

But the massive bombardment, in which Cromwell reported 'two or three hundred great shot' being blasted towards the Scots, could not long hide the disappointing reality. Cromwell's horse were prevented on both flanks from advancing by the marshy ground and an English attack proved to be 'no way feasible.'[29] Despite the intensity of the artillery duel the damage on each side was limited, not enough to draw the other into crossing the marshes. There were around twenty-five English casualties, perhaps more amongst the Scots as the English had a slightly more elevated position.[30] One Scottish cannonball smashed through an English pike division towards the left, killing two men outright and bowling three more to the ground. Most shot slammed into the soft ground however, spraying wet earth into the air as they ploughed the ground and then buried themselves in the slope.

---

28 Original Memoirs, p. 140.
29 Letter from Cromwell to the Council of State, 30 August 1650; Carlyle, p. 375.
30 Whitelocke, p. 237; Original Memoirs, p. 141.

The guns pounded on into the early evening, and local tradition preserved the memory by naming the fields 'the Flashes'.[31] Before the dusk, Cromwell drew his army back a little to invite the Scots forward; they 'stood all night in batallia' but Leslie remained still.[32] The following morning, Wednesday 28 August, Cromwell returned again to his former post and renewed the bombardment for a few hours. But with the clouds blackening and the men short of food, the English army was forced to accept that it had once again been thwarted. For all the smoke and noise, the attempt the swing west had failed either to draw the Scots into battle or to cut them off. The operation had been let down by a failure of intelligence, a lack of reconnaissance which had presumably come about through a reluctance to press scouts too far beyond the Water of Leith during the previous week. Cromwell could claim to have inflicted higher losses on his enemy, although his sources even for that uncertain; but Leslie had achieved his objectives and Cromwell had not.

Cromwell began his withdrawal in the late morning, but as the foot were ordered back towards Slateford the general appears to have led a cavalry vanguard in a more directly easterly direction as if making for the Coltbridge beyond Corstorphine. Leslie responded with speed to ensure the Ironsides did not cut him off from the capital, and skirmishing renewed between the troopers of both sides until Cromwell pulled his horse back towards the main army. It was a face-saving feint and little more. The main body of the English returned to their former camp at Galachlaw, but the general centred himself on Blackford Hill from which he could keep easier eyes on the Scots. Cannon were brought forward to Niddrie so as to command the road back to the garrisons at Musselburgh. The Scottish army, having finally moved from its trenches, was now more threatening than ever.

Leslie was marching on internal lines and therefore had the advantage of speed. Cromwell's men were tired and hungry, and despite their motivation they were surely demoralised to have achieved so little in more than five weeks of campaigning. To add to their discomfort, the sky now cracked once again and gave the weary soldiers of both armies 'a most tempestuous night.'[33] The rainfall continued in the morning as Cromwell urged his army back towards Musselburgh to prevent Leslie from cutting him off from the sea. The Scots had moved to the east of Edinburgh and lain overnight about Calton Hill, and now they seemed poised to interpose on Cromwell's supply line. Hodgson notes the threat to the right wing, as a result of which Cromwell's vanguard was thrown forward in haste towards Easter Duddingston and the Magdalene Bridge over the Niddry Burn. Two cannon near Duddingston Mill covered Cromwell's rear-guard, firing on Leslie's own right as it emerged from behind Arthur's Seat and enjoying a 'fair play' upon them.[34] But the Scottish regiments did not advance to provoke a general engagement and they resumed a defensive posture blocking the eastern approaches to Edinburgh. With some relief, over wet roads already churned up by repeated marches,

---

31 Douglas, *Scotch Campaigns*, p. 99.
32 Whitelocke, p. 236.
33 Letter from Cromwell to the Council of State, 30 August 1650; Carlyle, p. 375.
34 *Original Memoirs*, p. 142.

'ESSENTIAL AGONY'

Cromwell's army successfully deployed with Musselburgh to their back and the sea on their flank.

However, it may never have been Leslie's intention to cut off the English at all. Instead the priority was to oblige Cromwell to abandon all that he had so far achieved, removing the threat posed by the thrust into the Pentlands. In this light, David Leslie has scored a considerable success that day by forcing his opponent to dance to his tune. Hodgson recalls the Scots moving 'very briskly' within view of Cromwell, 'as though they designed to flank us.' Such a threat inevitably invited a rapid response, but then as the general himself reports the Scots became static, 'looking upon us but not attempting anything.' Whitelocke confesses that, 'the enemy got what they [the English army] had left on Pentland-hills.'[35] Put together, the Scottish movements on 29 August are clearly the fulfilment of a plan discussed three days earlier on Corstorphine Hill: 'the enemy keeps still in his leaguer betwixt Brads-Craigs and Pentland Hills. All possible means are and will be essayed to draw him out of that hold.'[36] Leslie had moved to threaten Cromwell's lines so convincingly as to force him to abandon his entrenched camp at Galachlaw, withdrawing his garrisons at Colinton and Redhall and pulling his whole force back to his forward depot at Musselburgh. As a result, Edinburgh was again secure and Cromwell was back where he had started.

28. The traditional site of the English camp at Galachlaw, now subsumed by the growth of Edinburgh.

---

35 *Original Memoirs*, p. 142; Carlyle, p. 375; Whitelocke, p. 236.
36 Letter from Loudoun to Argyll, 26 August 1650; Gardiner, p. 294.

The rain continued and Cromwell's army was weakening. Five hundred 'sick and wounded' soldiers were embarked at Musselburgh and sent off to England. Weeks of marching and camping through that miserable wet summer with short rations and unreliable supply lines were taking a toll. Dysentery was sweeping through the ranks, weakening the soldiers with the debilitating flux. Hodgson called it 'a poor, shattered, hungry, discouraged army.'[37] Cromwell called a council of war on Friday 30 August. Charles Fleetwood was in a maudlin mood, complaining that the Scots 'reduce us to a heart-broken condition by their alternate squatting on the fenny grounds and skipping like young goats on the mountains.'[38] David Leslie's success in reducing such an army to these straits should not be understated. The Scottish commander had not just hoped that Cromwell's army would suffer sickness and hunger, he had made it so. He had, however, deliberately left the door open to allow his unwanted guests to leave of their own accord. The English army abandoned Musselburgh and marched east.

The plan, according to Cromwell, was to return to Dunbar and turn the town into a fortified camp. With Leith secure in Scottish hands, Dunbar was the only harbour which could provide an all-weather haven for disembarking supplies. Musselburgh's harbour at Fisherrow was too small and the beaches only suitable for landings when the conditions were favourable. For a depot, it was also dangerously close to the Scottish lines as the previous day's marches had highlighted. More to the point, the battle-fitness of the men was diminishing just as the Scots appeared to be gaining in confidence: 'our army grew weaker every day,' recalled Hodgson.[39] The reports which reached Whitelocke in London were of much the same tone. 'The English were in a sad posture,' he wrote, 'very many of their men sick and wanting provision.'[40] In such circumstances, Cromwell's claim that his withdrawal was further designed to 'provoke them to engage' seems more of a cover, written with the benefit of hindsight, than a genuine motivation.[41] There was no way to gloss over the fact that the English army was now extremely vulnerable.

The Scots sensed the tide turning in their favour. Their own food supplies were dwindling, and the political pressure was mounting. East Lothian's rich harvest lay uncut but ruined, battered down by the rains and trampled by the armies. Profiteers were cutting crops early to sell on at a premium, prompting the burgh council in Edinburgh to threaten imprisonment and a twenty pound fine.[42] The Kirk Party was looking over its shoulder towards the king, who by showing signs of competence had earned their suspicion. For his part, Charles was chaffing and complaining of the 'villainy' of men who behaved little better than polite jailors: 'indeed it has done me a great deal of good,' wrote the king from Perth, 'for nothing could have confirmed me more to the Church of England than being here.'[43] The English were aware

---

37 *Original Memoirs*, p. 143.
38 Douglas, *Cromwell's Scotch Campaigns*, p. 107.
39 *Original Memoirs*, p. 143.
40 Whitelocke, p. 240.
41 Letter from Cromwell to William Lenthall, 4 September 1650; Carlyle, p. 584.
42 Wood, *Records*, p. 261.
43 Letter from Charles II to Sir Edward Nicholas, 3 September 1650; Bryant, *Letters*, p. 18.

of these divisions – Colonel Strachan had made no effort to hide them during his abortive conferences – and reported home that the Scots 'were not so a piece as they were, but their disaffection about the king, and other divisions, increase.'[44] With Johnston of Wariston breathing down his neck, David Leslie was braced to move off the defensive in search of a decisive result. He would settle for the triumph of shepherding Cromwell homeward and preserving the Scots army intact for the inevitable negotiations to follow.

Cromwell's weary army moved out of Musselburgh in the early evening on 31 August, firing the temporary huts which had been crafted by the enterprising soldiery as they went. The local minister's house was also burned, though whether by accident or malice is unknown.[45] A breakdown in discipline was a real risk under such strain: there had already been need for a gallows at the camp in the Pentlands, and deserters had been picked up at Berwick.[46] The ships sailed out into the Forth with their cargo of sickly soldiery, and this sight combined with the smoking encampment gave a sense of finality to the English retreat. Leslie moved off in pursuit, perhaps securing a quantity of grain which Cromwell was obliged to leave behind.[47] Leslie's vanguard pressed hard to ensure that the pressure on the English was sustained, reaching the west side of Preston village as Cromwell's rear-guard was barely clear of the east.

As night drew in, the English army settled into uneasy quarters in the market town of Haddington. West of the town, however, the Scottish horse reappeared and fell upon Cromwell's rear. As the general himself confessed, they 'put it in some disorder.'[48] In the darkness the swiftness of the light Scots lancers gave them an edge, striking out of the drizzle and darting amongst the ironsides to prevent them from forming their tight ranks. As the Cromwellian horse was obliged to stand and face them, they became exposed to more and more Scottish troops whilst their own army got further away. Then a cloud covered the moon, so reducing the visibility that the Scots were obliged to disengage. At midnight they attacked again, striking at Charles Fairfax's Regiment at the western edge of Haddington. This time Cromwell's men were more prepared and the attack was repulsed with the help of the old perimeter walls.[49] Hodgson believed it was Highland troops which had led the attack, but despite his protestations that they were forced to flee the reality remains that Cromwell's weary army had been denied a night's rest and was under greater pressure than ever.[50]

---

44 'A Letter from a Colonel of the Army, 31 August 1650', in *Original Memoirs*, p. 268.
45 Walker, E. *Historical Discourses, Upon Several Occasions*, (London, 1705), p. 179.
46 Whitelocke, p. 232.
47 This is uncertain, as the source states the supplies were taken at Leith although this had never been in Cromwell's hands. Douglas certainly thinks it more likely that Cromwell had left the supplies behind in Musselburgh for want of wagons, and presumably because the 500 men aboard reduced the capacity of the small fleet to evacuate all the supplies. However, if there were 20,000 boules of grain in Musselburgh then Cromwell ought to have been under less immediate pressure to retreat. Douglas, *Scotch Campaigns*, p. 107.
48 Letter from Cromwell to William Lenthall, 4 September 1650; Carlyle, p. 585.
49 *Original Memoirs*, p. 275.
50 *Original Memoirs*, p. 143.

At around 5am the following morning, Sunday 1 September, the English regiments formed in battalia in expectation of the once longed-for battle. Part of the army was posted to the west of Haddington, commanding the road into the town, whilst the officers debated where best to deploy for the expected battle. In the end it was decided to draw back and leave the settlement between the two armies. This suggests an expectation that the English would be fighting defensively, as they would hardly wish to place such an obstacle in their own path to provide shelter for the enemy. The south and east sides of Haddington are cradled by an angular bend of the river Tyne, which creates a challenge in identifying exactly where Cromwell intended to fight. Hodgson states that the regiments which had been posted to the west were withdrawn through the town, and his vague description implies an area to the east of the town and controlling the road to Dunbar. As it is unlikely the army crossed the river – it would surely have been worthy of a mention – this suggests the deployment was to the north-east of Haddington where the line could be protected by the Garleton Hills to the north and the river to the south.

Cromwell however describes the site as 'an open field, on the south side of Haddington.' This too would require the army crossing the river, but assuming the army then faced northwards it could still fulfil Hodgson's description of leaving the town between them and the Scots. Nothing would have suggested to Cromwell that Leslie would be willing to risk an

29. St Mary's Church, Haddington. Nestled in the corner of the River Tyne, which bounded the county town on its eastern and southern sides, the church had been caught in the crossfire during the great siege of the late 1540s. By 1650 only the nave was roofed and in use. It is said Cromwell stabled horses here.

engagement which required him to cross a river under fire, however, and by moving south Cromwell would have put the Scots in control of the road and cut himself off from the coast. It seems much more likely therefore that Cromwell's 'south' should not be taken literally as a compass point but rather as meaning 'on the road which leads to the south.' In other words, the direction which led to Dunbar in the east before the road could turn southwards towards Berwick and England. This is the interpretation which makes the most sense, and brings us back to the north-south deployment straddling the modern A1 motorway. The only factor in favour of a genuine southern movement is the folk tradition of Cromwell's army passing between Gifford, Garvald and Whittinghame. There is a story of cannon becoming enmired passing Danskine Loch (later drained). Such a route would however have marked a significant detour away from the main road, but no accounts record such a swing to the south and Cromwell's need to reconnect urgently with the coast seems sufficient cause to refute it.

For up to five hours the English regiments stood in their ranks and files awaiting the Scots. The wind brought drifts of fine rain across the open fields, soaking into woollen coats which had scarce been dry in weeks. As it was the Sabbath, officers led prayers amongst their men; parties of Scottish horse roamed without urgency in the fields immediately north of Haddington. It is unclear exactly where Leslie's army had quartered, perhaps the Gladsmuir when Cromwell had previously deployed to receive them on his first march to Edinburgh. A secondary road, basically a Haddington bypass, ran across the lower Garletons and gave an approach to threaten Cromwell's presumed right flank whilst the main road did the same on his left. No doubt the Scots officers were examining the options, but they made no move to threaten the English position. The English royalist Sir Edward Walker was unequivocal in explaining why: 'the Ministers would not give way to it, because forsooth it was the Lord's Day.'[51] By ten o'clock Cromwell had ordered his waggons to begin the journey to Dunbar, and shortly after the rest of the army was following them. Behind the army, the Scots.

Leslie kept his army at a discrete distance from the English, but the horse 'pursued very close' to keep Cromwell moving: 'our rearguard had much ado,' recalled Hodgson, 'to secure our poor weak foot.'[52] The Scots did not nothing to seriously hamper the English crossing of the Tyne at Linton Bridge, however, and it remained unclear whether Leslie's purpose was to fight or merely to sweep Cromwell before him. It was by no means a fast march, as the army reached Dunbar towards evening despite having only ten miles to cover over fairly easy ground. There were hundreds of sick men which the army needed to bear along with it, slowing them down considerably. The road itself will not have helped either, hundreds of wheels and thousands of feet and hooves churning ground already crossed by the English army three times previously. For the English soldiers, even if we consider Hodgson's repeated expressions of sickness and weariness as being at least partially exaggerated, this slog across the narrow bridge, over Pencraig Brae and past its standing

---

51 Walker, *Historical Discourses*, p. 180.
52 Original Memoirs, p. 144-5.

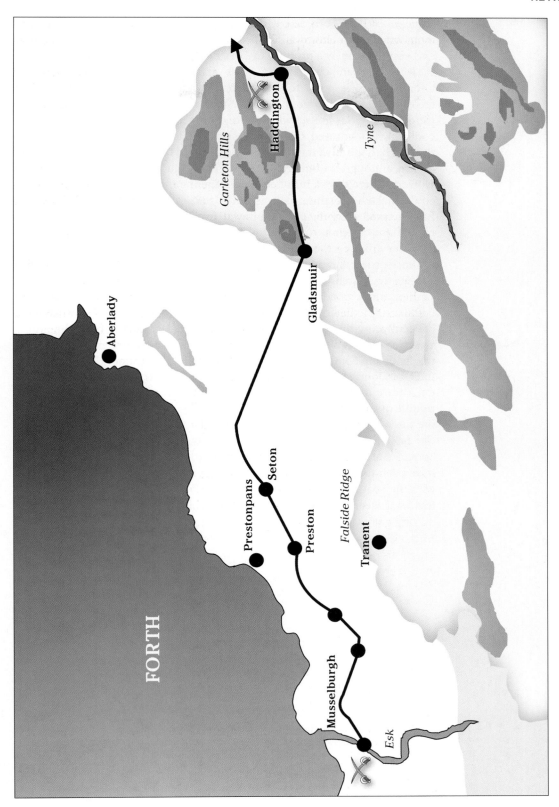

Map 5. Cromwell retreats under pressure from Musselburgh to Haddington, then on to Dunbar.

stone, must have been deeply demoralising. Dunbar lay visible before them long before they reached it, perched above a dark sea and beneath a brooding sky; simultaneously a promise of sanctuary and a symbol of failure.

It is unclear whether the Scots army initially followed directly in Cromwell's wake or else took a different road entirely out of Haddington. By crossing the stone bridge at the east end of the town, passing the remnants of the great religious houses which once dominated that side of the Tyne, Leslie could have shadowed Cromwell's army whilst keeping the river between them. It had the advantage of avoiding the mud thrown up by the army ahead of him, although it would have made it harder to pressure Cromwell directly. However there were a number of places along the Tyne were smaller parties could make a crossing, such as below the walls of Hailes Castle, allowing Leslie's cavalry to keep pressing the enemy; at one point the Scots were close enough for two guns to be unlimbered to keep them at bay.[53]

After crossing the Tyne the Scots main body eventually diverged from the main road and a gap opened up between the them and the English to the north. Marching over the Broxburn below the small village of Spott, Leslie's army 'gathered towards the Hills.'[54] The English army drew into battalia immediately south of Dunbar with the Lochend estate to their rear, concentrating their heavy guns on the knoll of the parish church where the view presumably also attracted the senior officers to make their base. But over the fields the Scots could be seen in the fading light mounting the western flank of Doon Hill from the approaches above Spott House. In response the guns were brought back out from the churchyard to 'a farmhouse in the middle of the fields where the army lay,' which may have been Newtonlees if the intention was to allow easy deployment to cover the main road east, or else Lochend if it was anticipated Leslie would attack via the crossing below Spott.[55] But if there was to have been a battle that day then it would already have been fought at Haddington. Instead, the first day of September ended with the Scots on the hilltop and the English with their backs to Dunbar and the sea. It seemed that the Scots held all the cards, recalled John Hodgson, 'having got us into a pound.'[56]

---

53 Original Memoirs, p. 144.
54 Letter from Cromwell to William Lenthall, 4 September 1650; Carlyle, p. 585.
55 Carte, *Original Letters Vol. I*, p. 381. Another alternative is Chesterhall, although this would only make clear sense if the army had already moved forward towards the burn. Lochend House there was likely more substantial than the mere farmhouse described by Cadwell; Firth, C. 'The Battle of Dunbar', *Transactions of the Royal Historical Society*, Vol. 14, (Cambridge: University Press, 1900), p. 19-52.
56 Original Memoirs, p. 144.

RETREAT

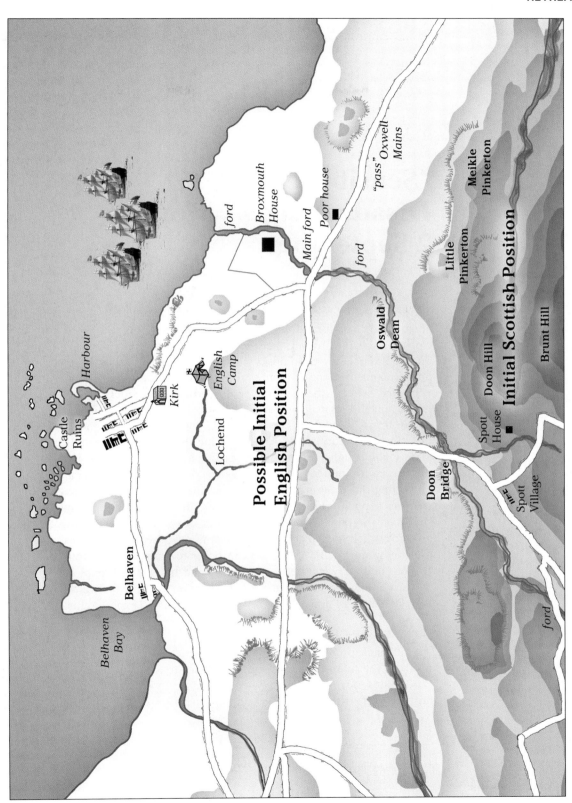

Map 6. Dunbar and the situation on the evening of 1 September 1650.

113

6

"Sensible of our Disadvantages", Monday, 2 September

The army of the Commonwealth of England stood in its battalia awaiting the enemy, red coats turned dark with the rain. Layers of mud caked hose and clogged shoes; sword hilts were red with rust and musket locks wrapped in dank strips of cloth. Cold noses streamed unnoticed, just as the water ran in little streams from the drooping brims of hats. Horses shook their mains and whinnied beneath the resulting sprays, whilst their riders pushed up their heavy bulks to stretch the backs. Forests of pikes three times the height of a man thrust into the black sky, buffeted by gusting winds and channelling the rain down tiny rivulets onto the numb fingers of the soldiers below. Here a man coughed his wretching cough; here a damp sneeze. Occasionally the breeze brought a muted laugh or a distant order; the slapping thuds of trotting officer along the rear of the lines. Vast flags made lazy by their wetness flapped suddenly on the gusts and cracked like whips as they shook off the rain. Grumbling teamsters slopped their feet in the churned ground as their hauled and shoved at cannon wheels, bringing the guns from their temporary park at Lochend in order to command the road between Dunbar and Berwick, between Dunbar and home.[1] In Broxmouth House, Oliver Cromwell's quill darted anxiously across his paper: 'we are upon an Engagement very difficult.'[2] This was not how he had expected his campaign to end.

The English army was drawn up in the town fields south of Dunbar, with the left flank protected by the defensible enclosures of Broxmouth House north of the main Broxburn ford. The line stretched west towards Wester Broomhouse farm, along a low ridge which sloped away gently along its northern side over the open grazing ground towards Lochend estate. There

---

1 The previous night the guns had been placed on the knoll of the parish church to the army's rear; the observation of Leslie's advance onto Doon hill made this caution unnecessary and the guns were then brought forward again.
2 Letter from Cromwell to Haselrigge, 2 September 1650; Carlyle, p. 377.

"SENSIBLE OF OUR DISADVANTAGES", MONDAY, 2 SEPTEMBER

30. The fields to the south of Dunbar, including in the mid-ground the town fields across which Cromwell initially formed his lines in case of an immediate Scottish attack. The army will have had its back to Lochend estate.

stood the tower house of the Baillies, where the Scottish army had briefly been based eleven years before as it had assembled for that first march against the late king which had triggered the start of the civil wars. The loch from which the grounds took their name had been drained, perhaps within living memory of some of the town's inhabitants, but parts of the area remained boggy. Indeed, although the soldiers formed on their low rise were spared the worst of the ground, the fields around them were so soft from the rainfall of that appalling summer so that Hodgson recalled a landscape of 'swamps and bogs.'[3] It was so bad that no tents had been erected on their arrival the previous night, and no effort was made to do so now.

This was a much weaker army than that which had crossed the Border in July. From the 16,354 soldiers present at the Chillingham Castle review, few more than 11,000 were now fit to fight. Of those 7,500 were infantry and 3,500 horse and dragoons.[4] As well as the sickness brought on by the weather and the poor provisioning, Cromwell's casualties over weeks of light skirmishing may well have been higher than he admitted in his dispatches. Although the worse had been embarked at Musselburgh, the English army was encumbered with hundreds of sick and wounded men, no doubt now scattered amongst the houses of Dunbar wondering if they would have to be abandoned in the case of defeat or an evacuation. Those capable of standing in their ranks were formed into brigades.[5] There were three infantry brigades, each comprising three regiments: Monck's (Monck's, Mauleverer's, Fenwick's); Pride's (Pride's, Comwell's, Lambert's); and Overton's (Coxe's, Daniel's, Fairfax's). There were

---

3 Original Memoirs, p. 144.
4 Letter from Cromwell to William Lenthall, 4 September 1650; Carlyle, p. 586.
5 The full order of battle is provided in the Appendix.

two cavalry brigades also, Lambert's (Fleetwood's, Lambert's, Whalley's) and Lilburne's (Lilburne's Hacker's, Twisleton's), with Cromwell's own regiment of horse in reserve and six companies of Okey's Dragoons. Each regiment was supported by two field guns, and there were a number of heavier cannon to provide additional support. This was a formidably trained and experienced army, united by the common experience of the campaign and united by the sense of danger.

Cromwell maintains that morale remained high amongst the rank and file, but the clock was ticking: 'our lying here daily consumeth our men.'[6] They had their backs to the sea and the enemy dominating the landscape before them; and the sickness would only continue to spread if the army remained together in a crowded pocket. The weather had been poor enough in July and August, and September had begun even worse. From now on the rains would be colder and the winds wilder, and the scarcity of resources would be exacerbated now that the armies had helped the weather in destroying swathes of harvest through the heart of one of Scotland's most productive landscapes. Dunbar would normally be in the midst of the vast herring drove, but the harvest of the sea would remain uncollated whilst rival armies were out in the fields and the manpower of Scotland remained in arms. So although the supply problem was just as acute for the Scots, and despite the opportunity for supply through the small harbour at Dunbar, there was in fact no realistic prospect that Cromwell's army could maintain itself there throughout the coming winter. The window of opportunity was closing.

The seriousness of the English position is revealed in Cromwell's letter to Arthur Haselrigge in Newcastle: whilst putting his faith in the Lord, the general advised his colleague to assemble whatever force he could to prepare, he adds ominously, for 'whatever may become of us.' So critical is the message that, short thought the letter is, the instruction is given twice. Significantly, Cromwell finishes by advising discretion: 'I would not make it public.' Defeat could lead to an immediate Scottish invasion of England, could reignite the civil war and bring down the republic. At the very least it would destroy Cromwell's fine army, his hard-won reputation, and his political power. He would pull some of England's most experienced and dynamic officers down with him. The stakes could not have been higher, and the risks were very real. Even for a commander like Oliver Cromwell, of whom Charles Harvey said that 'hope shone in him like a pillar of fire, when it had gone out in all the others,' there was no escaping that reality.[7]

Cromwell's army stood for hours awaiting battle, although it seems likely that the pikes would soon have been grounded and in due course the men will have rested themselves also onto the cold ground, huddling in their ranks and turning their backs to the wind. A sudden onslaught was now unlikely, the Scots army being visible between whenever the curtains of rain parted, still about a mile distant. Between the two forces lay the Brox Burn, running along the bottom of what Hodgson called 'a great clough' and Whitelocke 'a

---

6   Letter from Cromwell to Haselrigge, 2 September 1650; Carlyle, p. 378.
7   Harvey was later Cromwell's Groom of the Bedchamber; Carlyle, p. 377.

31. The old harbour at Dunbar, repaired with the aid of a grant during the Protectorate and now known as the Cromwell Harbour as a result. Its entrance was narrow and the coast around it rocky, making a large embarkation challenging. The small army of Sir John Cope would take several days to disembark here in 1745.

great ditch.'[8] Cadwell gives a fuller description: 'a great dyke about 40 or 50 foot wide, and as deep as broad, with a little rundle of water running in the middle of it, but very good grass growing on each side.'[9] The ravine runs like a scar through the landscape, and although the lower section is now heavily wooded this does not appear to have been the case in 1650. Instead, as with the main stretch of the valley still today, the high steep banks were of grass and gorse. In places the ravine is far wider than Cadwell suggests, often over a hundred meters, and although the burn itself is not wide its bottom is stony and uneven. After even just a few days of rain the depth can be unpredictable and inconsistent along the burn's length, reaching up the thigh in places. After the atrociously wet summer of 1650 the Brox Burn and its deep ravine was a serious obstacle to an attacking army.

The main crossing points of the burn were below Spott village in the west (now bridged), and where the main road into Dunbar crossed at Broxburn village in the east (where the road now is also carried almost imperceptibly over a stone bridge). A little upstream of this main ford was another at Brand's Mill, whilst the ravine flattened out beyond Broxmouth estate and allowed a crossing close to the sea at the burn's far end.[10] This last length was later straightened and landscaped with waterfalls when Broxmouth estate

---

8   Original Memoirs, p. 145; Whitelocke, p. 237.
9   Carte, *Original Letters*, p. 381.
10 The site of the Brand's Mill ford is again marked by a minor bridge close to the former mill buildings, which have been converted into private residences.

boundaries were extended to incorporate the burn, losing its original course and appearance. There was a further, lesser ford up at Oswald Dean, about halfway between Brand's Mill and Spott, where the banks slumped down just enough to descend into the ravine and tack back up the other side, although such a motion could be easily opposed from either bank as they overlooked the simple ford.[11]

Beyond the burn lay a band unenclosed agricultural land, bounded in the west by the little stream which curved around from the tower of Spott House to feed into the Brox Burn. To the south rises the great hump of Doon Hill, highest and steepest at its north-west shoulder, but with a long sloping eastern descent. The gorse-covered northern face was virtually impassable for a formed body of men.[12] At its narrowest, the distance between the ravine and the face of Doon Hill was only 300 meters, but as the burn turned northwards the landscape opened up considerably as it spread towards the coast at Whitesands. The crucial strip of ground between hill and burn was not flat: a long fold in the land created something of a ridgeline than ran parallel with the hill to the farmhouse at Little Pinkerton, which sat on its own small rise which created an uphill approach from the north before dropping away sharply behind the farm to the south. To the south-east of this spot was another farm, Meikle Pinkerton, which sat on an even steeper fronted rise at the eastern extremity of Doon Hill.

On the top of that hill was David Leslie and the Scottish army, which had ascended from the western and south-west the previous evening. The summit was crowned by an ancient hillfort, the raised ramparts forming a rough triangle of earthworks with the apex pointing west. which were far more defined in 1650 than they are today.[13] The plough has since laid them low, barely discernible except as a subtle shift in the ground, although satellite photography still reveals their faint echo. A second fort, perhaps an extension to the former, lay immediately to the east and is identified by the mid-nineteenth century as the site of Leslie's camp. Side-by-side to the south of Doon Hill were Brunt Hill and the lower Pinkerton Hill, and the space in between formed a long broad trough with a streamlet running in its basin. This was the landscape in which the Scottish soldiers spent the night of 1-2 September. It is an open and exposed space today, with just a few scattered trees clinging around the summit, twisted by the wind, as if standing sentinel above the camp.

---

11 This is marked on the first edition Ordnance Survey map as a ford, although it appears to have fallen out of use by the 1908 edition; the ground still hints at a former life as a minor crossing point, perhaps mainly for livestock as opposed to traffic. There is evidence of ancient settlements on both sides of the burn at this location, further suggesting an accessible routeway. The eastern bank is kinder than the Dunbar side, possibly because of localised quarrying.

12 There is currently a trackway which cuts up the north face diagonally, but as it does not appear in the mapping record it seems this may have been formed recently by livestock or farm vehicles passing through the gorse belt. In dry conditions it allows a relatively easy descent for a walker of average fitness, but is still sufficiently steep to be treacherous in the wet. It is unlikely a meaningful track existed in 1650 up the north face.

13 The forts in fact sit just below the highest point, defended most heavily on the southern side.

"SENSIBLE OF OUR DISADVANTAGES", MONDAY, 2 SEPTEMBER

32. Doon Hill, from the English army's side of the Brox Burn. The breadth and steepness of the ravine is clear from this perspective. The ridgeline running left to right beyond the stone wall is identifiable as the line where the ground changes from the darker to the lighter shade.

There are no descriptions of how the Scottish army deployed on Doon Hill, but as there was no possibility of Cromwell mounting an attack on such a position there was no need for the army to form in battalia. The ancient earthworks were probably used to contain the command post, giving a controlled area with spectacular views across the entire battlefield area. It may also have been used .[14] as an artillery park or to corral horses, as there were no other enclosures which could be used for such purposes. The waggon train was likely kept on the lower reverse slopes, to save the effort of dragging them up the sodden hillside in the fading light and to keep them available for any future motions. Whilst a screen of pickets lined the crest and the northern face, most of the men would have huddled in the hollow between the hills where they were less exposed to the lashing wind and rain. Without any natural source of fuel on the exposed open slopes, there was little comfort for the soldiers except where they could scoop themselves a shallow neuk in which to lay their shoulders. The winds on the hill were far stronger than those being experienced just a mile away to the north. Leslie himself probably stayed in Spott House even that first night: Doon Hill was no place for pitching a pavilion.

Oliver Cromwell believed his enemy at Dunbar was fielding 6,000 horse and 16,000 infantry, a vast total of 22,000 men. Sir Edward Walker gives a very similar figure, raising the horse to 7,000. This tallies roughly with

---

14 Carlyle, p. 386; Walker, p. 181.

the fifteen regiments identified in the 'List of Scotch and English forces in Scotland' as identified from subsequent identifications, assuming that those regiments were at full strength.[15] In fact they were almost certainly not at theoretical strength by the time they reached Dunbar, even if they had been in Edinburgh which is equally doubtful. It also seems the Harleian list is incomplete, failing to account for the brigading of sub-strength units, and there must also be an allowance made for anything up to 3,000 men being dismissed during the purges and others being incapacitated by sickness and skirmishing. With these factors in mind, Reid reduces the Scots army to 3,000 horse and 9,500 foot – a far closer match for Cromwell.[16] Grainger is also suspicious of Cromwell's numbers for the Scots army, noting that they are precisely double his own strength.[17] The discrepancy between Cromwell's figure and Reid's is itself the size of an army; but the reality is that there is simply no way of knowing anything with confidence except that Leslie commanded the larger of the two forces. Like their counterparts, the foot were arranged into brigades of three regiments each: Lumsden's, Lawers', Pitscottie's, Innes' and Holborne's.[18]

Leslie was up early on 2 September, issuing orders to ensure his army continued to maintain the initiative. 'Before sun rising,' a Scottish force was removed from the summit onto the lower slope in front of Doon Hill.[19] The size and composition of the force is unknown, as its exact placement. Firth considers that it must have been a 'considerable' body, although he bases that on no more than Cadwell's statement that it was 'part of their army'.[20] The move may have been intended to secure Leslie's left by ensuring control of the western ford at Spott. This kept open the road to Edinburgh, which also happened to be the quickest route to engage Cromwell's army in the town fields whilst it was drawn up in the open facing due south. Alternatively, this may have been to provide a tactical force capable of responding immediately to any attempt by Cromwell to break out towards Berwick, which regiments on the hilltop would have required time to descend and counter. Both possibilities suggested Leslie was in an assertive mood, determined to maintain the initiative rather than merely react to what the English might do.

A more significant move by Leslie was the despatch of a mounted force to Cockburnspath in order to secure the critical Pass of Pease where, as Cromwell well knew, 'ten men to hinder are better than forty to make their way'.[21] This cut Cromwell well off from reinforcement and resupply by land, and 'blocked up' the road to the Border should the English feel inclined to break out. The general opined that it would be 'almost a miracle' if he were

---

15 British Library: Harleian Manuscripts, Number 6844, 123.
16 Reid, S. *Dunbar 1650: Cromwell's Most Famous Victory*, (Oxford: Osprey, 2004), p. 39-40.
17 Grainger, J. *Cromwell Against the Scots: the Last Anglo-Scottish War 1650-1652*, (East Linton: Tuckwell, 1997), p. 40.
18 There were possibly also additional smaller cadres or companies from other units which were attached to make up numbers in the regimental units.
19 Carte, *Original Letters*, p. 381.
20 Firth, *Dunbar*, p. 30; Carte, *Original Letters*, p. 380.
21 Letter from Cromwell to Lenthall, 4 September 1650; Carlyle, p. 385.

"SENSIBLE OF OUR DISADVANTAGES", MONDAY, 2 SEPTEMBER

33. Detail of Fisher's illustration of the Battle of Dunbar, showing the parish church on its raised mound and a rather disorderly English encampment beyond. So prominent is the confused nature of the camp that it may be a deliberate reflection of the chaotic nature of erecting it in stormy weather, constrained further by what are presumably dykes and hedged enclosures rather than entrenchments. Alternatively, it could just be further evidence of the difficulties of accepting the plan at face value. (Ashmolean Museum, University of Oxford).

able to get the army out that way.[22] How he discovered that the Scots had secured the pass is unknown, although his pickets might well have seen the Scottish force ride off to the east and made the assumption. Alternatively, a messenger may have attempted to reach Berwick before returning to camp with intelligence. The news prompted Cromwell's anxious letter to Newcastle, which confirmed in the post-script that it was now difficult to communicate effectively with England.

During the course of that 'very tempestuous' morning, as their armies were lashed with yet more rain, the rival commanders each had critical decisions to make which would determine the nature of the events to come. Cromwell's mind, as his own letter to parliament makes clear, was already drawing parallels with the disastrous events of Lostwithiel in autumn 1644. There, the Earl of Essex had been bottled up in the harbour town by the army of King Charles I, who slowly tightened the screws until it was clear Essex was totally trapped. The cavalry managed to break out and reach safety, but Essex himself left the field ignominiously in a fishing boat. Eventually, demoralised and battered by rain, the remaining infantry had been obliged to surrender their arms and baggage. The men themselves were allowed to march free, but the hostile population harassed their column as sickness and desertion completed the humiliation. The reputation of Essex, once the senior military figure for Parliament's cause, never recovered and the disaster paved the way

---

22   Letter from Cromwell to Haselrigge, 2 September 1650; Carlyle, p. 378.

'ESSENTIAL AGONY'

for the Self-Denying Ordnance and the "new-modelling" of the army the following year. This could yet prove to be the fate of Oliver Cromwell.

In fact, Cromwell's options were limited. As he had explained in his letter to Haselrigge, the closing of the Pass of Pease had effectively removed the option of breaking out towards Berwick with only the cavalry as had been done at Lostwithiel. The force Leslie had brought down off the hill could be brought across to challenge a limited break-out as it tried to push through to the pass. To embark his infantry meanwhile would be a major operation, as Dunbar harbour was small and entrance narrow: embarking thousands of soldiers in poor weather under pressure from the Scots would require time and coordination. And as Hodgson agreed, there simply was 'no time to ship the foot... and we would lose all our carriages.'[23] This left the humiliating prospect of capitulation, surrendering the infantry and baggage. It was later reported to Whitelocke that the Scots had considered offering terms to the English, allowing them to leave with their swords but nothing else.[24] With Leslie's position too strong to assault, no sign that the Scots would now offer a general engagement in the open town fields, and the English army weakening daily and so unable just to wait events out, there were only too realistic options that remained: Cromwell could either sue for terms or attempt to break out with the whole army. Hodgson summed up the mood: 'we had great experience of the goodness of God to us, while we kept close together; and if we parted we lost all.'[25]

34. View of Doon Hill from the vantage point of Dunbar parish church. From the tower the view would have been ever more useful.

---

23 Original Memoirs, p. 145.
24 Whitelocke, p. 239.
25 Original Memoirs, p. 145.

"SENSIBLE OF OUR DISADVANTAGES", MONDAY, 2 SEPTEMBER

David Leslie's position was more complex. His army was exposed to a similar scarcity of resources as his opponent. The country had been experiencing food shortages even before the campaign, and the concentration of a large army in one place for weeks on end had exacerbated that situation locally in the Lothians. The removal of all supplies from East Lothian ahead of Cromwell's invasion and then the wastage of large portions of the ripening harvest as the armies crossed the landscape, all combined to ensure that Leslie's army only had what little it had brought with it from Edinburgh. Only by returning to the capital could the Scots reasonably expect to resupply. So whilst there is nothing to suggest Leslie's men were yet racked with the bloody flux like so many of Cromwell's they were certainly hungry, and in a large army of weakening soldiers sickness was never far around the corner. Staying in front of Dunbar and waiting for Cromwell to make a move was therefore not an option.

This leads to the crucial consideration of the army's position on the top of Doon Hill. Superficially, it looked like a strong one, dominating the landscape, road and town below. Despite being almost two miles from the High Street Doon Hill is seemingly omnipresent, rearing into view from the harbour, the church, the streets, the fields. It is not its height which gives it impact, for the hill is only in fact 177m (580ft) above sea level; it is rather the sheerness of its north face, which makes it thrust up so incongruously out of the surrounding farmland. But the modest height is deceiving as the hill's elevation is enough to expose those on its summit to weather conditions considerably worse than those being experienced in the town below; winds are strong and rain lashes rather than falls. The level of visibility also changes rapidly, and this is an important consideration which is often overlooked. In poor weather Dunbar can disappear completely from view, sometimes only for moments, sometimes for hours.

Doon Hill was therefore a position with considerable drawbacks. The men were exposed, without shelter or the possibility of resupply, and as they lay on the hill's back their experience was considerably worse than it would be if they were on the lower ground. If the wind was bad enough, as Hodgson reported it, for the English tents to be unable to weather it, then the situation on the top of Doon Hill must have felt severe indeed. Eventually Cromwell's men were indeed able to get their tents up, and a luck few were able to warm themselves around fires fuelled by the church pews. There was no such opportunity atop Doon Hill. More concerning to Leslie than his men's comfort however was the possibility that the weather could screen Cromwell's preparations or movements if he chose either to evacuate or break out.[26] If the Scots were to intercept him, there was a long descent to cut the road east or a shorter but steeper one to the south-west, the latter requiring a loss of visual contact and then a further march around the base of the hill. Too strong for the enemy to attack, too far from the town to apply direct pressure, Doon Hill seemed far less strong a position to David Leslie as it might appear to the casual observer today.

---

26 There was even a remote possibility Cromwell could strike unexpectedly west, cutting Leslie off from Edinburgh.

'ESSENTIAL AGONY'

35. The reverse slope of Doon Hill, between its south face (left) and Brunt Hill (right), in which most of the Scottish soldiers are likely to have attempted to shelter in the rocky red mud.

There are three parts to Leslie's decision-making on the 2 September: the personal, the political, and the military. The first is difficult to assess in detail as the Scots general did not wear his heart on his sleeve. His true personality remains elusive, leaving us to make general assumptions based on what narrow windows can be found in the sources. Certainly Leslie was more committed to the Covenanter cause than to the king's, which influenced which voices he would hear loudest in council. He could be both cautious and decisive as required, but he could also be ruthless and permit notable excesses. David Leslie combined the zeal of religious conviction with the ambition of the career soldier, and although he falls short of brilliance he was an able and proven commander. He was certainly no fool. In the context of his deliberations on Doon Hill, this brief and inadequate analysis is both informative and inconclusive. It tells us that Leslie could indeed fulfil the description given by Roger Boyle, Earl of Orrery, of being 'a general greedy of honour and impatient for delay', but also that he had sufficient self-control not to risk the army against his judgement and the experience to make that judgement count.[27]

---

27 Orrery, *Art of War*, p. 149. Leslie is not named but is clearly meant. Orrery, as Lord Broghill, was at this time serving parliament in Ireland, motivated by an aggressive animosity towards the Catholic rebels. He had fought against the Scots in the Bishops' Wars, but he would later seek to reconcile them to the Commonwealth. After Cromwell's death, Broghill sensed the tide turning and secured Ireland for Charles II and the restored king raised him to the earldom of Orrery.

Politically, Leslie's situation was complicated by the presence of the advisory committee which had attached itself to the army in Leith. Johnston of Wariston, despite all his personal anxieties whenever battle seemed imminent, remained convinced that the godly government of the Kirk Party had secured divine favour. The constraints placed upon the king, the persistent rejection of the Engagers, and the purges of the army, all supported by fast days, prohibitions against drunkenness and swearing amongst the soldiery, and an increased prosecution of witches, should have done the job. Besides, the Covenant had seen off all challengers to date, surviving even after repeated defeats on the field.[28] Even so, it was not godliness which motivated the committee to encourage decisive action; it was a determination that the defeat of the invader should be seen to be the work of the Kirk Party's army. It was they who had saved the country, not the king. The committee also understood well the limits of the resources available for keeping the Scots army in the field, and the costs to the country of prolonging the conflict.

Some of the military pressures working on the Scots have already been discussed. The Doon Hill position was exposed and uncomfortable; the supply line was extended and incapable of supporting protracted manoeuvres; the hilltop made it difficult to act quickly to intercept Cromwell if he moved; and in the poor weather the position lacked even the obvious advantage of a clear view of the enemy. In order to turn the screws on Cromwell, the Scots would need to control the road south and restrict his ability to move out. The first step had been to secure the Pass of Pease, the next was to block the coastal corridor carrying the road which led to it, bottling Cromwell on the north/west side of the Brox Burn and cutting them off from supplies and reinforcements. The weather, which could only deteriorate as the year wore on, would close the seas. If however the English did decide to see it out, fortifying the landward approaches to Dunbar and settling down for the winter as Cromwell professed to have intended, then the Scots were too poorly supplied to maintain a directly threatening position. There was no guarantee the Scottish political alliance could survive the winter either. It was therefore important that the Scots army denied the English the opportunity or space to dig themselves in.

Framed in this way, there were powerful personal, political and military incentives for David Leslie to order his army off Doon Hill. The only serious argument in favour of remaining was that it prevented Cromwell from attacking him directly, and that argument was totally undermined by the combination of the weather and the need for supplies. Nevertheless, what the Scots were about to do continues to be viewed in popular discourse as a classic military blunder. A large and capable army was about to leave an impregnable position and lay itself open to attack. The professional soldier is overruled by the amateur politician or the zealot minister. So where does this interpretation come from? Robert Baillie confirms in his correspondence that Leslie's decision was 'a consequence of the Committee's order, contrary

---

28 After his desertion from the Covenant, Montrose had been seen almost as a devil incarnate. Defeating him in 1645 had given David Leslie enormous status, which was only slightly diminished by the ease with which Strachan had then defeated Montrose again at Carbisdale.

to his mind.'²⁹ There are two points to note here: firstly, that the subsequent disaster does not mean that the committee's reasoning, assuming it was indeed their decision, was not sound in the context in which it was taken; secondly, this assessment is expressed by a government desperate to prevent Leslie's resignation as it needed him to continue serving through the crisis. It therefore had an incentive not to lay the blame at his door.

When Leslie himself accepts that he will likely be blamed, it is for 'drawing them [the soldiers] so near the enemy,' for which he expects to be criticised, which is not quite the same as for coming down of the hill.³⁰ The difference may be subtle, but it may also be significant. Gilbert Burnet, who was a boy of eight when the battle was fought, also blamed Wariston for forcing Leslie to attack, but he was writing over thirty years later about events he did not personally witness. Burnet was also an Episcopalian and a close associate of Charles II after the Restoration, with little reason to speak up for the Kirk Party despite the fact that Wariston was his uncle. By the time he wrote his history in the 1680s, Burnet was also living in England and therefore drawing on the dominant interpretations available there.

This is important, as the English accounts are fairly consistent where they ascribe motivations for the Scottish manoeuvre. Cromwell himself, naturally the most authoritative account, writes on 4 September that he has heard 'the Ministers pressed their Army,' and although the military men wished the English might 'have way made, though it were by a golden bridge. But the clergy's counsel prevailed.'³¹ Reese interprets the golden bridge as meaning some 'secret negotiations' were attempted on the night of 1 September, although there is no clear evidence any took place.³² It is in fact simply a metaphor, meaning that Leslie would have preferred to see Cromwell's army leave of its own accord, by whatever means, without having to face him in battle. More important though is Cromwell's accusation that the Scots ministers were to blame for the decision to quit the hill. In another letter written on the same day, Cromwell again faults the ministers: 'since we came to Scotland it hath been our desire and longing to have avoided blood in this business…; the Ministers of Scotland have hindered the passage of these things.' He continues to point out that 'some of the Ministers are also fallen in this Battle.'³³ Major White also claims 'the ministers did so importune them that they could not rest quiet till they had engaged.'³⁴

We should be extremely cautious of taking these accounts at face value. The shift from focusing on the committee to blaming the clergy is an important one, as it reflects the hostility of the Independents to the Presbyterians. If

---

29 Baillie, *Letters and Journals*, Vol. III, p. 111.
30 Letter from Leslie to Argyll, 5 September 1650; *Ancrum Correspondence*, p. 298.
31 Letter from Cromwell to the Lord President of the Council of State, 4 September 1650; Carlyle, p. 390.
32 Reese, *Cromwell's Masterstroke*, p. 72. Robert Blair does speculate that 'papers were interchanged' between Cromwell's army and some members of the Committee of War but this may just be an attempt to disassociate from those who later served under Cromwell's administration; Row, Robert Blair, p. 238.
33 Letter from Cromwell to Speaker Lenthall, 4 September 1650; Carlyle, p. 388.
34 Quoted in Firth, *Dunbar*, p. 30-31.

the English parliament had done right by the Solemn League and Covenant, or if the Engagement had succeeded, or if a Covenanted Charles II were triumphant over Cromwell, then Scots Presbyterianism would have been imposed in England. That is why it was so important to condemn as loudly as possible 'a kirk whose religion is formality, and whose government is tyranny.'[35] Since the coming of the king had so demonstrably not caused a royalist revolution in Scotland, the English could not brand their enemy simply as Malignants. Instead they set about making the kirk the target of their hostility, creating a narrative which gave renewed legitimacy to their campaign. The Scots who had opposed the Engagement had done so because it had not been backed by the kirk; resistance to the English invasion of 1650 *was* backed by the kirk. If the English could undermine the kirk therefore, and blame them not only for blocking Cromwell's peaceful overtures but also for leading the Scots army to defeat, then they could justify their invasion on the grounds that no Scottish government could be trusted whether it was led by Engagers or the Kirk Party. Within Scotland, it might also drive a wedge between the ministers and the congregations, between the government and the levies.

David Leslie was certainly under pressure from some of those around him. Wariston and the committee of war, representing the government, would have been echoed in their calls for action by assertive Kirk Party military officers like Strachan and Ker. Robert Blair, a senior churchman, certainly remembered 'division and dissension among the prime officers of the army.'[36] These discussions were however motivated less by religious zeal than by serious military pressures: fears that Leslie's army might fall apart even without a battle, or that Cromwell would steal back the initiative. If Leslie had indeed opposed moving the army into a more aggressive stance at Dunbar, which he would only have done if the tactical case was strongly against it, then it is likely that he would have been supported by the Earl of Leven, whose experience was frankly unrivalled. It is not an exaggeration to say that Leven was one of the greatest commanders Scotland had ever produced, and despite his age there is no reason to doubt his ability to read the situation at least as well as Leslie and probably better. Leslie, despite his pride and doubtless his desire to step out from beneath his namesake's shadow, knew Leven intimately and would certainly have weighed his advice. James Lumsden would have been another valuable voice of reason amongst the senior command. The combination of Leslie, Leven and Lumsden had the experience, competence and confidence to assert their views, and the counsel of caution had prevailed whenever it had been needed thus far.[37] It is hard to conceive of a situation which saw their collective wisdom overwhelmed against their express wishes, whether by a committee of war or by a gaggle of clergymen.

---

35 Letter reported by Whitelocke, p. 240.
36 Row, *Robert Blair*, p. 238.
37 What Major-General James Holborne might have thought is unclear, but his career will have left him fully aware of the capacity of the army they faced, and he may well have been wary of unnecessary risk.

'ESSENTIAL AGONY'

36. The view from the summit of Doon Hill in good conditions.

During the course of the afternoon, the Scots army moved slowly off the summit of Doon Hill. For the watching English soldiers, many of whom had only seen their enemy from a distance or in the chaotic darkness of fast-paced night attacks, the sight will have triggered feelings of anxiety and anticipation, even a little excitement in places. It did not happen quickly: as the hours passed, the grey-clad regiments dipped from view on the crest and reappeared again as they moved around onto the forward slopes. They descended from both flanks of the hill, the snaking easterly columns of cavalry more visible whilst most of the foot took the shorter but steeper route around the west. Thousands of men and horses in large formations negotiated the slick wet ground without the benefit of significant trackways to aid them, gusts of wind throwing fresh rain against their faces. Pikes were sloped over the shoulder to prevent the wind tugging and tangling at the formations, the path too steep for the shafts to be carried at the trail. The whole army did not move at once, but by a cautious and piecemeal descent which built through the afternoon. By 4pm the artillery and baggage were on the move too, iron-rimmed wheels sliding in the churned ground as teams strained on dragropes and cursed at their mud-splashed workhorses. Leslie and his staff came down too, leaving behind them a barren landscape of slopping brown mud, the rainwater pooling in the shallow abandoned nests of the weary Scottish soldiers.

Oliver Cromwell had drawn a garrison into the enclosure of Broxmouth House, manning its walls and hedges. Inside the ageing manor, the general had revitalised his customary optimism through prayer. He reassured his staff that God had surely heard him and would be sure to intercede. Now, peering though perspective glasses from the south-facing windows, Cromwell exclaimed: "God is delivering them into our hands, they are coming down to us."[38] It was the sight of the artillery and baggage descending at 4pm which

---
38 Fraser, Cromwell, p. 263.

"SENSIBLE OF OUR DISADVANTAGES", MONDAY, 2 SEPTEMBER

finally confirmed that the Scots were committed to a total redeployment. Cromwell's own army was moved forward to the Brox Burn, occupying the raised fold which ran parallel with the ravine a little way back from its lip. The left flank arced northwards and was anchored at Broxmouth, around which most of the cavalry were massed to control the road and crossing points. Fleetwood detached a small picket of twenty-four men from Pride's Regiment, supported by six troopers, to occupy the 'poor house' around 400m east of the main ford.[39]

As the Scots army began to mass on the sloping ground to the north of Doon Hill, officers riding along the line with instructions whilst sergeants dressed ranks and sodden soldiers shuffled and muttered, Leslie observed the tiny English outpost at the cottage. Humble though it was, this little house sat in the basin of the 'shelving pass' as Cadwell called it, the gap between two banks of rising ground through which the road to Berwick ran.[40] The six horsemen were presumably posted on the hillocks, from which they had an uninterrupted view of the Scottish deployments. These lifting folds in the ground are an important feature of a landscape which is often simplified into a flat plain: in fact the land between the ravine and Doon Hill rises almost continuously as you move inland, whilst a series of folds and dips mean that whole formations could disappear out of view from certain perspectives.

37. The ground into which the Scots army now moved, between the ravine and the hill. They occupied a subtle ridgeline which can be discerned in this image by the line of the bushes in the centre. Little Pinkerton is on the left. The view is from Cromwell's new position along the bank of the ravine, near Oswald Dean (on the right, where the bank is broken down and access to the burn easier).

---

39 Carte, *Original Letters*, p. 382. Carlyle asserts the house may be a shepherd's hut.
40 This corresponds roughly with the site of the present battlefield monument, although the lie of the ground has surely been affected on the south-western side by the construction of the railway. As a result the actual "pass" talked of in the accounts is less obvious that it might have been at the time, although the word is used with considerable freedom in accounts of battlefield landscapes and need not imply major features, just the easiest places to move formed bodies.

Understanding this means that the isolated English picket near the poor little house at the roadside makes a little more sense: the hump of ground beside it gave Cromwell's staff their closest view of the Scottish deployment, for once the latter had descended the hill their intentions were less easily discerned from the windows of Broxmouth. By the same token, this ground would give Leslie a much better vantage point for interpreting the English dispositions around the fords.

Accordingly, the Scottish commander detached two troops of horse to clear the ground ahead of his army. This occurred around 4pm, just as the English were observing the definitive motions of the Scottish train as it descended to a new position between the two Pinkerton farms. This was the height of the Scots descent, and for the six English troopers on the little hillock there was plenty to observe and therefore to distract the eye. The sudden advance of two troops of lancers may not therefore have drawn immediate urgent attention; certainly they Scots were bearing down on the outpost before there was any hope of evacuating it safely. The English troopers, unable of course to oppose such a large force, 'gave way' and galloped back across the burn to safety.[41] This left the remaining twenty-six soldiers of Pride's Regiment, most likely to be musketeers, totally exposed. A full troop of Scots horse should, according to the levy instructions, have contained 75 men, giving a theoretical total detachment of 150 lancers attacking the outpost.

The Scots were enthusiastic, falling on the outpost and quickly killing three foot-soldiers. We can imagine their backs pierced with lance points as they fled in vain from their posts towards the turf-roofed hut, whilst the odd musket cracked to provide some futile cover for them. Such a lowly building as the 'poor house' probably had no windows or enclosures from which to mount any serious form of defence, and thus served only to prevent the soldiers from being overwhelmed from all sides. It seems likely that they attempted to flee, keeping what order they could, but that the lancers rode over them, bowling many to the ground and slashing at others. It seems clear that many of the English soldiers were wounded, perhaps only superficially, but that the Scots did not over-play their hand and were content to have driven them off so ignominiously. They had cleared the road, ensuring there were no enemy eyes on their side of the burn, and taken several prisoners who could potentially enlighten their commanders as to the mood in the English army. This was probably one of their key objectives. The Scots had won first blood at the Battle of Dunbar.

Some English accounts claimed that the Scots mistreated the English picket after rounding them up, first offering quarter and then cutting up their prisoners 'in a most barbarous manner' before releasing them.[42] But Cadwell's early report only mentions that they 'took three, and wounded and drove away the rest,' and does not mention any 'cruel usage.'[43] Cromwell does not report the incident at all, perhaps at least in part because there had been

---

41 Carte, *Original Letters*, p. 382.
42 Rushworth, *Old Parliamentary History*, xix, p. 342.
43 Carte, *Original Letters*, p. 382; *A True Relation of the Routing of the Scottish Army*, in Original Memoirs, p. 279.

"SENSIBLE OF OUR DISADVANTAGES", MONDAY, 2 SEPTEMBER

38. Broxmouth Lodge, which may mark the location of the 'poor house' around which the first blood of the battle was shed. It marks a later entrance point into the estate, which in 1650 was restricted to the western side of the burn. Its position would therefore have been isolated at the side of the road.

39. Detail of Fisher's plan, showing what is probably the 'poor house' on its own to the left and soldiers crossing the ford towards it. Note the garrison on the wall beneath Broxmouth, and the baggage wagons drawn up behind. (Ashmolean Museum, University of Oxford)

an oversight in that no covering force had been sent to extricate the picket. The *True Relation* mentions that the soldiers at the poor house were 'not seconded by those appointed to bring them off,' indicating that somebody somewhere had failed in their duty.[44] If the Scots did indeed attack men who were at their mercy after being captured, then it was reprehensible and indicative of the hostility felt by the common soldier towards an invader who had caused them considerable hardship. But had such an outrage occurred it would surely have been worthy of mention by the commander. It seems entirely possible that the story grew in the telling, perhaps beginning with the men of Pride's Regiment who had both suffered the indignity of being driven off and, potentially, failing to cover their comrades' retreat. Certainly the True Relation says Pride's claimed to have gotten even with the Scots the next day.

One of the soldiers captured by the Scots was a character of the sort which often emerges to enliven such moments in history. Despite having only one hand, this worthy veteran showed a defiant courage and brazen audacity which must have created quite a scene when he was brought before the Scots general. There followed a memorable exchange, as reported by Cadwell. The soldier had, despite his disability, fired three times during the short skirmish with the lancers.[45] Leslie interrogated him personally, asking if the English army still intended to fight. "What do you think we came here for?" the prisoner replied. The general, apparently unabashed by this tone and determined to test his captive for information, continued by asking how the English expected to fight with half their men and all their great guns embarked for evacuation. "Sir," the soldier retorted carefully, "if you please to draw down your army to the foot of the hill, you shall find both men and great guns also." By this time the Scots had already brought themselves down to the forward slopes, but was still holding ground considerably higher than their opponents. Another Scottish officer intervened: "How dare you answer the general so saucily?" "I only made answer to the question asked," maintained the stubborn soldier, who was dismissed with a trumpeter for escort back to his own lines. When he reported what had occurred to his own general, the veteran further claimed that he had lost twenty shillings as a result of the skirmish. Cromwell, no doubt amused by the audacity, gave him some coins for his troubles.

Oliver Cromwell had quit Broxmouth after observing the Scots descent, securing his army's position along the burn. He may well have brought forward guns to cover the road out of Dunbar, as once the Scots detachment had driven off the picket they declined to stay in the vicinity of the poor house; they would have been in range of any artillery posted on the bluff above the ravine where the burn rounds towards the north, where its banks finally shallowed beyond Brands Mill towards the sea. After ensuring all was in order, Cromwell 'with his officers went and supped at Dunbar for refreshment.'[46] Where he actually went is unknown, but Cadwell's phrasing

---

44 Original Memoirs, p. 278.
45 Without apparently hitting anyone, it should be added.
46 Carte, *Original Letters*, p. 382.

suggests that it was not at Broxmouth but within the town itself, presumably because the cupboards were as bare at Broxmouth as in all other houses they had visited. Cadwell puts the supper at just after 4pm, the same time he gives for the skirmish at the cottage. Perhaps that explains how nobody was immediately available to order the extraction of the picket. 'Before five of the clock', perhaps triggered by the sounds of the distant skirmishing, 'they took horse and went into the fields.'[47]

Over the next few hours, as day turned to evening, Cromwell and his officers observed the final crucial manoeuvres of the Scots army. 'The Enemy,' reports the general, 'drew down to the right wing about two-thirds of their left wing of horse. To the right wing; shogging also their foot and train much to the right; causing their right wing to edge down towards the sea.'[48] This description is of crucial importance to our understanding. Leslie was clearly massing his cavalry on his right (east) flank, leaving only a small force of horse on the left over towards Spott House. The foot also shifted to the right, recognising in their redeployment that the fords near Broxmouth were now the critical corridor of action, since the steepness of the Brox Burn ravine prevented any serious possibility of a battle being fought across it. The baggage train was concentrated with a strong guard between the two Pinkerton farms, where the low ramparts of ancient earthworks might yet have stood to give some basic enclosures for the waggons.[49]

David Leslie's army, after much movement and re-alignment in the early evening, now extended along the whole ridgeline below Doon Hill. In the west, his extreme left lay close to small burn running from Spott House, able to control the crossing point of the Brox Burn below Spott village. The centre of the infantry line covered the Oswald Dean ford and, further east, gazed down the open sloping ground towards with Little Pinkerton farm immediately to their rear. To their right, the line of the right wing of the foot bowed slightly into a north-easterly direction, the ravine of the burn turning more directly northwards away from them. This brought the line across where the modern A1 motorway runs, beyond which the old road to Berwick was controlled by the massed Scottish cavalry which comprised the army's right wing. The extreme right lay on ground which sloped away towards the sea, and it seems likely it did so near Whitesands bay since this was where the sea came closest into the landscape, closing the flank.

This alignment matches both Cromwell's detailed description and also Hodgson's: 'a great clough was between the armies, and it could be no less than a mile of ground betwixt their right wing, near Roxburgh house, and their left wing; they had a great mountain behind them.'[50] In fact the whole span of available space on this alignment was just short of two miles, and calculations by Historic Environment Scotland have estimated the Scottish line, based on contemporary military manuals and the estimated numbers,

---

47 Carte, *Original Letters*, p. 382.
48 Letter from Cromwell to Speaker Lenthall, 4 September 1650; Carlyle, p. 386.
49 It is possible that it was closer to Meikle Pinkerton, placing it far to the rear.
50 Original Memoirs, p. 144. Roxburgh house refers to Broxmouth, which was owned by the Earl of Roxburgh as has already been mentioned elsewhere.

'ESSENTIAL AGONY'

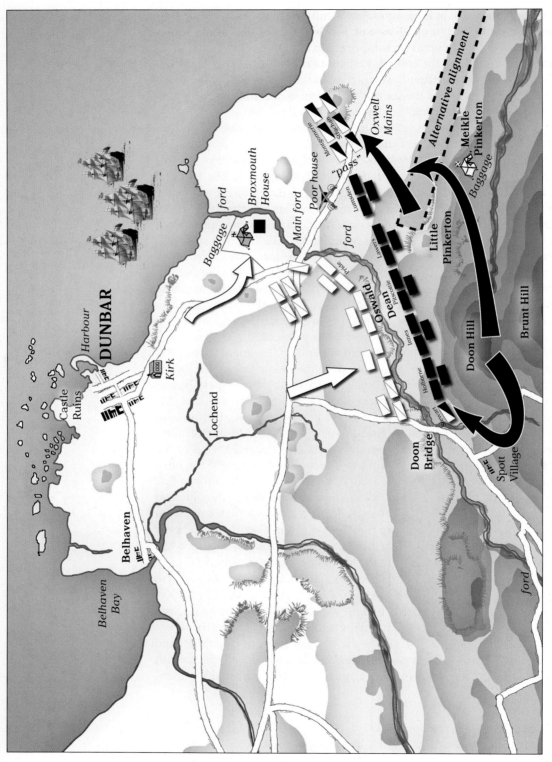

Map 7. Both armies redeploy along the Brox Burn. Also indicated is the alternative Scottish position proposed by Historic Environment Scotland (based on Firth's interpretation of Fisher's plan).

at around a mile and a half in length. Any infantry attack by Cromwell's men on this line would face an uphill assault, and likewise for the cavalry if they were to be turned on the seaward side. This again satisfies descriptions of the coming engagement.

There is no need therefore to swing the axis of the battle-line back until it is formed at right-angles to the burn, with Little Pinkerton now on the left rather than centre, as the recent Historic Environment Scotland plan has done. This is based on Firth's analysis, which is based almost exclusively on an interpretation of Fitz-Payne Fisher's illustration.[51] This proposed alignment fails on a number of point as will later be shown, not least in the fact that the Scots line cannot draw up here and still be described as having 'shogged' right towards the sea. In fact the Scots right would have been totally open, somewhere beyond the modern Easter Pinkerton. This line also fails to fulfil Cromwell's assessment that the Scots were planning 'an attempt upon us, or to place themselves in a more exact condition of interposition.' On the contrary, such an alignment would have placed no increased pressure on Cromwell's army at all as it did not close the road or threaten assault.[52] As a result, the alignment of the Scots army must have been as described above, closely linked along most of its length by the line of the ravine.

40. Spott House was to the rear of the extreme left of the Scottish position and therefore too distant from the danger-point on the right. It remains a private estate.

---

51 Firth, *Battle of Dunbar*.
52 It also left the Oswald Dean and Spott village crossing points completely undefended behind the Scots line. The Scots right would have been almost 1.5 miles to the south-east of Broxmouth, over undulating ground, meaning Hodgson's report must be wrong. Cromwell could not have seen its deployment.

This leaves our two armies, as the rain continued to gust over them whilst the gloomy daylight faded into darkness, facing one another in close proximity. Cromwell's men had managed to erect their encampment, but with the enemy so close it is unlikely any expected that they might gain much use of it. As such, Walker's comparison – 'Cromwell in a Town and Tents, and the Scottish army exposed in the fields' – might in fact be a false one.[53] Darkness brought no safety, just the increase fear that the threat might now develop unseen. The new Scottish position may well have been lower and out of the worst of the wind, but it was certainly no drier on that 'very rainy and tempestuous' night. They still stood to arms in their positions, and twice there were alarms which justified their vigilance.

David Leslie retired to his bed in the early hours of Tuesday morning, riding the short distance to Spott House satisfied that the enemy would not now attempt a breakout under cover of the lashing rain. Spott was the largest house in the vicinity, and although it has evolved considerably since it was once possible for local guides to point out the room in which Leslie slept that tempestuous morning. It seems likely that the Earl of Leven was already there, since there will have been little purpose in the ageing veteran spending long hours out in the rain getting under the feet of a protégé he considered perfectly capable. Leslie had made his dispositions and given his orders, and shortly before daylight on 3 September he expected his cavalry to begin tightening the knot on Cromwell by moving up and threatening the fords.

If Leslie then chose to continue aggressively, this would probably be the prelude to a major attack on the fords at Brands Mill and Broxburn. Although Broxmouth House and its walls were a significant strongpoint below the main ford, a massed assault on the flank of the main army could potentially split the latter from the garrison and isolate the men there. The Scottish artillery could probably deal with the garrison from the rising ground to the east and south-east of its grounds; if not then the infantry would have to 'storm Broxmouth House.'[54] Their numerical advantage would give the Scots huge impetus on the attack, especially against a weak and demoralised opponent. If successful, the Scots assault on the fords would force Cromwell to pull back from the protection of the ravine to avoid having his flank turned, withdrawing to form a new line in front of Dunbar itself. This would probably be anchored on the parish church and its prominent knoll, but it would require the abandonment of the English camp and made any form of breakout impossible. and the Scottish army would then have the freedom to cross the burn and deploy their full force in the town fields. Cromwell would

---

53 Walker, *Historical Discourses*, p. 165.
54 Baillie, *Letters and Journals*, Vol. III, p. 111. It is worth noting that some modern plans of the battle appear to show Broxmouth as a house standing in isolation, which makes dealing with a garrison seem like short work. However, as we have already seen, travellers in recent times had commented on the thorn plantations at Broxmouth and Fisher's plan very clearly shows an enclosed estate with trees, hedges and a stone wall manned by musketeers. The estate perimeter was certainly smaller than it is today, but we would surely be surprised to find an estate such as Roxburghe's not to be enclosed. This makes a difference in understanding how Cromwell's men crossed the burn, as they could not have done so in the enclosed area.

be forced to seek terms to save what remained of his army, or fight to the last against formidable odds.

If the Scottish intentions were this aggressive, then the plan was not without risk. If Cromwell's men stood firm at the ford, the battle would be intense and costly. But even if the attack failed, Leslie's army would still remain and it would have closed the road to England decisively with its new position. Besides, Cromwell could not afford the losses of a stubbornly fought defence even if it was a successful one. Whilst pinning him down at the ford, the Scots might even be able to detach forces from their left to go via the Spott ford to fall upon Cromwell's flank and rear. It would be like a reversed version of the battle at Winwick in 1648, only it was Cromwell holding the narrow roadway beside a ravine, and the Scottish horse which would work around his flank and force him back to a final defence around the churchyard. That same engagement had also shown Cromwell that the Scots, even when in dire circumstances, could hold their own for hours against a narrow frontal assault. But these comparisons and possibilities will never have occurred to the English commander: Cromwell was not planning to defend.

According to Hodgson, the English command assembled for a council of war at around 9pm on Monday evening. By then the extent and nature of the Scottish redeployments had been observed and analysed throughout the day until darkness ended the chances of seeing anything further even in the unlikely case that something major was attempted. Although the options for evacuating the foot and breaking out with the horse were discussed,

41. Broxmouth House, showing Cromwell's Mount to the left with its iconic Cedar of Lebanon. The present house is 18th Century but appears to stand on the same site.

apparently being the preference of some regimental colonels, it was accepted that even if this was the best option the window of opportunity had already closed. Hodgson, writing with the benefit of hindsight of course, has Lambert providing five reasons why the army should attack the Scots. Firstly, it was important to keep the whole army together to maximise its strength rather than dividing horse and foot. Secondly, embarking the foot would take too long and require an abandonment of the baggage. Thirdly, the Scottish alignment restricted the ability of the left and centre to support the right in case of attack there, giving the English an opportunity to secure the road. The fourth point was that the Scots 'had left intervals in their bodies' which could allow units to be defeated in detail. Finally, the English artillery could pin the Scottish left and centre down whilst the attack went in on the right.[55]

This was persuasive argument, and its eloquence was a result of planning. Cromwell is believable when he reports that both he and Lambert formulated the same appreciation of the opportunities as they watched the Scots deploying: 'I told him [Lambert] I thought it did give us an opportunity and advantage to attempt upon the enemy. To which he immediately replied, that he had thought to have said the same thing to me.'[56] Such was the synergy between these two highly capable and experienced commanders, the same conjoined awareness which had wreaked havoc on the Engagers' plans in 1648. 'We called for Colonel Monk,' continues Cromwell, a sign of the confidence the general placed in his advice. These three men had then presented their plans, quite probably with Lambert as their mouthpiece, to the council of war at Broxmouth that night. This allowed Cromwell, with due propriety, not to express his own judgement until others had freely expressed theirs. Faced with Lambert's rehearsed logic, however, the regimental colonels all 'cheerfully concurred.'[57]

The first two of Lambert's arguments, the reasons not to evacuate the foot by sea, have been discussed elsewhere already. The three remaining points are all highly significant however, and amount to an explanation of the English battle-plan. The third argument used to support an attack was that the Scots 'had not great ground to traverse their regiments betwixt the mountain and the clough.'[58] This primarily affected their left and centre, which lay in a corridor of ground which was roughly 275m wide between the Brox Burn and the northern face of Doon Hill. This was indeed an extremely narrow space for manoeuvring large formed bodies of men, especially since brigades were drawn up with two battalia to the fore and a third behind covering the space between the front two. For a brigade to redeploy in battle order to face ninety degrees to its right was therefore no simple task, and once it had done so it would then fill the corridor and prevent any of the units behind from moving up in support.[59]

---

55 *Original Memoirs*, p. 145.
56 Letter from Cromwell to Speaker Lenthall, 4 September 1650; Carlyle, p. 386.
57 Letter from Cromwell to Speaker Lenthall, 4 September 1650; Carlyle, p. 386.
58 Original Memoirs, p. 145.
59 This challenge would not have existed if the deployment was as HES have interpreted Firth's article, as most of the Scots frontage would have been unhindered by the landscape as they had left the ravine off to the left.

The two-up-one-back formation was a standard one, designed to allow a fresh formation to move forward in support of the front line when the latter came under pressure or to form a reserve line should it be driven back. The battalia were each a self-contained block of pikemen supported by two sleeves of musketeers, capable of operating independently as well as within the bigger unit. The men it contained often came from more than one regiment, as a brigade usually comprised three regiments and the ratios of pike to shot in the battalia were far more important than the integrity of a regiment as a tactical unit. Command and control was therefore more complicated at the tactical level than is often appreciated. Nevertheless, this was a battle-winning system which had been honed through decades of experience in European and then British theatres of war, to all of which the Scottish senior commanders had been proactively exposed. This formation did however mean that there were, as Hodgson tells us that Lambert had pointed out in council, 'intervals in their bodies, on the brink of the hill,' and if the Scots army was not alert and under tight control then these gaps could be exploited, particularly by cavalry, to sow confusion. Clearly this is what was meant by Lambert's fourth point. The brink of the hill was surely the ridgeline which ran parallel with Doon Hill on its northern face, atop which sat Little Pinkerton farm.

Lambert's final winning argument was the potential to make decisive use of the English artillery. Hodgson is clear: 'our guns might have fair play at their left wing, while we were fighting their right.' Between Oswald Dean and Brands Mill the ravine of the Brox Burn turns northwards in a wide arc, creating a protected salient which allowed the English guns to be brought quite close to the Scottish line without fear of counter-attack. It was effectively a giant half-moon battery, about 350m across, onto which Cromwell could mount his heavier guns. These were the guns which Leslie hoped might already have been embarked, despite the bluffs of his one-handed captive. The lighter guns had been distributed along the lines, two to a regiment, as infantry support weapons earlier that day. From the salient in the line of the burn, Cromwell's cannon would indeed be able to fire directly on the Scottish right ahead of the main attack, and then when the lines were engaged here they could easily switch their fire to the Scottish centre and left. Combined with the points above, this meant that the Scots formations there would have to try wheeling to face the threat to their right whilst exposing their flanks to raking artillery fire from barely 500m away.

There is, however, one critical issue which is not decisively cleared up by either Hodgson or Cromwell in their accounts of the decision making: was the intention to decisively defeat the whole Scots army; or simply to use the whole army to break out rather than just the cavalry. Nothing which either report says confirms either, although Hodgson goes so far as to say 'if we beat their right wing, we hazarded their whole army, for they would ne all in confusion.' This could well be the benefit of hindsight however. One important piece of evidence lies in Fisher's engraving, which clearly shows the English waggons clustered under guard in the enclosures at Broxmouth. As they had previously been corralled at the churchyard, there must have been an order to bring them forward and this is indicative of a particular intent. As Reid has also identified, it would have been an extremely unusual decision to bring the baggage train forwards towards the area of contact in anticipation of a planned general engagement.[60] It makes far more sense, however, if the intention was to have the waggons ready to move rapidly onto the road ahead of a successful break-out.

Once the decision had been taken to mount the attack, the detailed arrangements had to be made. Cromwell's army would form what amounted to a single massed column, which would only be able to form proper battalia for action once on the other side of the burn. There were three places the army could cross: the upper ford where Brands Mill now stands; the main ford where the road crossed; and the lower ford beyond Broxmouth estate, which was probably just a wide stretch of shallow water unrestrained by the banks which formed the ravine higher up. How wide the corridor was between the sea and Broxmouth's enclosure cannot now be known, as the latter's boundaries have clearly changed; but even now there is a belt of land between the perimeter of the park and the coastline.[61] This was probably the widest crossing point but it was also the furthest from the enemy and required a detached march through what is now Deer Park and around the north side of the estate, all of which was out of direct contact with the rest of the army and would take longer. The crossing would have to be crossed quickly and efficiently as they were not wide. Command and control would be critical, and every unit would need to be positioned correctly in the column so that redeployment for action was efficient.

The vanguard was to be six regiments of horse: Lambert's, Fleetwood's and Whalley's to the fore; Lilburne's, Hacker's and Twisleton's close behind. Next came the infantry van, which perhaps surprisingly was to be Monck's brigade despite it being nominally the weakest: Monck's own regiment, Mauleverer's, and Fenwick's half regiment. Perhaps these units had been less depleted than others by sickness, making the disparity in numbers an administrative illusion. It was certainly an expression of confidence in Monck, and a real chance for him to make is name under Cromwellian colours. Behind this brigade came Pride's, comprising Pride's own, the Lord General's and Lambert's regiments of foot; and finally Overton's brigade comprising Coxe's, Daniel's and Fairfax's regiments. Cromwell's own Regiment of Horse brought up the rear as the final reserve, with those companies of Okey's Dragoons which were mounted. Okey's other companies continued to line the bank of the ravine, where their presence could cloak the major redeployment happening beyond during the night and, come the battle, ensure the minor ford at Oswald Dean was covered.

The English began preparing for their redeployment around 10pm, soon after the conclusion of the council of war. The Scots detected movement and stood ready, but nothing came of it.[62] It was not until the small hours that the regiments were ordered to draw up their column. Tents were left standing,

---

60   Reid, *Crown, Covenant and Cromwell*, p.165.
61   Now filled by links belonging to Dunbar Golf Club, which contrary to the implication in a recent fictional account of the battle was obviously not there in 1650.
62   Row, *Robert Blair*, p. 238.

orders given than personal baggage was to be left behind and only the essential waggons loaded at Broxmouth for movement. The night continued as filthy as the preceding day, and in this landscape already churned up by marching feet and the rolling of waggons the roadway was probably indistinguishable from the broad muddy slicks along its flanks. It was hard going for the soldiers, the darkness compounded by rainstorms which reduced visibility dramatically. Men bunching close together for shelter and support, and so as not to become separated in the darkness and confusion, exacerbated the impact of slipping and sliding in the mud by disordering those around them. Pikes became entangled, hands grappled for support, voices cursed and muttered; vigilant officers hissed back at them. The ground between the ravine's banks and the line of the road was far from flat, further complicating the coordination as the whole army, eleven thousand men, moved onto a new axis and prepared for a major operation.

The men were cold, wet, exhausted and hungry, but the prospect of imminent action had a steeling effect. Hodgson, on seeing a cornet speaking his earnest prayers, gave the care of his troop over to a subordinate and rode to hear the words. Inspiring the young officer must have been, for Hodgson 'met with so much God' on hearing him that the coming action held no fear; when he returned to his 'poor weak soldiers' he was able to encourage them greatly.[63] No doubt similar scenes were experienced elsewhere, as the veteran soldiers found what comfort they needed from their faith, their companions, or their shared experiences. The weather helped to shield their movements, but the enemy was close at hand so there was no room for complacency even if it was generally accepted that silence was impossible. Whilst Lambert took the lead in ordering the column, Cromwell bit his lip with anxiety until it bled. As the hours passed, he itched with impatience and nervous energy. He knew the stakes could not have been higher. As Thomas Carlyle would later put it, imagining that fateful night: 'the Harvest Moon wades deep among clouds of sleet and hail. Whoever has a heart for prayer, let him pray now, for the wrestle of death is at hand.'[64] And pray they might, for on both sides of the Brox Burn the generals have been planning for an assault.

---

63 Original Memoirs, p. 146.
64 Carlyle, p. 381.

7

"The Wrestle of Death", Tuesday, 3 September

After a long day cautiously shifting themselves of the summit of Doon Hill, then redeploying and redressing at its foot, the Scots army had spent long hours standing in battalia in the darkness. Buffeted by the cold rain, hunger gnawing at their stomachs, the grey-clad regiments waited for an attack that they never really believed would materialise. The wind carried ghostly sounds on its disorientating gusts, but with tens of thousands of men stretching across the landscape there was no way of interpreting them. After the early alarm at 10pm there was at least one other anxious moment; pikes were raised and the army stood ready to repel whatever came out of the darkness. But a ravine which was virtually impassable in daylight was completely impossible to cross in the night, so the risk could only come on the right and there the army was furthest from the enemy. It must have been the regiments withdrawing from the lip of the burn which the Scots had heard, or perhaps even deliberate attempts by the English to remind the Scots that they were still in position, a screen for their planned redeployment. Perhaps they were withdrawing altogether, the more optimistic Scots might have hoped.

The order for the army to stand down, coming sometime between 12am and 3am, was understandable. The chances of anything dramatic occurring before dawn were negligible, and the Scots were anyway confident that they held the initiative. The army was tired and hungry, and faced the prospect of launching a potentially difficult assault in the morning; there was little to be gained by keeping them in arms all through such a wet and tempestuous night. According to Walker, many of the troopers unsaddled their horses; wet and chafing, their mounts were suffering as much as they were.[1] Soldiers found little comfort among the trampled corn, but exhausted meant that sleep came quickly as they huddled together against the elements. Many officers looked to their own comforts and retired from the line.

Leslie later complained that he had given orders that the men 'stand to their arms' all night, but neither he nor his senior staff were on hand to see

---

1 Walker, *Historical Discourses*, p. 180.

"THE WRESTLE OF DEATH", TUESDAY, 3 SEPTEMBER

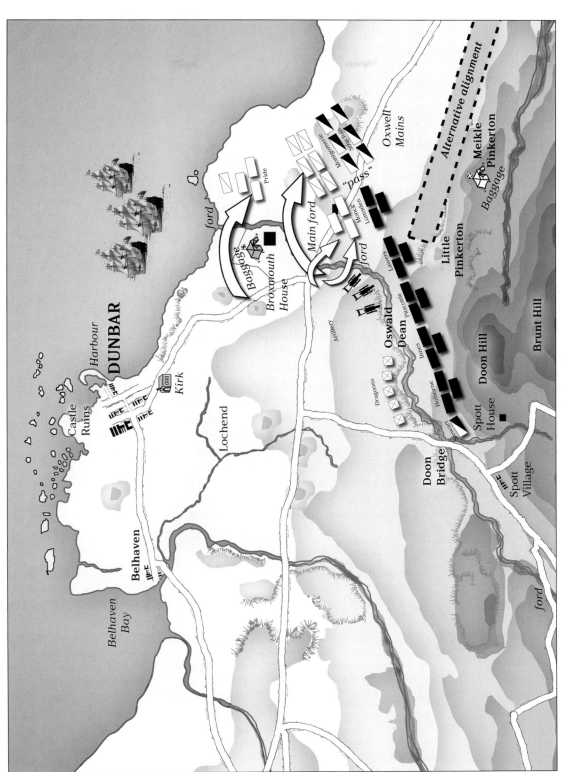

Map 8. Cromwell launches his army forward against the Scottish right.

to it.² Walker blames the committee of war, although it seems far more likely that its members had long since sought shelter themselves, possibly at Spott House with Leven. What seems more likely is that Major-General James Holborne, to whom the blame is usually attached for giving the order to extinguish the musketeers' match, found himself to be the only officer of note in the vicinity and may well have simply allowed the soldiers to yield to their inevitable desire to rest.³ If regimental officers were absenting themselves also, there was no chain of command to prevent it. Leslie officer corps had let him down, but they had done so by following his own lead.⁴ It was a lapse in leadership and a failure in discipline. No fault should be attached to the soldiers themselves, for their miseries had been faced with stoic endurance. Besides, despite the alarms, there was a general sense in the Scottish lines that they could rest 'in great security.'⁵ Their biggest problem was the weather, but they could hardly have got any wetter than they already were.

Most of the Scottish soldiers will not have moved far to find rest, and although they were no longer standing in readiness the men will still have clustered in their companies close to their positions. On the far left was William Stewart's small regiment of horse, in the relatively safe nook behind the Brox Burn to their fore and its little tributary to their west. The rest of the Scottish cavalry were on the right, massed into two brigades led by Robert Montgomerie and Archibald Strachan, the team which had led the raid on Musselburgh which had caused such havoc. The foot regiments were arrayed in standard fashion according to the seniority of the brigade commanders: Lumsden's took the right and Holborne the left; Colin Pitscottie's brigade formed the centre, with James Campbell of Lawers' to their right and John Innes' to their left. The artillery seems to have been massed towards the right, presumably in expectation of being deployed against Broxmouth once daylight came.⁶ But by the time the sun rose in the east, the Scots army would already be teetering on the brink of disaster.

Cromwell's plan was for the 'falling-on to be by break of day,' which would have been sometime between 5am and 6am. That would give the advanced preparations the cover of darkness, and then sufficient light for the main engagement to be coordinated. The various English accounts are muddled

---

2 Letter from Leslie to Argyll; see Appendix III.
3 Walker, *Historical Discourses*, p. 165. Reid has interpreted the order to extinguish the match as evidence that the Scots were not in fact planning a major offensive operation for the morning. This seems an unnecessary leap: if the Scots were controlling the timetable they would have plenty of time to relight their match before moving out. Reid, *Crown, Covenant and Cromwell*, p. 166.
4 Perhaps the purges had weakened the sense of professionalism amongst the officer corps, but they should have heightened rather than reduced the fear of dismissal. Indeed, Leslie should have been (and probably was) making use of the purges to remove the least qualified officers as well as the least politically desirable. It was not therefore the system which was at fault, it was the officers themselves and their senior role models.
5 It was a lapse in leadership and a failure in discipline.
6 Reese believes the artillery would have been of little use in Leslie's planned attack on the ford, because the walls of Broxmouth estate would been in the way of their line of fire. That is precisely why they *would* have been of use, to cannonade the garrison there and clear the flank of the attacking column at the ford. The reality is that the location of Leslie's guns is not at all clear, although Walker does allude to them being on the right of the Scottish line.

"THE WRESTLE OF DEATH", TUESDAY, 3 SEPTEMBER

42. The main ford over the Broxburn, today replaced with a low bridge.

over the precise timings, which suggests that it was the growing light which was the critical signal rather than a pre-arranged hour on the clock. At last, after that long and wearying night and a campaign of seemingly unending wet, hunger and disappointment, the moment of action was drawing near. Cromwell himself was agitated, his impatience transferring to his horse as it stamped its hooves and whipped its main. Perhaps he was now at the top of the mound beside Broxmouth House which gave him a vantage point from which to look over his army beyond the estate enclosure, massed in a dense column and coiled for action.[7] With each minute he could discern more detail in the tableau, soldier's faces coming into focus, sounds rising clearer. The rain had stopped and the wind was breaking up the clouds, revealing glimpses of a large bright moon on a lightening scale. It was past 4am; now was the time.

But Lambert was not there. Cromwell led his horse down to the lines, letting it turn in anxious circles as he bit his lip and rose in his saddle to look along the lines. Here were the English, after all their caution and planning, 'in disorder and the Major-General a wanting.'[8] Cromwell had, according to Hodgson, agreed at the council of war the previous night to delegate the

---

[7] "Cromwell's Mount" is today crowned with a magnificent Cedar of Lebanon, which is likely to be a later garden feature. Whether the mound itself is natural or not is unclear, but it sits on rising ground and its elevation would have given Cromwell a clearer view over to the Scots than even the upper windows of the house itself.

[8] Original Memoirs, p. 146.

complex arrangements for the assault to Lambert. The latter was now at the rear of the column, somewhere back along the road towards the parish church, organising the regimental guns which would follow the army over the fords before deploying rapidly in support of the attack. The bigger guns were in position in their salient. It is easy to imagine the exasperation and strain felt by Lambert after a full and frustrating night trying to manage the redeployment, watching the sky anxiously and sensing the increasing need to move before the day broke and gave away the element of surprise. In the distance, across the ravine, a Scots trumpet warned that the enemy was stirring. The army could wait no longer.

Now at last this tired by confident subordinate came riding down the line and set the forlorn hope of horse forward across the ford. The watchword was "The Lord of Hosts"; an essential precaution ahead of the coming confusion, when friends could be mistaken for enemies as they emerged from the fog of war. The cavalry forlorn rode out to clear the open ground between the Brox Burn and the Scots flank, ensuring that that the main body could cross in safety behind them and deploy into battalia unhindered. Their trotting hooves splashed noisily through the shallow water and its stony base, changing to wet thuds as they slopped off into an arc heading towards the rising ground and the poor house where the pickets had been mauled the previous afternoon. They disappeared into the eerie light of the pre-dawn and silence again enveloped the waiting column. Then, in the distance along the road, an explosion of sound.

Pistol shots split the cold fresh air of the morning, the flash of powder bright and startling. Voices rang out too, and the firing quickly intensified after those first sporadic shots. Cromwell's forlorn had run straight into its Scottish counterpart, 'a party of theirs who came to alarm us.'[9] These were the Scots horsemen whose trumpet had sounded earlier, whose task was to push the Scottish front right up to the fords ahead of the general's later offensive. What followed was a rolling cavalry fight across the line of the road, mainly focusing around the little 'shelving pass' below which stood the hovel.[10] Caught by surprise, the Scottish cavalry pickets were driven back and the ironsides penetrated towards the enemy's main line: in places Cromwellian troopers rode over tents and shelters, and even overran some of the Scots cannon which had been brought forward ready to threaten Broxmouth.[11] But the element of surprise was now gone and the sounds of pistols and carbines spitting their fire would soon rouse the whole Scots line. The Battle of Dunbar had begun.

The English accounts of this phase of the battle are something of a jumble, and as modern historians have attempted to distil from them a sensible timeline of events there has emerged a curious picture. The skirmishing

---

9 *True Relation*: Original Memoirs, p. 277.
10 The skirmishing probably extended over a broad front from the near the modern stables and along the rising ground east of the battlefield monument.
11 Walker, Historical Discourses, p. 180. Curiously, a trooper in Stewart's regiment is said to have had his tent cut down around him, but he should have been on the extreme left flank and there's no clear way this could have occurred so early in the battle as to catch him sleeping.

"THE WRESTLE OF DEATH", TUESDAY, 3 SEPTEMBER

43. Detail of Fisher's plan, showing Pride's men crossing the burn below Broxmouth, ready to come up in relief of Monck's brigade.

between the cavalry pickets is interpreted by some, such as Reese, as being the occasion of the delay at the ford which caused Cromwell such anxiety. But Hodgson is plausible and explicit in blaming this on the Lambert's prolonged efforts to order the rear of the column, not his absence because of the cavalry action.[12] This is largely based on what is probably a misreading of Cadwell and the *True Relation*, who begins by stating that the forlorn gave the enemy 'a strong alarm' after 4am. He then goes on to describe the main cavalry action which opened the general engagement, which he describes as lasting an hour and creating the space for the infantry columns to come up.[13] The description of the latter has been interpreted as relating to the preliminary skirmishing, but actually the latter has been dismissed concisely with the 'strong alarm' comment. If it is not taken this way, then we end up with a strange set of circumstances which requires two implausible events: first, Cromwell waits for an hour until the skirmishing concludes before crossing with the main body; second, for that same hour David Leslie and the Scots army do not react to the now clear and present danger of an assault. Far more likely, the initial delays were caused by the challenges of ordering the column, and the main attacks went in hard on the heels of the forlorn.

---

12 Reese, p. 84-5. In conflating the admittedly unclear description in Cadwell, Reese is forced to dismiss the latter's report that the artillery were exchanging fire at this point, since it does not make sense at that point for them to do so. This compromise hints at the error.
13 Carte, *Original Letters*, p. 383.

'ESSENTIAL AGONY'

44. The area of the shelving pass, a relatively subtle feature in the bigger picture of folds and creases in this deceptively complex landscape.

As the cavalry pickets clashed, the vanguard moved forward. First went the massed cavalry brigades of Lambert and Lilburne, giving the English something like three thousand heavy horse to deploy behind the skirmishing forlorn. Behind them came Monck's brigade, splashing mud-caked shoes through the rain-fresh stream before immediately plunging them back into the broad mud slick which was once the road to Berwick. They would need space and time to form their battalia, and the cavalry would have to win them both. Lambert wasted little time in dressing his ranks and drove his horsemen forward to relieve his pickets and crack the Scots flank. Meanwhile Cromwell had sent his own Horse under William Packer along with two regiments of foot on the wide arc around the seaward side of Broxmouth. They had furthest to go if they were to reach the enemy, but the move eased the pressure on the other two fords and would bring them out into open ground cleared by the cavalry. Every passing moment was giving the Scots crucial time to recover, so there could be no delay.

The Scottish command were, undoubtedly, caught unaware. The army was not prepared for a general engagement and therefore lost critical time which could have been spent reordering the battle line to greater advantage. Leslie was probably not caught in his bed, since his cavalry pickets were already moving forward as we have seen; but his location at this crucial moment is unknown. If he was still at Spott House then he was about as far from the epicentre of the developing crisis as he could possibly be, perhaps as much as a mile and a half from where he was most needed. It seems likely, since if he were further to his right then we would expect to find more of his army up and ready under his gaze. For the Scots soldiers as the intensifying gunfire shook them suddenly from their short and restless sleep, the instant uncertainty was compounded by the absence of the men they needed the most, their regimental officers. For most of the infantry as they sprang up from the battered and trampled crop, dazed and damp and aching, there was simply nothing to see. Surely this was the sound of their own right flank moving up against Broxmouth? Staff officers flew eastwards, buffcoats flapping untied, the unmistakable faces of deep-seated concern. Then the ground rumbled with the eruption of Cromwell's great guns.

The Scots cavalry were the first to recover from the attack. Crucially, their forward pickets had given them enough warning for saddles to be thrown onto the backs of horses before the full weight of Lambert's main attack could come crashing down on them. Strachan was up and galvanising his brigade, and as the Scots lancers launched their counter-charge there began an intense broiling cavalry battle for control of the open ground between the road and the sea. This was the main grapple for control of the road, the critical fight which would give Monck's foot brigade the room to advance against their counterparts. Cadwell reported that the Scots 'charged very resolutely,' and Cromwell admired their 'gallant resistance.'[14] At first Lambert was pushed back by the stubborn Scottish counterattack; Major Lister was briefly but Lilburne came up in close support and the Scots troopers now had a clear view of Monck's infantry moving and therefore threatening their flank. The superior weight and discipline of the veteran English horse began to tell.

The lancers charged, disengaged then charged again; the ironsides drew their knees together and themselves charged hard at their lighter Scots opponents whenever they drew back. Over eight thousand horses, thirty-two thousand pounding hooves, thundered across the landscape through the growing fog of acrid smoke as drawn by Fisher. Pistols and carbines burst fire at close range; lance-points rang off iron plates or snagged on straps; heavy sword blades splintered shafts, chopped down on bonnets and turned their blades on steel rims. Lambert and Strachan, both zealots to their cause and veterans of their craft, were in their fiery element as they clashed in what Cromwell called this 'very hot dispute at sword's point between our horse and theirs.'[15] But despite their heroism, little by little, the Scots were being pushed backwards; backwards away from the protection of the sea, back from the road, back from the foot.[16]

As the cavalry battle raged to their left Monck's brigade was forming its battalia, presumably with Fenwick's companies forming as its second line support. As they dressed their ranks with professional urgency, the soldiers were screened from the Scots infantry by the folding ground to the south.[17] As soon as Monck was satisfied the battalia were ready he moved his men forward without delay. The marched up the gentle slope with the road on their left, bending away from them as they marched south-south-east. The

---

14 Carte, Original Letters, p. 383. Letter from Cromwell to Speaker Lenthall, 4 September 1650; Carlyle, p. 386.
15 Letter from Cromwell to Speaker Lenthall, 4 September 1650; Carlyle, p. 386.
16 The cavalry engagement occurred across the area now covered by the limestone quarry and the artificial loch, the Scots horse eventually being driven back through where the cement works stands.
17 They formed in the area directly east of the Brand's Mill ford, their left flank roughly where the monument now stands.

'ESSENTIAL AGONY'

45. The cavalry battle raged across the open ground between the road and the sea, an area partially covered today by an artificial loch (a filled quarry in this case). The loch is out of the picture to the left, as is the cement works which created it. The Scots horse were driven back across this ground, breaking up as the ground rose beneath them.

ravine of the Broxburn protected their flank to their right. The brigade crested the fold with drums beating; green flags unfurled above each advancing company of Monck's regiment, six feet of silk whipping on the cold gusts. It was now almost 5.30am and the blue light of the moon was giving way to the grey light of day.

Lumsden's infantry brigade was posted on the Scots right because its commander was the senior infantry officer. But the position of seniority belied the fact that the brigade contained some of the least experienced units in the Scots army, fresh regiments which had only reached the army after it had commenced its march east and had not therefore benefitted from the battalia training which had surely been undertaken over the long weeks at Leith. For these men, on the crest of the sloping ground between Little Pinkerton and Oxwell Mains, their first taste of battle was to be a bitter one. Musketeers desperately attempted to light their match with shaking fingers, hundreds of burning lengths hurriedly passing through hands numbed with cold and fear. They fumbled cloth covers off the locks of the muskets. Pikemen pushed and shoved, eyes once creased with exhaustion now widening with a growing realisation. Officers stumbled forward, bellowing hoarse instructions, leadings staffs waving. Halberd shafts pushed uneven rows of men into rows. The cavalry battle roared to their north-east; they may even have initially formed their ranks to face it. Then Monck's brigade came over the fold ahead and began ascending the slope, heading straight for Lumsden's shaky line.

Monck's regiments did not hesitate. Pikes were levelled to the charge, a bristling phalanx presenting with uniform timing which sent a shiver through the Scots. The men of the levies were becoming oblivious to the cries of their officers, to the desperate calls of their own drums, dumfounded by the sight of Monck's two forward battalia advancing beneath their colours. James Lumsden himself was here now, bellowing from his saddle as he tried to brace his untested men for the coming shock. The first crashing volleys came in from the four blocks of muskets facing them, the sound punching the air and sending led balls whipping through the air. Firing up the slope favoured the attackers, and before the smoke had cleared the next line of firers had advanced to the fore; four more crashing volleys. Two great pike divisions advanced between the sleeves of shot as the musketeers rolled forward in support. The first Scots muskets cracked in ragged volleys, the complexities of tactical procedures too new to have become instinctive. Men fired when they were ready to fire, eager to retire for the reload as it took them further from the enemy, further from death. Monck sensed their weakness: the English charged.

At the first shock Lumsden's brigade recoiled. Their static lines could not absorb the momentum of Monck's attack, pikes piercing forwards towards unarmoured bellies and brass-mounted musket butts swinging to shatter teeth and jaws. Scottish hands dropped their pikes, the lines instantly yielding to the incoming pressure. The white banner bearing the bright Douglas heart, the heart of the Bruce himself, plunged to the filthy ground as Sir William Douglas of Kirkness fell mortally wounded as his regiment disintegrated. Yellow banners crossed with black saltires fell amidst the falling forests of pikes. Lumsden himself was struck, his horse slamming to the ground amidst the chaos and devastation; enemy hands grappled at him, blood and mud spoiling lace and leather alike. As the front two battalia broke in flight they carried the third behind, a brigade of over two thousand Scotsmen shattered in moments.

If Monck's men felt 'they had discharged their duty' by destroying Lumsden's raw brigade, they were now in for a shock of their own. To their right, James Campbell of Lawers was swinging his brigade around for action pivoting around Little Pinkerton farm. Unlike the brigades to his left, Lawers' position was unconstrained by the ravine of the Brox Burn as it curled around to the north ahead of him. It did mean that he was exposed to the fire of the batteries in the salient, but he understood the immediate concern was stabilising the flank. The core of Lawers' brigade was his own veteran regiment, which had been in service continuously since the Bishops' Wars. It had been tested in extremes, suffering heavy losses against Montrose at Auldearn, where the colonel Sir Mungo Campbell had fallen amongst his men; but his son James had inherited the command of the remnants and, after backing the Kirk Party during the Engager crisis of 1648, had rebuilt it to around six hundred men. Beneath their classic blue and white saltires, Campbell of Lawers' Regiment was the steely heart of his brigade, David Leslie's 'stoutest regiment'.[18]

The Scots now wasted no time. Monck's men had been disordered by their success against Lumsden and the sight of Lawers' brigade will have left their commander in no doubt that this was an altogether more solid

---

18   Letter from Cromwell to Speaker Lenthall, 4 September 1650; Carlyle, p. 387.

opponent. In order to reform to receive the developing counterattack, Monck probably gave ground, eager not to put the Scots cavalry out of sight at their backs and perhaps hoping to regain the protection of the ravine on their right flank. Green flags flourished as rallying points and drums called out furiously. Fenwick's companies had perhaps rotated forward to cover the other battalia as they reformed. The ranks reformed as the Scots volleys crashed out; Lawers's Regiment, supported by Preston's and Haldane's, fell on with all their strength. In the shock Monk's brigade, as Cromwell coolly recalled, 'received some repulse.'[19]

The Scottish foot now held the advantage as they were able to drive Monck back down the slope into the bowl between the Scottish ridgeline and the fold which screened the fords. Tired and probably outnumbered, Monck's men struggled to maintain their footing in the slick ground, the fallen corn shifting on the mud beneath as they churned it up with their endeavours. For the soldiers the world now narrowed: all appreciation of the wider tactical situation was lost in the bitter struggle 'at push of pike and the butt end of musket.'[20] Where the press was tightest men reached for their short swords, seized hold of bandolier collars, grasped musket stocks and grappled. To the left of the Scots the remorseless pounding of the great guns sounded from across the ravine, the banks lost in thick smoke illuminated by flashes of orange and red. In the shallow hollow the infantry fought on oblivious to the cavalry battle off to their right, and Lawers' brigade pushed Monck relentlessly back towards the ground on which he had formed his battalia barely half an hour before. Here they had to push them upwards, losing momentum as they pressed towards the road.

Meanwhile the Scots cavalry were in trouble. Despite their earlier success the weight of the ironsides was too much to resist. As Lambert recovered the initiative and drove back the Scots, troops began to break. Cadwell makes the turnaround sound rapid: as the English cavalry recovered they, 'put them [the Scots horse] to the run very suddenly, it being now near six of the clock in the morning.'[21] The Scottish horse had performed prodigious feats in reacting to the unexpected English assault. They had been the most aggressive and formidable part of the Scottish resistance throughout the campaign, distinguishing themselves in the daring and swiftness of their sallies. But their forward lines had been overrun before the battle had properly been engaged, and their light mounts and mobile tactics were unsuited to the slogging full-frontal engagement on this sloping coastal battlefield. They were driven back, fragmenting as they went, just as Lawers' brigade was pushing forwards, opening a route into the Scottish rear.

Lawers' Brigade, by its very success, was becoming isolated. The English artillery ensured that it remained so. The nearest Scots support was Pitscottie's brigade, but its attempts to wheel its battalia round to the right were constrained by the narrowness of the land, just a little over 300m wide. It would have been a taxing redeployment even for an experienced force,

---

19 Letter from Cromwell to Speaker Lenthall, 4 September 1650; Carlyle, p. 387.
20 Original Memoirs, p. 147.
21 Carte, *Original Letters*, p. 383.

"THE WRESTLE OF DEATH", TUESDAY, 3 SEPTEMBER

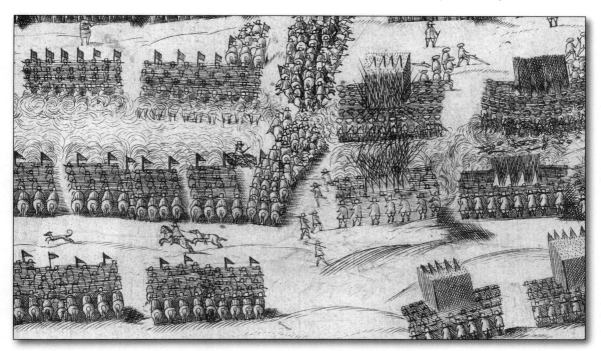

46. Detail of Fisher's plan, showing the massed cavalry battle on the left and the furious infantry fight on the right. In the centre is Cromwell, directing his own regiment into the flank of infantry engagement. (Ashmolean Museum: University of Oxford).

and the brigade's cohesion was still weakened by the lack of senior officers to coordinate the army's response to the deteriorating crisis. Lumsden was badly wounded, and even if Monck's men had been obliged to abandon their prize for the moment, he was lying helpless amongst the wreckage of his brigade. Holborne was presumably with his own brigade on the far left, and as the last senior officer recorded in the lines overnight was presumably exhausted. Leslie's position remains unknown, but he must by now have been trying to reach the right of his line to assess the extent of the enemy's attempted break-out.

But as Pitscottie's centre brigade struggle to redeploy, it was obliged to do so under fire from English guns across the ravine. If they wheeled to face the east, then the battalia would be raked by cannon fire. Iron shot, already able to slash through the formations from the front, would tear through whole ranks. The formation would be decimated, order shattered by the sprays of mud and blood as the shot tore through. Even if Innes had prepared to risk exposing his men to this hazard, it is doubtful they would have followed for long. The wet ground absorbed much of the artillery shot and reduced the terrifying skipping balls which took down soldiers' legs even deep within formations, but the cannonade was shocking enough even without the prospect of turning your flank to it. Innes brigade was pinned down, which meant so too was everything to its left. James Campbell of Lawers was on his own.

On Cromwell's side of the ravine, the gun teams toiled to maintain a rapid rate of fire. If the Scots' great guns were indeed assembled over to the right, where the flow of the battle prevented their effectiveness and where, according to Walker at least, they were swiftly overrun, then the English heavy battery was virtually unopposed. The Scots regiments across the burn could probably call up nothing but small leather guns in response, light cannon designed

153

'ESSENTIAL AGONY'

47. The artillery salient, formed by the bowed line of the Brox Burn, showing clearly how the English cannon could enfilade any attempts by the Scots to reinforce their right.

for close infantry support but not for prolonged counter-battery fire. They presumably fired anyway. The English gunners were overseen by an artillery expert, Colonel Richard Deane, but at each firing the cannons' recoil gouged their trails into the soft earth. Considerable effort was needed to manhandle them back into position, although the rate of fire was more important than the precision of the shot: artillery was as much a psychological tool in battle as it was a killer. It was the fear of the death-dealing explosions, untouchable across the ravine, which kept the Scots fixed in their places as the shot fell around them and furrowed the earth.

Beside the gunners was an arced line of Okey's dismounted dragoons, lining the gorse on the lip of the burn. They were stretched thin, but there was no real threat to them except if the Scots dared attempt to cross the steep-banked ford at Oswald Dean. It seems likely that the dragoons maintained a sporadic fire on the Scottish centre and left: too long range to cause any damage but sufficient to fixate attention to the north whilst the main battle raged to the east. It might even have been an audacious raid by Okey's men, taking to their mounts, which had overrun the forward tent lines of part of the Scottish left earlier in the morning, cutting the tent of Bannatyne of Corhouse down about his head. It would have been a risky diversion, which could only have gone in via Oswald Dean, but it appears to be depicted in Fisher's plan of the battle.[22] Reese's interpretation has Overton's brigade still

---

22 Conceivably, a raid could have been mounted or extracted over Doon Bridge below Spott. If it happened, Okey's Regiment's mounted raid would have sown considerable confusion over where the real threat would come.

lining ravine as well, based presumably on the lack of direct reference to its exploits in the main engagement. These threats from across the burn, however illusory, further explain why two thirds of the Scots army stood facing northwards whilst the battle was being lost to their right.

Oliver Cromwell was now riding across the ground east of Broxmouth (now occupied by a caravan park), putting himself at the head of the flanking column which had crossed the burn below the estate. This comprised his own regiment of horse under William Packer, his regiment of foot led by William Goffe, and the infantry regiments of both Pride and Lambert. This considerable force had emerged from the burn into an open landscape cleared by the success of the English cavalry. Ahead and to their right, however, Monck's brigade was under intense pressure; Cromwell drove Pride's forward to support it. Their battalia crossed the road close to the battlefield monument 'to fall upon the enemy's flank, which was done with a great deal of resolution.'[23] The last cavalry reserve was meanwhile sent forward in the wake of the main horse brigades where their fresh weight might break what remained of the Scottish resistance there.

Pride's brigade were fresh; Lawers' brigade had been fighting hand-to-hand in the churning mud for some time. Cromwell reports that they came 'seasonably in,' supported in their efforts by 'the courage the Lord was pleased to give.'[24] Under the fresh threat Lawers' men gave ground, but the slope came back into their favour as they were pressed back towards Little Pinkerton. As Hodgson admiringly remembered, 'one of the Scots brigades of foot would not yield.' But without support Lawers' brigade was hopelessly exposed: whilst its left flank was protected by the ravine, the artillery prevented from targeting them by the risks of striking their own men, their right flank hung open now that the Scots horse had been driven decisively back. The latter had finally lost all hope of holding, troops and regiments scattering back around the eastern shoulder of Doon Hill. Others tried to avoid being cut off from their homes, and instead rode around the rear of their lines along the face of Doon Hill. According to Robert Blair, the routing horse 'running through the foot, put the whole army into confusion.'[25] The English horse would soon follow in their wake.

This was the moment of critical decision for Cromwell, whose lack of hesitation in the field gave him so often the edge. Lumsden's brigade was destroyed and scattered; Lawers' was holding but unsupported and exposed; the Scots horse had been driven off. The routing cavalry were sowing confusion in the Scottish rear, whilst the English artillery pinned them down. The break-out had been a total success: the road to Berwick was clear and the whole army could now withdraw from Dunbar having badly mauled their enemy. But, as Walker succinctly put it, 'if his Design were formerly but to have made his way [to the border], he now altered it.'[26] Cromwell saw the chance to turn a tactical success into a devastating victory.

---

23 Original Memoirs, p. 147.
24 Letter from Cromwell to Speaker Lenthall, 4 September 1650; Carlyle, p. 387.
25 Row, *Robert Blair*, p. 238.
26 Walker, Historical Discourses, p. 180.

'ESSENTIAL AGONY'

48. The area around Little Pinkerton farm (on the rising ground to the right), with the ravine on the left. The fields in the centre of this image saw the bitterest of the infantry fighting and the smashing of Lawers' brigade, into the back of which we would now be looking. Cromwell's charge came in from the right. In the background is the artificial loch, across which ground the cavalry battle had raged until the Scots were driven back beyond the right of the frame.

The decisive move is captured in the famous illustration of the battle by Fitz-Payne Fisher, a former royalist who opted to flatter his former enemies by celebrating their most famous triumphs. His intended masterpiece, an illustrated account of Cromwell's victories, was never completed, but he did interview veterans of Dunbar whilst they still served and created an engraving of the battle which was later presented to the general. Its depiction of the landscape is, on the whole, faithful and informative, although the lack of a key leaves the identification of individual farmhouses open to debate. The illustration shows in a single image events which clearly did not occur simultaneously, the Scots depicted in their bonnets and the English in round hats. It should not be taken as a precise plan of the deployments, as Firth first attempted and Historic Environment Scotland have more recently taken to the extreme. Instead, as most modern authors have also concluded, it should be accepted as a well-informed illustration but nothing more. To those who argue that its veracity is confirmed by its presentation to Cromwell, it must be pointed out that neither Cromwell nor his officers ever saw the Battle of Dunbar in its entirety. They certainly never saw it from the air, revealing the evolving action over a distance of almost two miles, through the obstructions of the undulating ground and the fog of war. An eye-witness looking at Fisher's plan would have recognised the church, the fords, Doon Hill and the massed attack on the Scots right, and accepted that this was the Battle of Dunbar. That was all his illustration required; it was not a forensic analysis. But the moment which Fisher *does* give us with striking clarity, is the figure of Oliver Cromwell himself, commander's baton in hand, diverting his ironsides into the flank of Lawers' brigade.[27]

---

27 There is only one character drawn by Fisher in the English army who faces directly towards the viewer, standing in isolation amidst the fray and directing the bending column of horsemen. It is clearly Cromwell.

Campbell of Lawers' brigade was now the extreme right of the Scottish army; everything beyond them had been broken up. They had beaten Monck back, but the weight of Pride's fresh regiments pushed the Scots back up the slope towards Little Pinkerton. The battalia were now disordered, all three engaged as the Pride relieved the pressure on Monck by working onto Lawers' flank. The Scots fought doggedly, pressed together, unable now even to fall when they lost their footing in the churned earth. The pike yielded only by inches, lunging with their shafts as the thrusting heads of their enemies' sought to exploit any gap. Wicked points snagged in thick rolled plaids, or else tore through grey wool; but considerable force was needed to penetrate even through coats and doublets, five layers of wool and linen between skin and steel. Both sides had lost the momentum needed to drive back the other, it seemed, their phalanxes locked together. Then, unseen and unforgiving, an immense impact struck the Scots formation from the right. A wall of horseflesh, massive force, smashed into the exposed and flank. The musketeers broke beneath the charge, unable to defend themselves against the English horse; pistols flashed amongst them as they streamed back for safety, laying open the pikemen to their left. Cromwell's Horse pulled back, reformed and surged forwards into them.

Locked in the push of pike to their fore, there was nothing the Scots could do to oppose the charge. Pikes splintered as unbraced men were bowled sideward against them, heavy shafts smashed into the heads of their comrades, whilst feet stepped back onto tumbled bodies and tripped. The formation was blown open in seconds: the cavalry 'charged from one end to another of them.'[28]. As the Scots reeled and fractured, the English infantry seized the moment and surged forward with renewed vigour, exploiting the confusion in the Scottish lines to ensure the damage was irreparable. The whole brigade was ripped apart, and with resistance now impossible the shattered broke in flight, Cromwell's cavalry riding amongst them as they ran. Lawers' own regiment lost around a third of its men.

For the fleeing men the options were few; the looming mass of Doon Hill's northern escarpment meant that the only way to run was west, past Little Pinkerton on their left as they headed straight towards Pitscottie's brigade. Cromwell's horsemen and the English infantry came behind. But defeat was turning now towards disaster, as Lambert and Lilburne's two battered but triumphant brigades of heavy horse were now riding parallel with the fleeing Scots. After driving off what remained of the Scots horse, the disciplined English cavalry regiments had swing round to the south west beneath the steep hillock of Meikle Pinkerton, overrunning the Scots baggage guard with ease. Without pausing for plunder their advance rolled on towards Little Pinkerton, threatening to drive a wedge between the Scots centre and Doon Hill which would roll them back into the ravine.

But the Scots did not wait for the threat to develop. The rearward battalia had already been disordered by routing Scottish troopers, and if Pitscottie's brigade had managed to wheel even in part, its front was now

---

28 Original Memoirs, p. 147.

thrown into chaos by hundreds of fleeing comrades. The shock of seeing the most experience units in the army in flight, and the double threats of the ironsides reforming behind them and the even bigger column of horse advancing towards their flank, was too much to bear. Cromwell kept his men in tight order, making sure at this crucial stage that the discipline of his cavalry told. He ordered his regiment around the wreck of Lawers' valiant stand, 'to be clear of all bodies,' and as the sun rose over the sea to his left the general proclaimed: "Now let God arise and his enemies shall be scattered!"[29] Cromwell's horsemen had gained the ridgeline and now filled the eastern end of the corridor between Doon Hill and the Brox Burn. The line halted and with their general they sang Psalm 117, before advancing steadily with the morning sun behind them like some agent of divine wrath.[30] They must have looked terrifying, unstoppable.

Pitscottie's brigade broke. Disordered, shocked, thrown into confusion by their routing comrades and under constant artillery fire, men began first to edge backwards, then to turn, and then to throw down their weapons and run. As in so many battles before and since, the collapse of an army happens quickly as panic spreads like fire. To Hodgson's eyes the Scots 'routed one another,' each fragmenting company disordering the next until who battalia were disintegrating. "I profess they run," laughed Cromwell. The cavalry charged across the line, ensuring there was no possibility that the fleeing Scots could recover and reform. As formed bodies turned to a fleeing tide of individuals the field presented a cavalryman's dream. Cromwell watched his men as the Scots were 'made by the Lord of Hosts into stubble to their swords.'[31]

David Leslie desperately needed to take a grip of his collapsing army. His surviving regiments were caught in a trap between the ravine and the hill, with the only exit point the bottleneck at Doon Bridge below Spott.[32] Exactly what took place is unrecorded, but it is possible to reconstruct from the flow of events elsewhere. As the centre fragmented, or perhaps even before, William Stewart's cavalry were sent across the burn. They were too few to offer any hope of resistance even they could have forced their way through to the west, and besides they were needed now to cover the retreat. Okey's Dragoons surely mounted up and rode west to harry the escaping Scots, and Stewart's men had a chance of keeping them at bay. Holburne's brigade, untouched by the fighting so far was brought into column and marched down into the ford. With them presumably came the committee of war and perhaps the Earl of Leven too. We can imagine the urgency of this desperate evacuation, jostling companies splashing through the burn where the trackway to Spott cut through the banks of the ravine before ascending through the sodden corn and passed Wester Broomhouse. John Innes will have been ordered to

---

29 Original Memoirs, p. 147. The words are from Psalm 68.
30 "O praise the Lord, all ye nations: praise him, all ye people. For his merciful kindness is great toward us: and the truth of the Lord endureth for ever. Praise ye the Lord." Original Memoirs, p. 148.
31 Letter from Cromwell to Speaker Lenthall, 4 September 1650; Carlyle, p. 387.
32 In 1650 it was more likely, although not definitively, a ford.

"THE WRESTLE OF DEATH", TUESDAY, 3 SEPTEMBER

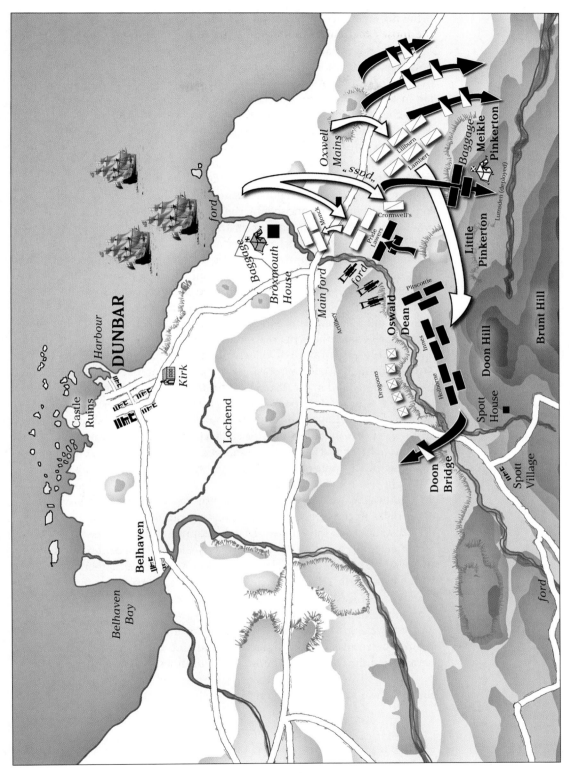

Map 9. The Scottish right is decisively defeated whilst the English artillery pin down the centre-left. The English cavalry complete the destruction of the Scottish resistance.

bring his men out too, but as he was attempting to extract them the rout of Pitscottie's brigade threw the whole centre into disorder.

The role of the Scottish officers now was to keep as many men together in bodies as they could. All sense of company cohesion was lost, colours falling by the dozen before Cromwell's relentless advance. The safety of the Scots lay in keeping together, but in attempting to do so whole clusters of men were cut off by the rampaging horsemen who herded them up like sheep. Their only hope then of preventing a bitter massacre was to throw down their arms. With Okey's dragoons remounted and skirmishing to the west, Oswald Dean provided another exit point for fugitives. Men cast away their weapons to scramble down its bank, splashing across the burn, tripping and turning ankles, grasping at gorse bushes to pull themselves up the steep track beyond. They fled towards Belhaven, desperately hoping that the English would concentrate their pursuit on the main column, although most were soon rounded up by English patrols.[33]

The main Scots column had to keep its nerve: Cromwell pressed it hard with his cavalry. Cutting cross country and heading due west, Leslie's men were horridly exposed to their enemy in an open landscape. The English horsemen were relentless, 'killing and wounding them all the way,' to ensure the maximum damage was done to the army which had so long defied them.[34] When they could, the Scots rear-guard attempted to hold off the enemy; the sporadic thunder of ragged volleys rolled like a distant storm over the East Lothian countryside. The occasional battered troop of Scottish horse could be seen riding hard in the distance, riding hell for leather towards Edinburgh after circling around the back of Doon Hill to hook back west. But with every harassing English surge and with every passing mile, the column fragmented further as exhausted men took the chance to look to their own safety, or gave up the flight altogether and surrendered. They looked more like refugees than regiments, most of their drums and colours having been abandoned in the flight.

Cromwell gave his men the freedom for 'chase and execution' over almost eight miles in the direction of Haddington, riding with them as they did.[35] That distance took the English as far as Traprain, where the vast Law rose up to protected the Scots on their left just as the River Tyne bent round to do on their right. This was a natural place for Cromwell's exhausted but exhilarated troopers to finally reign in. Leslie now rode on ahead hard for the capital city twenty miles west, perhaps taking Stewart's cavalry. He had to ensure the Committee of Estates was prepared for whatever was coming in his wake; he had to be there to ensure the remnants of his army held together when they returned. Cromwell had won the Battle of Dunbar, but that did not yet mean he had won the war.

When Oliver Cromwell returned to the field of battle later that morning, the scene was very different to the one he had left. The ironsides presumably

---

33 There is a tradition, unsubstantiated, that some were cut down and buried near Battleblent House.
34 *True Relation*, Original Memoirs, p. 277.
35 Letter from Cromwell to Speaker Lenthall, 4 September 1650; Carlyle, p. 287.

"THE WRESTLE OF DEATH", TUESDAY, 3 SEPTEMBER

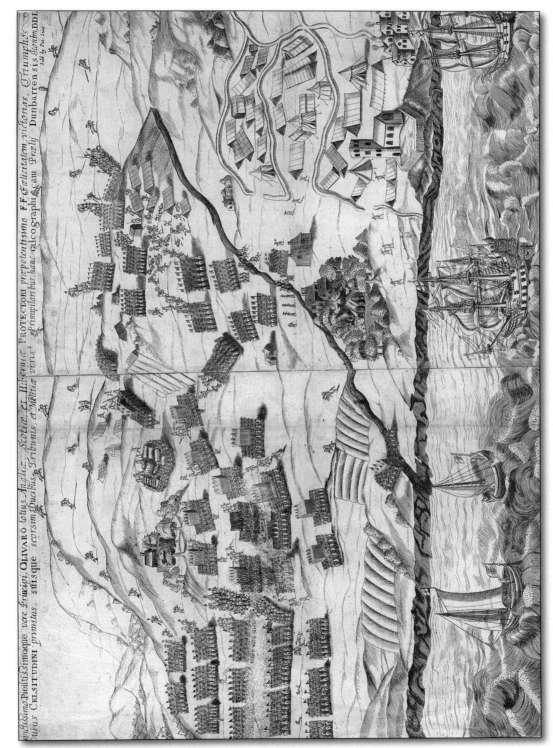

49. 'The Victory at Dunbar' by Fitz-Payne Fisher, published by Peter Stent. Contrary to some interpretations, the illustration does in fact show a Scots line parallel with the burn but set back from it along the lower ridge, being driven back on its far right (our left) towards the higher ground behind near Meikle Pinkerton. It is not intended to show a starting deployment at right angles to the ravine. (WA.Suth.C.3.293.1 © Ashmolean Museum, University of Oxford)

retraced their steps back to the western end of the battlefield, where a party no doubt broke off to search Spott House for any papers or valuables left behind by the Scots commanders and their political overseers. As he trotted up onto the ridge below Doon Hill, Cromwell could look for the first time upon the landscape of his victory. It was a landscape still filled with people, but with a strange and uneasy calm. Large groups of grey-coated figures, sat amongst the flattened corn, red-coated captors standing watch. English soldiers shoved and jostled hundreds of bonneted prisoners into lines, pulling off bags and jackets, slitting seams in search of hidden coin. Here and there small parties of Englishmen laughed, striking one another across the shoulder; the sound more incongruous than the distant bark of an order or shout of recognition between comrades. To the east, waggons were searched and inventoried.

Horses with empty saddles nosed the corn storks and grazed lazily. Others whinnied and stamped, darting this way and that; traumatised by the fight and frightened by the smell of blood and death. A group of officers supervised as dozens of fallen flags were thrown onto a waggon, whilst work parties across the field gathered armloads of muskets or slung bundles of pikes over their shoulders. Others poked at silent corpses with their feet, or rolled them onto their backs. Soldiers pulled at muddied boots, cast aside grey coats to salvage doublets from beneath. Stockings, shirts, bonnets: everything had a value to a soldier. Every now and then a hand reached up in agonised protest, stilled with the thrust of a sword or knife, or a musket butt as a coup de grace. The occasional pistol shot rang out, but nobody stirred but the birds. The dirty white sheets of trampled tent-lines stood out against the browns; overturned carriages lay amongst the littering pike shafts. Men groaned. They sat dumbly staring at their blood covered hands; or lay in the weak heatless sun clutching their damp clothes tight across their open wounds for fear of seeing the damage. Shapeless masses writhed amongst the dead, pulling themselves vainly forward to who knows where. A soldier kneels, offers water. Men sobbed.

There was no doubting the extent of Cromwell's victory. 'Upon the place and near about it, were about three thousand slain,' tallied the general. Amidst the wreckage and detritus of their defeat, up to ten thousand Scots had been rounded up and disarmed.[36] Most of those killed died once their ranks had broken, and they lay like the litter of the tide in a long corridor between Doon Hill and the Brox Burn. A large haul of officers, headed by the badly wounded Lieutenant-General Lumsden, were already being sifted from their soldiers and listed; then they were probably taken to Broxmouth estate, where William Douglas of Kirkness died of his wounds. He lies there still, covered by a simple stone slab. It is the only marked grave on the battlefield, although there is a tradition that at least some of the fallen were buried in the corner of Spott kirkyard.[37] George Winram, Lord Liberton, took a little

---

36 Letter from Cromwell to Speaker Lenthall, 4 September 1650; Carlyle, p. 387.
37 It is unlikely those who fell on the right flank were moved such a distance. Most were probably buried in groups at the nearest field boundaries. No convincing evidence of battlefield burials has yet been found.

longer but also died of his wounds; Lumsden would recover and remain in captivity until 1652.

Cromwell's figures should be treated with caution. If taken at face value then they account for almost as many men as Reid believes the Scottish army contained at the outset.[38] Reid's recent revisions of the Scottish strength may well be too conservative; Cromwell's contemporary figures may well be exaggerated. Walker revises the numbers to '2000 Common Souldiers' slain, and 'five or 6000' taken as prisoners.[39] Robert Blair does not concern his account with numbers: 'it was a lamentable defeat,' he records. Many were killed, many captured.[40]

Cromwell's army had not come through unscathed. His report to Parliament was as follows:

> I do not believe we have lost twenty men. Not one Commission Officers slain as I hear of, save one Cornet; and Major Rooksby, since dead of his wounds; and not many mortally wounded: Colonel Whalley only cut in the handwrist, and his horse (twice shot) killed under him.[41]

This should be treated with considerable scepticism. Whitelocke doubles the figure to forty, and in a different letter written the same day as his first estimate Cromwell says thirty.[42] All his horse and at least two thirds of his foot brigades had been heavily engaged, often in hand-to-hand action. The answer may lie in the lack of detail as to the wounded. 'Not many mortally wounded,' could well be a cover for a larger number of walking wounded, which would better reflect the realities of the engagement. Cadwell appears to confirm this: 'we lost none but at the dispute of the pass, which we esteemed to be about twenty; many wounded.'[43] But victory was not measured solely in lives and limbs lost. There is less reason to doubt Cromwell's figures for the materiel captured: 'the whole baggage and train taken, wherein was good store of match, powder and bullet; all their artillery, great and small – thirty guns.' In addition, there were more than 15,000 weapons recovered, presumably a mixture of those cast away on the field and those in the captured stores. Finally, Cromwell sent on more than 200 colours as an unmistakable visual embodiment of the scale of his triumph. They were to hang in Westminster Hall beside those taken from the Engagers two years before. No parliamentarian would miss the message that the republic owed its survival to the army, to Cromwell.

And parliament was overjoyed: Bulstrode Whitelocke was on his way to Chelsea when a messenger drew up with news of the victory. Abandoning his plans, Whitelocke followed him to Westminster and heard Cromwell's letter read. The messenger's report was ordered to be proclaimed from the

---

38 Reid, *Dunbar 1650*, p. 39-40.
39 Walker, *Historical Discourses*, p. 181.
40 Row, *Robert Blair*, p. 238.
41 Letter from Cromwell to Speaker Lenthall, 4 September 1650; Carlyle, p. 387.
42 Whitelocke, p. 237; Letter from Cromwell to Richard Mayor, 4 September 1650, Carlyle, p 391. Either ten more men had died of their wounds since the first letter was written, or Cromwell has no reliable casualty figures for his own men and is guesstimating inconsistently.
43 Carte, *Original Letters*, p. 384.

'ESSENTIAL AGONY'

50. Grave of Sir William Douglas of Kirkness in the woods beside Broxmouth House. It is the only marked grave on the battlefield, probably marked because the widow of the 1st Earl of Roxburghe was also a Douglas. and Queen Victoria mentions in her diary that she visited it during her stay at the house in 1878.

pulpits the next day, being a Sunday, so that all the congregations of London could give thanks to the Lord. Within days the Scottish flags were being hung, and instructions being given for the striking of medals for the men who had achieved such a triumph.[44] Fresh reports from the battlefield were read out whenever they arrived, the messengers were rewarded. 'The Scots were driven like turkeys,' ran the news, 'and went along cursing their king and clergy for ensnaring them in misery.'[45] Instructions were sent north for Haselriggege for the disposal of the prisoners, and incentives offered for volunteers joining the army. So great was the extent of Cromwell's victory, it seemed, that a determined push would now settle the issue once and for all. Those who thought so would be disappointed.

---

44   Contrary to popular belief, this was not the first such medal to be struck. Nor, from the relatively small numbers of survivals, does it seem likely that the general distribution to all Dunbar veterans was ever actually made. Cromwell protested against the use of his own image, but in truth Dunbar had set him up for the role of first among equals. His road to dictatorship was opening up.

45   Whitelocke, p. 237-9.

8

All the King's Men

Back in Scotland, Cromwell had no time to rest upon his laurels. Despite its success, and the vigour with which the men had fought, the army was still sick and under-supplied. There is no mention of any great stores of food being found amongst the Scots baggage, indicative of Leslie's situation before the battle and providing no relief to his triumphant opponent. Yet despite the need for rest and resupply, Cromwell needed to maximise his current opportunity. If he applied enough pressure now the façade might at last crack. He called on Haselrigge to send urgent reinforcements, holding back only the rawest new levies for garrison in the rear.[1] If Cromwell were to move forward then the large numbers of Scottish prisoners were a major concern. The army would be hard pressed to guard them let alone feed them. Since there was no chance of the Scots joining his army, as captured English royalists like Monck might once have done, Cromwell needed to get rid of the prisoners without them being a drain on his own resources.

The first step was to discharge the wounded and the infirm, those who were least likely to take up arms against him again after they had returned to their homes. There must have been many such men, bones smashed by musketballs, great slashes across their backs or chests, limbs mangled. Five thousand are said to have been released on parole, although the true figure is unverifiable and may have been considerably lower.[2] Those who survived limped off to uncertain futures. Streams of wounded men could be encountered on the roads, like those Anne Murray tried to help in Kinross.[3] These survivors became burdens on their families and parishes, but despite the nation's economic weakness many communities did what they could, raising sums at parish level to pay for surgeons and support the wounded until they were able to work once more.[4] Beyond that point, however, there was little that could be done. If a survivor could not work, they could not eat. The body counts of battles rarely account for those who die in the weeks and months that follow, far from the sound of the guns.

---

1 Letter from Cromwell to Haselrigge, 4 September 1650; Carlyle, p. 389.
2 Whitelocke, p. 238.
3 Plowden, A. *Women all on Fire: the Women of the English Civil War*, (Sutton: History Press, 2004), p. 187.
4 Gerrard et al, *Lost Lives, New Voices*, p. 134-5.

For those who could not make their own way off the field to this vulnerable freedom, Cromwell issued a proclamation permitting civilians to recover the wounded in carts. It seems unlikely that many could have taken up such an offer, however altruistic it might appear, as carts were hard to come by with rival armies both desperately in need of support vehicles. The simple reality is that many will have died upon the field at Dunbar for want of anyone else to save them. Across Scotland thousands of women were destined to linger in hopeless limbo for news, unable to know if they were widowed or simply waiting for a loved one to return. Fathers, sons, brothers failed to return, their absences impacting rural communities particularly hard. After a decade of war, these losses were increasingly hard to bear.

Cromwell sent the rest of the prisoners down the road to Berwick with an escort of four troops from Francis Hacker's Regiment. If they had stayed in Scotland then they would either have to be released or they would have starved to death, 'neither of which would we willingly incur,' says Cromwell. If released, there was nothing to prevent these same men standing in his way once more. Sending the prisoners southwards took them away from the theatre of war and placed the burden of their future onto parliament and, in the immediate term, Arthur Haselrigge. The prisoners taken at Preston had been sold into military service overseas or into indentured service, establishing the precedent for those from Dunbar. Whitelocke repeated rumours that the Scots had boasted they would send Cromwell's army 'to Barbadoes' if it was forced to capitulate, a threat which was so clearly beyond the capacity of the Scottish forces that it can only have been propaganda to help justify the parliament's own intentions.[5] In London a committee was established to make the arrangements for what to do with the prisoners, and the instructions were accordingly sent north to Haselrigge.

Hacker's troopers took the prisoners south without adequate supplies and without any particular understanding of the challenges. They probably also lacked a great deal of sympathy for their charges, men who had forced weeks of hunger and hardship onto the English army.[6] The same might well be said of Hacker's friend Haselrigge, who in fairness was no better prepared from the sudden appearance of 4,000 prisoners than anybody else. Those Scots who marched south into an infamous captivity were already undernourished, demoralised and exhausted. Some will also have been suffering from the psychological trauma which followed their experiences of the sudden and terrifying defeat.

They then began a march of around thirty miles to Berwick-upon-Tweed, over roads ruined by weeks of persistent rain, over a landscape stripped of supply and support. For men weakened with hunger, the passage of the Pass of Pease – now abandoned by the defenders – posed a wearying challenge. Hacker's men had nothing to give them except the goad. At Berwick, having

---

5 Whitelocke, p. 240. The English settlements in the West Indies were largely built on the back of indentured service, in which context the idea of transporting prisoners of war for such tasks is less shocking to contemporaries than it is to us.

6 Hacker himself had stood on the scaffold at the execution of the late king, having signed his death warrant.

now entered England, some of the prisoners refused to go further until they were fed. Thirty were shot to encourage others to their feet. Overnight, before the prisoners were driven across the arches of Berwick's long bridge over the Tweed, those who could slipped away into the darkness.

From Berwick to Newcastle the prisoners had an increased escort but no more supplies. They were faltering, starving. At Alnwick, thirty miles further on, they were housed between the 'middle and upper gaite' of the mighty but crumbling castle. Robert Watson, one of the officers in the garrison, wrote that there was now 'no feare of Scottes invasion.'[7] The threat had always been illusory. Another day, another gruelling thirty miles brought the weary column to Morpeth, where they were herded through the town and across the Wansbeck and 'put into a large wall'd Garden.'[8] Here, in the lee of the derelict castle, the Scots tore up the planted cabbages, falling on the bitter harvest and eating roots and all in their desperation. In doing so they 'poison'd their Bodies,' reported Haselrigge. On the road to Newcastle they began dying, men falling by the wayside as the march went on.

At Newcastle, twice occupied by hostile Scottish armies in the 1640s, Haselrigge had the prisoners housed in the church of St Nicholas, now Newcastle Cathedral. John Knox had once served the congregation here. Now, beneath a lantern spire so reminiscent of St Giles' in Edinburgh, the bloody flux was spread through the weakened prisoners. Some were so sick that they could not go any further; others were already dead. Already segregated, the officers were now completely removed from the main body. Some were lodged in private or commandeered houses in the city, but most eventually ended up on the windswept promontory at Tynemouth. There, in the ancient castle, they would remain for the next few years. The rest were sent on to Durham the next morning,

The vast cathedral at Durham, perched above the looping river below, was no longer required for worship under the republican regime. According to puritan theology, buildings however grand could not in themselves be holy; the concept of God's house was dangerously close to that of the Roman temple. Durham Cathedral was therefore a large, convenient and secure structure in which to accommodate the Scots prisoners. They appear to have slept in the nave to the west, where evidence of the fires they lit for heat can still be discerned. They broke up whatever they could find for fuel, Scots Presbyterians having as little regard for the sanctity of such buildings as their captors. Some prisoners even seem to have broken through to the library and seized valuable manuscripts for their fires, although weak and unarmed prisoners are unlikely to have inflicted the damage to the stone tombs of which they are regularly accused.[9]

---

7   Letter from Robert Watson to Hugh Potter, 11 September 1650; quoted in Gerrard et al, *Lost Lives, New Voices*, p. 125.
8   Letter from Haselrigge to the English Parliament, 31 October 1650; Pugh, *Swords, Loaves and Fishes*, p. 385.
9   Their predecessors may well have done so, however, when Leven's army was clearing the north of royalists. The best analysis of the experience of the prisoners in Durham is Gerrard et al, *Lost Lives, New Voices*.

Haselrigge sent a daily bread ration down from Newcastle, but the spread of dysentery was compounded by the squalid conditions and men continued to die. For starving men, food can itself be fatal if not carefully moderated; it is unlikely such risks were appreciated, and men who did not seem poorly suddenly died. Over the coming weeks, as the toll continued to rise to the equivalent of nearly thirty losses per day, the sickest prisoners were moved to better conditions in the adjacent castle with cooks preparing improved rations for them. But as Haselrigge's defensive explanations expose, a humanitarian tragedy was unfolding which was simply beyond the authorities to remedy. Hundreds of stripped emaciated bodies were buried without ceremony in a growing open pit between the castle and the cathedral. Over 1,600 perished. When a small corner of their mass grave was accidentally discovered some 263 years later, the full extent of their suffering gained worldwide attention at last. A plaque inside the cathedral and another above the burial place stand silent tribute to the tragic stories of these unnamed prisoners. Those few whose remains were excavated, although representing a tiny sample of the full Scottish army, have provided us with an unrivalled insight into its rank and file. Most had lived hard lives, accustomed to periods of shortage, but nothing could have prepared them for their experiences in captivity. Their remains were reinterred with great dignity in 2018.

Parliament sent orders to Haselrigge that 2,300 healthy prisoners should be sent to Chester and Liverpool from which they could be shipped to Ireland to join the fight against the Catholic rebels. Others were requested to serve against France, and the rest to be sold into indentured service. The plans were based on what Cromwell had reported: four or five thousand physically fit prisoners. Haselrigge's long letter back to them at the end of October reads as an uncomfortable explanation as to why he could not fulfil their instructions: most of those prisoners were no longer alive. Of the survivors, small parties were sent to work in the salt-pans at South Shields and to kick-start a linen cloth industry in the north-east of England. If those excavated at Durham were representative, then there were plenty of prisoners who were experienced at such work. The less skilled were assigned as labourers. Some, presumably those with greater military experience, were indeed sent to fight in Ireland and on the continent; yet others were sent to drain the Norfolk fens. Some were transported to Barbados, where they joined Irish prisoners in creating a community of low status "redlegs". Most famously, a hundred and fifty were sent to Augustine Walker and taken aboard the *Unity* to North America. Many ended up in sawmills or industrial operations like the Saugus Ironworks, working their way through seven-year contracts. Beyond that, they were able to forge new lives at last.[10]

Whilst the human tragedy was unfolding on the road to Durham, the war continued in Scotland. Cromwell ordered the breaking of any pikes and muskets captured from the Scots which could not be put to immediate use. The

---

10 The latest research relating to the names of prisoners reaching New England can be found in the appendix of *Lost Lives, New Voices*, p. 245ff, and in the comprehensive website of the Scottish Prisoners of War Society: https://scottishprisonersofwar.com. With so much excellent work being done in this field, there is little need for us to go into it further here.

51. Memorial plaque in memory the Scottish prisoners who lost their lives at Durham.

reason, according to Whitelocke, was simply that there was no 'conveniency to send them for England,' presumably meaning the Cromwell needed every available cart and waggon for his army as it resumed its operations.[11] The thousands of captured pike, up to eighteen feet long, provided the triumphant soldiers with far more firewood than even they could make use of once the discarded weapons had been broken up. Fire may have been the used to spoil captured muskets too, as it would destroy both the wooden stocks and metal locks.[12] Meanwhile, as Cromwell oversaw events at Dunbar

---

11 Whitelocke, p. 239.
12 The fire-fused wreckage of burned Scottish weapons and equipment may yet lie within the fields around Dunbar, as might evidence of large fires. Regrettably, we have no corroborating detail and so any such discovery will emerge only by happy accident.

and as the soldiers returned to their tents to thank God for their salvation, Lambert rode on to occupy Haddington, securing the road for the march on Edinburgh. The day after the battle, Cromwell wrote letters to parliament, to Haselrigge, to Henry Ireton over in Ireland, and to friends and family. That same day Lambert pressed on to Edinburgh with seven regiments of horse supported by a regiment of foot.

The English were too late to catch Leslie, who had gathered the shattered remnants of his army, several thousand men including a good many horse. Then, carrying with him most of the people required for the continuing function of the government, he fell back further to Stirling. Despite the effort and expense laid down for its fortification, the repeated instructions for which had already suggested less than adequate progress, the capital of Scotland was effectively indefensible without the support of a large army. Certainly Cromwell would now be able to cut it off from reinforcement and resupply if Leslie had attempted to cling on. So if Scotland was to continue its resistance, Stirling was the next line of defence. With a castle equally as formidable as Edinburgh's, with gun-looped town walls rooted in the bedrock, and with control of the strategic crossing of the River Forth which protected its flank, Stirling was the link between the south and the north.

On reaching Stirling, however, the Scots' first priority was to consolidate the command structure. The most pressing issue was Leslie's position: whilst blaming the slackness of his own officers, he claimed the defeat at Dunbar represented 'the visible hand of God.'[13] His offer to resign was rejected: the Kirk Party could not afford to replace their champion. There was, understandably, an urgent inquiry into Dunbar but it laid no blame on the army command. Responding to circulating criticism, the Scottish parliament later formally exonerated the Earl of Leven and James Holborne of any culpability.[14] The Earl of Loudoun was already writing on 6 September that the government was making 'utmost endeavours with all diligence to draw together the remnant of the scattered forces, and to strength the army with the addition of some new levies of horse, foot and dragoons.'[15]

The Committee of Estates, having expressed its continuing confidence in Leslie, quickly sent his most vocal critics – the zealous cavalry officers Strachan and Ker – to a semi-autonomous command in the west. Here, in the lands which had given birth to the Whiggamore Raid in 1648 and which would become the heartlands for the later Covenanter movement, the Western Association began assembling fresh levies of particularly godly supporters. They felt sure it was Scotland's adherence to the king which caused the loss of the divine support which had protected the Covenant until Dunbar. They had sympathisers in government, including Johnston of Wariston, but Strachan and Ker refused to deal any further with David Leslie. The extreme wing of the Covenanter cause was breaking off from the centre.

For King Charles, therefore, a real risk was emerging that the Scots might now turn against him. On the very day of Dunbar he had written to his agent

---

13 Letter from Leslie to Argyll, 5 September 1650; *Ancrum Correspondence*, p. 298.
14 Formally recorded on 13 December 1650, *RPS*, M1650/11/17
15 Letter from Loudoun to Charles II, 6 September 1650; *Ancrum Correspondence*, p. 299.

ALL THE KING'S MEN

52. The Covenanters, represented by "Jockie", hold King Charles II to the grindstone to extract concessions in return for their support. This famous image, showing the standard dress for lowland Scots at the time, may well reflect Charles' own private feelings as much as those of the satirist. The king had a long memory.

Sir Edward Nicholas asking for a ship to be sent from the Netherlands in case he needed to make a rapid exit.[16] London heard rumours that the king 'thanked God that he was so rid of the Scots.'[17] From Stirling the government sent an eye-witness from the battlefield to give the king a full description of events at Dunbar in person, sadly denying us the opportunity to read what might have amounted to an official Scottish account. The messenger also carried a letter from the Earl of Loudoun which echoed the views of men like Strachan: 'feare the Causes of the Lord's fierce anger, which is manifest against your Majesty and your people, that it may be removed.' Loudoun asked the king to apply himself to 'repairing this breach' with God, which Charles will have read as a thinly veiled instruction to do as the committee told him, even if it required additional restraints on the royal freedom.

There was however a subtle shift in Loudoun's language towards the second half of his letter. He asked the king to 'interpose your Royal authority, by your letters to the shires, for giving ready and exact obedience to public orders.' Although those orders were still to come from the Kirk Party, here was an overt acknowledgement that there were those in Scotland who were looking now to the king for guidance. The ruling party, already at risk of splitting from those who Hodgson called the 'Remonstrators' of the Western Association, 'a party that could not agree with the rest,' was afraid that it was also losing ground towards the royalists. In Stirling, and despite the explicit acts of parliament forbidding it, there were those who now openly argued

---

16 Bryant, *Letters*, p. 18.
17 Whitelocke, p. 241.

that former Engagers 'should in this present exigent be permitted to join with the rest.'[18] The pressure was mounting to reverse the purges of the army and repeal the Act of Classes, but there was a convenient excuse to delay as such a decision required a sitting of parliament. Dunbar had badly damaged the Kirk Party's authority; it remained to be seen whether the wound was mortal.

At Stirling, Leslie was busy enhancing the fortifications and cutting the fords which might have allowed Cromwell to try bypassing him. This allowed the safe flow of supplies from Fife now that the harvest had been collected, as well as the passage of 'green new levied soldiers.'[19] Recruitment in the south was hampered not only by Cromwell's success in the south-east but also by competition with the Western Association forces in the south-west. Raising an army had been hard enough in advance of the invasion, but winter was now coming and it was hard to gloss the disaster at Dunbar except by emphasising the scale of the emergency. By mid-September most of the nobles and politicians had gone, both to avoid becoming entrapped at Stirling and to facilitate the required action in the shires. Loudoun stayed to support Leslie as much as he could, lamenting 'the divisions and factions amongst the officers of our armie.'[20]

The king remained at Perth, eager to play a much more direct role but closely guarded by his watchers. He renewed contact with the Duke of Hamilton, who as the Earl of Lanark had led the Engagers against Leslie, and who was currently in a sort of internal exile on his island of Arran. Charles was also talking to the Marquess of Huntly, whose family had been in arms for the royalist cause since the birth of the Covenant, and to the Earl of Atholl with his great territory straddling the Highland line and giving access to the clansmen beyond. The king had found a potential powerbase, a source of manpower which had been untapped by the Kirk Party who doubted their reliability in the cause of the Covenant. Engagers on the continent were making ready to return too.

Whilst these uncertainties were splitting the Scottish leadership, Oliver Cromwell had meanwhile occupied Leith and Edinburgh without incident. Securing the port, a far more substantial harbour than Dunbar, greatly strengthened the English army's position. The capital city itself was a disappointment, with many of the inhabitants having fled with their belongings, but they did seize a magazine of weaponry which Leslie had not been able to evacuate. The military situation was not straightforward even in victory, however. Leslie, whose forces sat at around five or six thousand men according to Walker, of which a thousand were cavalry, blocked the road north. The Western Association was a growing threat to the west, challenging Cromwell's flank if he moved north. Edinburgh Castle, held for the Scots by Walter Dundas, had been supplied for a long siege and Cromwell's artillery train was hardly designed for reducing one of the mightiest fortresses in the kingdom. He sent for heavier guns from England and began a protracted correspondence with the isolated castle governor.

---

18   Row, Robert Blair, p.
19   Letter from Loudoun to Lothian, 16 September 1650; *Ancrum Correspondence*, p. 306.
20   Letter from Loudoun to Lothian, 16 September 1650; *Ancrum Correspondence*, p. 306.

Cromwell also issued a proclamation guaranteeing the safety of all citizens who came to Edinburgh 'with their cattle, corn, horse or other commodities.'[21] With the burgh council refusing to meet under occupation, there was no civil authority in the capital. Cromwell maintained order through the army, from his headquarters at Moray House on the Canongait, but he was keen to get the markets running again. Not only did the soldiers want access to supplies, but the economic life of the city needed to be restarted even in a limited form to prevent the risks of shortage and diseases amidst the remaining citizens. Hodgson recalled the affect: 'we had considerable markets kept in a little time, and provisions brought in plentifully.'[22] It was an important chance for the English army to recuperate from the trials of the summer.

Armies of occupation are never popular however, and despite Cromwell's express desire to maintain strict discipline there were complaints that all empty houses in the city were plundered.[23] Others were obliged to provide quarters for soldiers. Most of the foot were posted in Leith, but a large force was also centred on Holyroodhouse and the adjacent royal park. A series of kirks, including Greyfriars, the High School and the College were all stripped of their furnishings and records, mostly to fuel the fires which warmed the soldiers. On Wednesday 13 November one such fire got out of control, gutting the renaissance palace of the Stuart kings. If some were pleased with the symbolism, others lamented the shelter its historic rooms had provided them. Holyrood would eventually be completely redesigned for Charles II, creating the splendour which can be visited today, but that lay a number of long hard years into the future.

By the time of the palace fire, Cromwell had already marched on Stirling and then, as if to repeat the duels of the summer, returned again to his base. He left on 14 September, leaving Overton's brigade to hold Edinburgh and maintain the blockade of the castle. The army marched through Linlithgow, camping at another Stuart palace, and on towards Falkirk. A herald was sent to the garrisoned tower of Callendar House, seated between the old Roman wall and the historic battlefield of 1298. The commander refused to yield whilst Stirling yet held out, but agreed to offer no harassment to the English passing by. Once again Cromwell's soldiers were obliged to march in pouring, relentless rain. On Wednesday 18 September the English formally summoned Stirling to surrender, but the herald was not admitted. The regiments were drawn up before the walls that afternoon 'in order to a storme, ladders and all things that we could possibly expect being provided for that purpose.'[24] But if this was intended to unnerve the garrison, the demonstration failed. Cromwell called a council of war and the attack was called off; the army pulled back and encamped.

The defiance of Stirling was, as it had been with Edinburgh in the preceding campaigns, based on the presence of Leslie and the modest Scottish field

---

21 Proclamation, 14 September 1650; Carlyle, p. 403.
22 Original Memoirs, p. 149.
23 Walker, *Historical Discourses*, p. 187.
24 *A Diary of all the Proceedings in the Army from their March out of Edinburgh*, in Original Memoirs, p. 318.

'ESSENTIAL AGONY'

53. The walled town of Stirling, dominated by its castle, viewed from Abbey Craig to the north. In the foreground loops the River Forth, where the bridge and fords were controlled by Leslie's army.

army. The general had drawn entrenchments between the town walls and the riverside, and then formed his army north of the river so that the only approach was over Stirling Bridge, of which any English army was wise to be wary. The powerful castle, discharging its cannon to signal its intent to resist, dominated the small city on its rocky outcrop. Suburbs beyond the walls had been cleared, denying the enemy shelter on their approaches. Stirling, where the Engagers and Whiggamores had come to uneasy terms in 1648, was more than ready to receive Cromwell's best efforts.[25] The English withdrew to Linlithgow, which they fortified as a forward strongpoint, and then the main army returned to Edinburgh. There, on 21 September, Cromwell was informed that Lord Liberton – one of his most senior prisoners from Dunbar – had died of his wounds.

Edinburgh Castle offered little by way of a proactive defence: the occasional crackle of musketry, the odd brief cannonade when English pickets made themselves visible. The garrison was hindered by the fact that in order to do anything more aggressive they had to be prepared to inflict collateral damage on the capital. Instead they could just hope to sit it out, and Cromwell was advised they had supplies enough for fifteen months or more. He was more than frustrated: 'I thought I should have found in Scotland a conscientious people and a barren country: about Edinburgh, it is as fertile for corn as any part of England; but the People generally are so given to the

---

25 Walker, Historical Discourses, p. 188.

most impudent lying, and frequent swearing, as is incredible to be believed.'[26] By 9 October he was writing to the Scots government, inviting them to come to terms rather than suffer the 'sad consequences of blood and famine.' God had chastised them, he said, and would do it again.[27]

The danger for Cromwell was that the further he moved into Scotland the more his army had to be diluted by the need to place holding garrisons. With the Scots still in the field the English needed to hold a sufficient bridgehead to deny them space to recruit and resupply in the richest regions of Scotland, and to provide security and supplies for themselves. Cromwell had to detach units to clear out isolated Scottish garrisons in the towers and minor castles which dotted the counties around the capital. There were harassing forces forming along the supply lines, based out of castles such as Borthwick, Dirleton, Tantallon and Hume. These moss-troopers revived the tactics of the reivers, and their numbers were boosted by survivors of Dunbar who could not get through to the main army. These problems would only get worse unless the war could be brought to a formal settlement.

The situation in the west provided Cromwell his best chance, as the Western Association was led by men whose hostility to Malignants was shared with their republican enemy. Cromwell's appeal for a resolution offered greater hope to some than continued service in the king's name. The more extreme Covenanters in the west were, despite instinctive patriotic opposition to the invaders, deeply unhappy at the apparent drift towards royalism. From Dumfries they began preparing a remonstrance arguing that the king was the problem not the solution. It demanded the king completely abandon any association with so-called Malignants, as they could only support a king free from the influence of royalists. Until Charles agreed they would not fight in his name let alone under his orders. Archibald Strachan wanted to go even further: getting rid of the king would end the war overnight, he insisted. Always ready to exploit division, Cromwell planned a march on Glasgow to apply pressure on the westerners.

Behind the Scottish lines, King Charles had also finally lost patience. The country needed leadership. The Marquess of Argyll was needling him constantly, ensuring the king had no space to develop his own party and controlling access as much for his own advancement as for that of the Kirk Party. The king promised a dukedom but still could not bring the dour Campbell onto his side. After seeing Cromwell off from Stirling, there was a sense that the immediate crisis had passed and to appease the more radical elements the Committee of Estates proposed another clear-out of the royal household and a tightening of control of his personal guards. Enough was enough: Charles' supporters had prepared an elaborate scheme to seize Perth and Dundee through the agency of Atholl, Huntly and Viscount Dudhope. The king informed George Villiers, Duke of Buckingham, on 2 October of his intention to authorise the scheme. But Buckingham, the most senior English royalist in the slimline court, saw that the plan was too complex to succeed

---

26 Letter from Cromwell to the Lord President of the Council of State, 25 September 1650; Carlyle, p. 405.
27 Letter from Cromwell to the Committee of Estates, 9 October 1650; Carlyle, p. 408.

'ESSENTIAL AGONY'

and endangered all their work to bring the Covenanters together under the king. Charles was unsure how to proceed, his frustrations and his cautious judgement in fatal conflict, but on the night of 3 October he managed to wriggle free from his watchers.

What followed was an utter debacle. The king travelled over thirty miles to Cortachy Castle, where he successfully linked up with John Scrymgeour, Viscount Dudhope, a veteran of the Preston campaign. There he was disappointed to find so few royalists were ready to move, and although he sent a message calling Atholl to meet him at Clova, 'with all your friends and followers, foot and horses,' Charles may have already convinced himself that the project had misfired. The Kirk Party responded quickly to his absence, perhaps informed by Buckingham. They called together the Committee of Estates and sent a commissioner to bring Charles back with the minimum of fuss. Robert Montgomerie, who had fought with Strachan on the right at Dunbar, rode out with a large force of cavalry to break up any emerging royalist assembly. He caught up with Charles in isolated discomfort in a shepherd's hut at Clova. Only forty-eight hours after encouraging him, the king ordered the Earl of Atholl to 'lay down arms and let every man return to his home.'[28]

This incident, known as The Start, left the Kirk Party 'grieved and amazed with his Majesty's sudden and inexpected behaviour.' Charles' relatively passive acquiescence in the face of their demands seems to have been mistaken for a genuine meekness. But the tone of Loudoun's instructions to the commissioner reflected a recognition of the king's strengthening hand: Sir Charles Erskine was sent to 'assure him [the king] of the constant loyalty' of the government and the army.[29] More significantly, it was also agreed that the king would appear in person at the next meeting of the Committee of Estates. Although Charles would be required to accept the error of his attempt, the conjunction of king and government was actually an important improvement in the king's political position.

It was in the context of these disturbances that Cromwell issued his letter to the Estates and commenced his march on Glasgow. The move had a number of objectives, not least the attempt to bring the Western Association to the table. It would also disrupt their military preparations by interposing English forces across their primary recruiting grounds, whilst showing the Scots that he could move at liberty across central Scotland. Leslie might even be drawn out of Stirling to threaten the Linlithgow garrison or relieve Edinburgh. Indeed, it was the false rumour that he was doing so which lured Cromwell back. But although there was no battle to be had – the English contented themselves by thoroughly clearing out a ring of small garrisons – the combination of his appeals for peace and the news of The Start were working on the Western Association. But even the Remonstrance they drafted, which Robert Blair described as being 'in a high strain,' did not

---

28 Letters from Charles II to the Earl of Atholl, 4 and 6 October; Bryant, p. 19.
29 Instructions from the Committee of Estates, 5 October 1650; *Ancrum Correspondence*, p. 306.

go far enough for Strachan, who entered into direct correspondence with Cromwell.[30]

Meanwhile The Start had created a confusing situation behind the Scots lines. Although the planned coup had been a flash in the pan, it had brought a number of Charles' supporters out into the field. Desperate to avoid the risk of civil war, the government proposed an Act of Indemnity for all those who had risen. This was not without controversy, from both ends of the spectrum. Some feared it would be an encouragement to the royalists whilst those to whom it was addressed objected to the suggestion that they could be in rebellion whilst they were serving the king. The Earl of Middleton, veteran senior officer from the doomed Preston campaign, re-emerged from the wilderness and headed a sizeable force in Angus. When Sir John Browne, acting on behalf of the government, sent him a peremptory summons, Middleton detached a force of cavalry and fell on Browne's encampment at Newtyle. They 'killed an Officer or two, and about fifteen others; took 120 prisoners and most of the horse.'[31]

The day after the skirmish, 22 October, Loudoun wrote to the king's secretary, the Earl of Lothian, entreating that Charles should publicly confirm his approval of the Committee's decision to send Leslie north to disperse any who remained in arms.[32] To those who refused the Indemnity, Loudoun promised 'fire and sword till they be totally suppressed,' but the reality was that the government desperately needed to avoid the outbreak of any more fighting. Two days later James Livingstone, the cantankerous Earl of Callendar who had served as Hamilton's second at Preston, wrote from Amsterdam that 'in this time of eminent danger,' it was his duty to return from exile to serve his country. David Leslie reached Perth that day to subdue the Highland royalists with 3,000 men, but on 26 October an Act of Pardon was issued. As Whitelocke reported in London, 'David Lesley's army have no mind to fight with Middleton's men.'[33] The political momentum was swinging towards the king.

As November began, with the royalists in the north accepting the indemnity and the risks of a major Scottish split abating, Cromwell was having problems of his own. His best hopes of forcing an open fracture in the opposition still remained with Strachan and Ker in the west, but there was little to show for the discussions so far and the Remonstrators were looking increasingly isolated from the political mainstream. Even Wariston was moved to block their attempts to agree terms with Cromwell.[34] In the meantime, the moss-troopers were increasing the pressure on Cromwell's men as they went about their business of trying to control the landscape. Despite 'all our tenderness to the Country,' the general wrote, with all the self-righteousness of a confident invader, 'divers of the Army under my command are not only spoiled and robbed, but also sometimes barbarously

---

30 Row, *Robert Blair*, p. 246.
31 Walker, *Historical Discourses*, p. 203.
32 Letter from Loudoun to Lothian, 22 October 1650; *Ancrum Correspondence*, p. 317.
33 Whitelocke, p. 257.
34 Whitelocke, p. 255.

'ESSENTIAL AGONY'

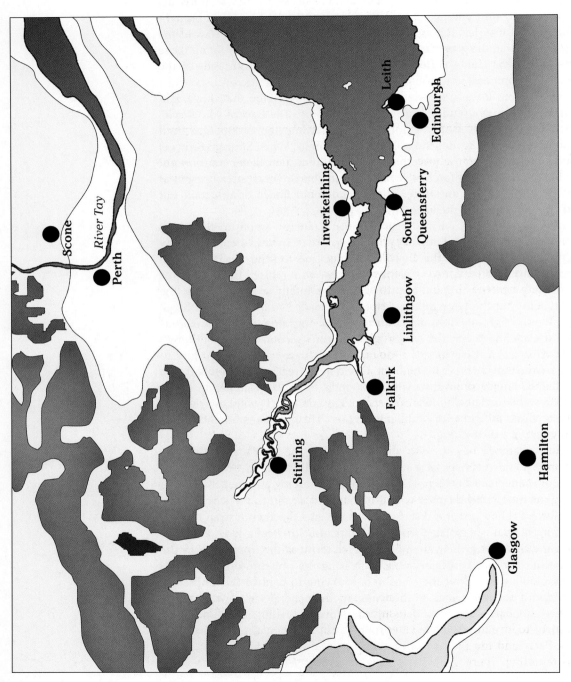

Map 10. South-central Scotland: the theatre of war opens up.

and inhumanly butchered.' Heriot's Hospital, not quite completed, had been commandeered as a military hospital for Cromwell's sick and wounded. As frustrated in most of his aims after Dunbar as he had been before, the general was losing his patience: 'I will require life for life, and a plenary satisfaction for their goods, of those parishes and places where the fact shall be committed: unless they shall discover and produce the offender.'[35] There was a real danger that the war might degenerate into the brutal cycle of raid, reprisal, and repression.

Edinburgh Castle continued to hold out, and even the deployment of Derbyshire miners could not increase the effectiveness of the futile attempts to undermine the forward defences. After weeks of labour, however, Cromwell successfully raised batteries which could at last threaten to bring fire upon the walls on the crag above them. Crucially, mortars had been brought up from England and, as Hodgson rather inadequately reports, 'some few fireballs were thrown in.'[36] The castle guns returned fire on the batteries but did little damage. Equally however, the garrison had little to fear in the short term if they remained resolute. The year was drawing towards its close and Cromwell was still only sixty miles from the Border, David Leslie still had an army, and the Covenanters were still standing by their king. On the surface, Dunbar had hardly improved Cromwell's lot at all.

Something needed to be done to break the deadlock, as there was a real risk that the effects of Cromwell's victory were being blunted by time. For ten days the Committee of Estates and the Scots clergy debated the content of the Western Remonstrance. The original National Covenant had, although directed against the late king's religious policies, never been intended as anti-monarchy. In many ways it had been a fairly conservative revolution, which had helped it to become such a successful national movement. Even the great Montrose had originally taken up arms in its cause, although as civil war spread across all three kingdoms attitudes had hardened and perspectives had evolved. Viewed in this light, the Engagers of 1648 were closer to the original tenor of the Covenant than the Remonstrators of 1650. This goes someway to understanding how the men who had nurtured and defended the Covenant since its birth, fighting a vicious civil war against the royalists along the way, found themselves drifting into the arms of a Stuart king.

Charles II had gone further than his father would have done in acceding to their political and religious demands, after all, and a Covenanted King had been their theoretical ideal all along. Other motivators included personal ambition, the breakdown in confidence after Dunbar, and the immediate problem of an invading army. Most importantly, the person of the king provided a focus for national unity. Even Gilbert Ker professed that he desired, if Charles Stuart proved sufficiently earnest in his commitment to the kirk, 'to love the king and serve him.'[37] In the coming conjunction of the Kirk Party and the Engagers, the middle-ground of the Covenanter cause was reuniting. There was also an urgent military need to reintegrate those

---

35 Proclamation, 5 November 1650; Carlyle, p. 412.
36 Original Memoirs, p. 149.
37 Letter from Ker to Lothian, 22 November 1650; *Ancrum Correspondence*, p. 320.

with experience and those who could raise substantial manpower, including royalists in the Highlands.

In this context, the Remonstrators of the Western Association were isolated. Their refusal to work with David Leslie alienated Strachan and Ker militarily, just as their demands relating to the king were increasingly out of step with the drift of events. The kirk assembly's response to the some of the issues raised was equivocal, finding some 'sad truths' in its words, but there was no appetite for risking a national breach. Accepting the demands of the Remonstrators would 'breed division in this kirk and kingdom' which the English could then exploit.[38] With the kirk unable to support it, the Western Remonstrance was rejected: 'the king's party carried it to vote colonel Strachan's declaration to be scandalous.'[39] Strachan had in fact refused to sign the remonstrance since it had not gone far enough; he was dismissed from his command. For Cromwell, there was now little to be gained from wasting more time attempting a settlement with the Western Association.

With Ker increasingly isolated, Cromwell turned his strength against him. Here was an opportunity to knock out the threat to his flank and deny Leslie any support or supplies from south of Stirling. Not knowing exactly where Ker would concentrate, Cromwell opted to lure him on by dividing his forces. A cavalry detachment under Whalley struck down through Lauderdale to open the campaign, drawing Ker towards Peebles. On 27 November, Lambert rushed off towards him with several thousand horse, linking up with Whalley and pushing Ker back westwards. That same day, Cromwell took the direct road to Glasgow, staying 'on the north side of the Clyde.'[40] In danger of being trapped between the two enemy columns, Ker withdrew to Bothwell Brig on 29 November to block the English from crossing the river. Cromwell was apparently thwarted, for after tarrying into the following morning he ordered a retreat. Ker pulled back to Rutherglen.

On 30 November, however, Lambert and Whalley slipped across the Clyde and encamped outside Hamilton with around 3,000 men. Distracted by the political situation, the Western Association forces had not done a great deal to proactively threaten the English. Now, facing political and military isolation, Colonel Ker was feeling the pressure to prove the value of his Western Association forces. After losing Strachan, he was also keenly conscious of the vulnerability of his own personal position. But he now seemed to be faced with a golden opportunity: Lambert had presumably come west expecting to link up with Cromwell, but the latter already withdrawn. Underestimating Lambert's strength, Ker decided to attack.

In the very early hours of Sunday 1 December 1650, beneath an icy cold moon, the Scots cavalry pounded across the frozen ground toward Hamilton from the north. A forlorn hope was detached to clear Lambert's pickets from the town, which they did with astonishing success. Total confusion reigned as English troopers shut themselves up into houses, carbines cracking loudly in the crisp air. Lambert himself had to scramble through the back doors

---

38 *RPS*, A1650/11/3.
39 Whitelocke, p. 276.
40 Letter from Cromwell to Speaker Lenthall, 4 December 1650; Carlyle, p. 413.

of a tavern to get out of Hamilton and gather up his forces. Ker was slow in exploiting the initial success of his advance guard however, and by the time the main body of the Scots came riding up the English had recovered. The troopers recovering their discipline, Lambert's men formed on the far side of the Cadzow Burn. Ker charged, losing his own cohesion crossing the brook, but Lambert beat him back. The English counter-charge resulted in a rolling and disjointed battle back through Hamilton as Kerr's men were tumbled back. As his little army collapsed, Kerr was wounded and overwhelmed.

Dawn revealed over a hundred Scots dead, along with an English toll which was undoubtedly higher than the six admitted by Cromwell. Lambert pursued, breaking up the remnants of the Western Association army. Most of the senior officers were taken amongst the hundred or so prisoners. Hearing of the disaster Archibald Strachan attempted to rally a party of the Remonstrators, but immediately gave up the prospect of continuing the fight. With a small party he rode out to offer his services to the English, convinced at last that Cromwell represented a lesser evil than the king. It was a move which undid all the previous valour of his performance at Dunbar and ensured that he would forever be remembered as a turncoat.

The fight at Hamilton is known locally as the Battle of Heiton, in reference to the fighting in the town centre or "high town". There is a plaque tucked away under the later bridge over the Cadzow Burn, but the landscape has been consumed by the growth of Hamilton and the engagement largely forgotten.[41] But Ker's defeat was a significant moment: the Western Association was finished as an autonomous force. Although Hamilton was hardly a national disaster on the scale of Dunbar, the radical party's military credentials were now as tarnished as the Kirk Party's and the loss of both Ker and Strachan took the momentum out of the movement. Besides, before the defeat the Committee of Estates had despatched Robert Montgomerie west with a large force of horse to relieve Ker of his command. Survivors of the Hamilton fight joined up with him.

The extent to which Cromwell's retreat from Bothwell Brig may have been a calculated lure to bring Ker into the field is a moot point; his campaign in the west had successfully knocked out one of the sources of opposition and increased his own freedom of movement. But Montgomerie's appearance in the west meant that the strategic flank was still not fully secured. A field victory towards the end of the year was however good news to send home, and Cromwell now sought to crown his achievements with the capture of Edinburgh Castle. On 12 December he sent Dundas a formal summons: 'my duty presseth me, for the ends aforesaid, and to avoid the effusion of more blood, to demand the rendering of this place to me upon fit conditions.'[42]

The governor asked for ten days in order to consult the Committee of Estates, since he held his commission by their orders. Cromwell refused, on the grounds that the Scottish government no longer represented the same

---

41 At the nearby Bothwell Brig, another army of western Covenanters would face defeat – this time at the hands of King Charles II's government forces – in the summer of 1679; an event far better remembered in the area today.
42 Letter from Cromwell to Dundas, 12 December 1650; Carlyle, p. 416.

cause as it had when Dundas had been appointed. 'I hear,' said Cromwell, 'those that are honest amongst them enjoy not satisfaction, and the rest are now discovered to seek another Interest than they have formerly pretended to.' In other words, the Kirk Party were turning into royalists, Malignants, which helped Cromwell to paint a more simplistic picture of friend and foe. Dundas replied again on the morning of 13 December, repeating his request but also inviting Cromwell to elaborate on his point. In his willingness to enter into the discussion Dundas had already compromised himself, exposing that he was open to political persuasion. Cromwell talked more of the growing Malignancy at the heart of Scottish policy, and allowed a ceasefire of a few hours on 14 December for Dundas to seek other voices in Edinburgh who could confirm it. Alexander Jaffrey, the provost of Aberdeen, had been captured at Dunbar and seems to have been found useful by Cromwell; Dundas sought his advice, but he replied that it was too high a matter for him to meddle in.

There now occurred a most extraordinary intervention. A certain Captain Augustine Hoffman, a German mercenary in Scottish service and now leader of a band of highly efficient moss-troopers, succeeded in bluffing passage through Bristo Port. Riding straight through the centre of Edinburgh to the castle gates, Augustine inserted thirty-six men and a cache of supplies into the garrison, before riding out without interference. For the English this was a deeply humiliating episode, exposing the ineffectiveness of their military blockade of the castle. It should have given the soldiers within a considerable boost in morale, which even Cromwell's renewed cannonades could not easily quench. The English batteries were concentrated, blasting at the defences from the town-ward side, but the damage seems to have been largely superficial and there was nothing to suggest the castle could be rendered indefensible any time soon.

Nonetheless, negotiations resumed a few days later. By now Cromwell was unwilling to discuss the matter further and gave Dundas an hour to reply with his nominations as to who would come out to agree terms. The spirit of resistance was extinguished, and Dundas said Major Andrew Abernethy and Captain Robert Henderson to treat with Monck and Lt-Colonel Francis White. The articles of surrender were agreed and the greatest fortress in the land was opened up to Oliver Cromwell. For days the citizens of Edinburgh watched as a steady stream of trunks of valuables were brought out of the castle, goods which had been deposited there for safekeeping before the arrival of the enemy. The English permitted the owners to recover their belongings but that did not help those who had fled.

Cromwell and his officers looked on with immense relief, as their losses in attempting to force the castle must surely have been considerable. Dundas marched out on 24 December with 120 musketeers behind a single drum and a billowing red ensign. Their plan was to sail to Fife out of Leith, but the winds were against them and they were obliged to sit under guard in the port overnight. There most of them 'laid down their arms and will not engage anymore.'[43] White occupied the castle with companies from the Lord

---

43 Original Memoirs, p. 351.

General's Regiment of Foot. Cromwell and his officers spent the afternoon exploring the ancient fortress.

Carlyle would later write that, 'all was handsome, just and honourable' in the surrender of Edinburgh Castle.[44] For Dundas and his garrison, the terms had indeed been generous; they had left with their arms and belongings and their matches lit. They had however left behind them five 7, 9 and 24 pounder cannon, two culverins, two demi-culverins, two minions, two falcons, three brass 3 pounders, and Mons Meg, plus 'ten thousand arms, and a great store of ammunition and provisions.'[45] But even this material loss was nothing compared to the psychological one: Edinburgh Castle had changed hands during civil crises, but falling to the English was a different matter altogether. More to the point, it had gone down with barely a whimper. To the Committee of Estates, the Scots army, and the king, the capitulation was an outrage. Dundas was no grizzled veteran but nor was he a fool, and it must have been clear that he could held out far longer yet. Politically however, Dundas sympathised with the Remonstrators more than the royalists, and Cromwell's words will have carried weight. Strachan was in Edinburgh too by this time, and it is not without possibility that he was in private correspondence with the governor, whom he knew. Walter Dundas, his subordinate Andrew Abernethy, and Archibald Strachan were all charged with treason the following March.

Oliver Cromwell knew that he had achieved an enormous success for minimal loss. He knew that if the defence had been prosecuted effectively then Edinburgh Castle, 'would have cost very much blood to have attained, if at all to be attained.' A full siege would have tied up most of his army and prevented any serious operations against Leslie until it could be resolved. With great relief he was able to report the castle's capitulation to parliament: 'I must needs say, not any skill or wisdom of ours, but the good hand of God that given you this place.'[46] Thus 1650 ended well for the Commonwealth of England: the Spanish had formally acknowledged the republic; the faltering Irish rebels had removed Ormond from command and he had returned to exile in France; the Scottish garrisons in the south were being reduced one by one, leaving Leslie bottled up in the north facing a hard winter; and Edinburgh Castle was in their hands. The Scots had obligingly aligned themselves ever nearer the king, making it easier to cast them all into the mould of Malignants. Come the spring, Cromwell could return to the offensive and finish them off.

Meanwhile, momentous events had been occurring in Perth's burgh chambers. On 25 November 1650, King Charles II had taken his place behind the Honours of Scotland and addressed the opening of his first parliament. He spoke of the 'great many difficulties' which had overcome to reach this moment, and of his aim to work with those gathered before him for 'the general good and common happiness of these three covenanted kingdoms.' It was humble speech, expressing his pride at being the first king to be able to

---

44 Carlyle, p. 421.
45 Original Memoirs, p. 355; Whitelocke, p.281.
46 Letter from Cromwell to Speaker Lenthall, 24 December 1650; Carlyle, p. 422.

claim he had entered into a covenant with his people and his willingness 'to live and die with my people in the defence of it.' He also regretted his error in supporting The Start.[47] The tone was right: the king sensed his moment had come but did overplay his hand.

Parliament was in the process of discussing what to do about the western remonstrance when news came of Ker's defeat at Hamilton. Loudoun sent orders to what remained of the Western Association to put themselves under command of Montgomery so that resistance in the region could continue. 'Nothing shall be wanting for your encouragement and assistance,' he wrote.[48] Montgomerie merged what remained of the Western Association's 'broken regiments' into his own. The sitting of parliament reinvigorated the war effort. Leven and Holborne were officially exonerated of any blame for the disaster at Dunbar. David Leslie, retaining the full confidence of king and committee, was ordered to gather in all stores of corn about Stirling. Arms were ordered from Gothenburg in Sweden to replace those lost at Dunbar and Edinburgh. Two days of public humiliation were held to appease the Lord and bring the nation and the king back into his favour. Then on 23 December a new Act of Levy was issued, ordering the whole nation into arms once more. Unlike the summer levies, this one included the clansmen of the north, including Cameron of Lochiel and the MacDonalds of Keppoch and Clanranald.

Three days later William Hamilton wrote to the Earl of Lothian from his domestic exile on Arran. He had been informed that parliament had at last rescinded the penalties it had placed upon him after he disbanded his army in 1648. The duke understood the gravity of the national situation, in which 'so much of the blood of Scotland is daily spilling.' He knew there would still be those who would object to his return, and he sought Lothian's advice on how he should act. 'I know not how with conscience and honour,' he wrote, 'I can forbear to contribute my endeavours, even in the capacity of a trooper, in this common cause.'[49] The committee of the kirk was holding a meeting in Perth alongside that of the parliament, and they finally concurred that 'it's a necessary duty, both by the law of God and of nature, to use all lawful means for the defence of the liberty, lives and estates of the people.'[50] The road was now open for the Engagers and royalists to return to arms in the national service. 'By the blessing of God,' wrote Robert Baillie, 'this may be a greater beginning of union among ourselves, and of a more happy acting against the enemy than formerly.'[51]

On Saturday 1 January 1650, Charles II was crowned king beneath a velvet canopy in the small but ancient church at Scone. He listened to a powerful sermon by Robert Douglas before the crown was placed on his head by none other than the Marquess of Argyll. Loudoun guided him to the chair of state. It was a ceremony which blended traditional ritual with

---

47 *RPS*, A1650/11/1.
48 *RPS*, A1650/11/6.
49 Letter from Hamilton to Lothian, 26 December 1650; *Ancrum Correspondence*, p. 324.
50 Row, *Robert Blair*, p. 250.
51 Baillie, *Letters and Journals*, Vol. III, p. 107.

54. The Coronation of Charles II at Scone, showing Argyll placing the crown upon his head and Robert Douglas in the pulpit. Attributed to Jacob van der Ulft. (Royal Collection Trust © Her Majesty Queen Elizabeth II, 2019)

covenanter moderation, and though Charles may later have grumbled about the lecturing sermon the coronation was the perfect compromise for the moment. As his nobles crowded around the king in the cramped environment, to swear their oaths with their fingers touching the crown upon his head, the ceremony represented the personal intimacy Scottish lords looked for from their monarch. Charles too swore his oaths, arising with full legitimacy if not total authority. His ancient royal pedigree was recounted, stirring the hearts of patriots as the list of kings was read, binding those present in the sense of national cause. It was done, said Robert Baillie, 'so peaceably and magnificently as if no enemy had been among us.'[52]

This was a moment of longed-for unity, of pride and self-confidence amidst a context of relentless of turmoil, sacrifice and fear. Now the nation could put behind the divisions of the civil war and of the Engagement crisis of 1648; could move on from the disaster at Dunbar. As Charles II was presented to his people at Scone, as that dread year of 1650 died behind

---

52 Baillie, *Letters and Journals*, Vol. III, p. 128.

him at last, those who had crowned him might even have believed that a covenanted kingdom might work.

But they were witnessing a false dawn, a prelude to yet another disaster, and to nine years of military occupation. Not until 1660 would Charles II be restored to power in his three kingdoms; and then he would rule them from London. When he thought of Scotland it would not be to remember those who had fought at Dunbar, however, but those who had dared to bargain over the terms of his inheritance.

Epilogue

Worcester, England, 3 September 1651

This day twelvemonth was glorious at Dunbar; this day hath been glorious before Worcester; the word was then 'The Lord of Hosts', and so it was now, and indeed the Lord of Hosts was wonderfully with us.

Robert Stapleton

At midday on the first anniversary of the Battle of Dunbar, three hundred and forty miles from that historic field, the quiet calm of a clear bright day was split by the thud and crackle of musket-fire. It began at Powick Church south-west of Worcester, its warm yellow stones ringing with the impact of lead balls. Scottish matchlocks flashed back from the narrow windows. The firefight was brief but intense; the English assault determined not the be held up at the church as it swept northwards towards the stone bridge across the River Teme. There, in 1642, the opening engagement of the civil war in England had been fought. Now, the last battle of the Wars of the Three Kingdoms was beginning after twelve long years of increasingly bitter conflict.

At Powick Bridge the Scots held firm, the enemy's assault funnelled along the narrow stone crossing where it lost momentum and cohesion. The dispute 'lasted a long time, and was very hot.'[1] But Oliver Cromwell had anticipated that problem: in parallel with Colonel Richard Deane's assault marched a larger column under the command of Lambert and Fleetwood to turn the Scots flank. Where the Teme met the Severn, two pre-fabricated pontoon bridges were being dragged forward to link Cromwell's left and his centre, and to allow Lambert to outflank the bridge at Powick and drive the Scots back towards the defences of Worcester itself. Rushing up to repulse Lambert's crossing was Colin Pitscottie, two brigade commanders from Dunbar facing each other once again.

The campaigns of 1651 had extended the theatre of war dramatically, and the Scots-Royalist invasion which the English republic had so feared had at last materialised. King Charles II, taking personal command of his army in

---

1 Letter from Stapleton, in Whitelocke, p. 345.

'ESSENTIAL AGONY'

55. Powick Bridge, from the bank possessed by the English.

Scotland, had led it out of Stirling to a line of new defences between Torwood and Airth and defied Cromwell to attack. The latter had tried, skirmishing around the river crossing at Larbert and storming Callendar House at Falkirk, but the Scottish positions were too strong to challenge directly. In July, Colonel Overton had led a landing party at the Queensferry crossings west of Edinburgh, creating a bridgehead into Fife which Lambert then filled with 4,500 men. James Holborne rushed across the block them, assembling a mixed force of Highland and Lowland levies which was placed under overall command of the Sir John Brown whose quarters had been beaten up by Middleton's royalists six months before.

On 20 July 1651, Lambert had launched his breakout. The Scots were driven back from their initial positions closing the neck of the peninsula, and Holborne fled with much of the horse. Brown managed to reform his line across a ridge of hills overlooking the English positions, but their cohesion had been fatally compromised. Lambert drove on relentlessly, pushing the Scots back ever further. The battle fragmented into a protracted running fight as the Scots broke up, the dramatic climax of which was the desperate heroism of the MacLeans as they fought a last stand over the body of their fallen chief. The Battle of Inverkeithing, between that town in the east and Rosyth in the west, opened a new route into the north of Scotland and undermined Leslie's policy of containment. The main army had pulled back from Torwood, but their position their position at Stirling was still too strong from Cromwell to risk assaulting. As a result, the latter followed Lambert across the Firth of Forth and marched north to seize Perth.

EPILOGUE

56. The Maclean monument on Inverkeithing Battlefield.

This was the critical strategic moment for the Scots at Stirling, but the king persuaded his commanders that it was time to take the war into England. Historians have long debated whether Cromwell had anticipated the move and deliberately left the road to England open, but if so he had gambled deep by pushing as far north as Perth. When the Scots struck south, Cromwell had to throw his weight after them 'in all haste.'[2] Lambert went first, to get ahead of the Scots to restrict and harry their movements as he had done in 1648; Cromwell came in his wake with the foot. George Monck was left behind to continue the reduction of Scotland, beginning an autonomous command which would last until 1660.

Charles II had led his army down the same roads as the first Duke of Hamilton had chosen on his fatal march to Preston. Hamilton's brother and successor was with him. As before, the Scots had hoped to connect up with English royalists as they went. Also as before, most of the English royalists were intercepted and knocked out of the main fight. To the king's bitter disappointment, it seemed all England was rising against him: the memory of Preston and the Scottish army's poor discipline were too strong. After two years of predictions that the Scots would invade with a Malignant army, reigniting the civil wars, the Council of State's messaging succeeded in convincing the people that this was an invasion not a liberation. Militias mobilised, fresh forces springing up to join with the veteran regiments

---

2 Hodgson, in Original Memoirs, p. 153.

'ESSENTIAL AGONY'

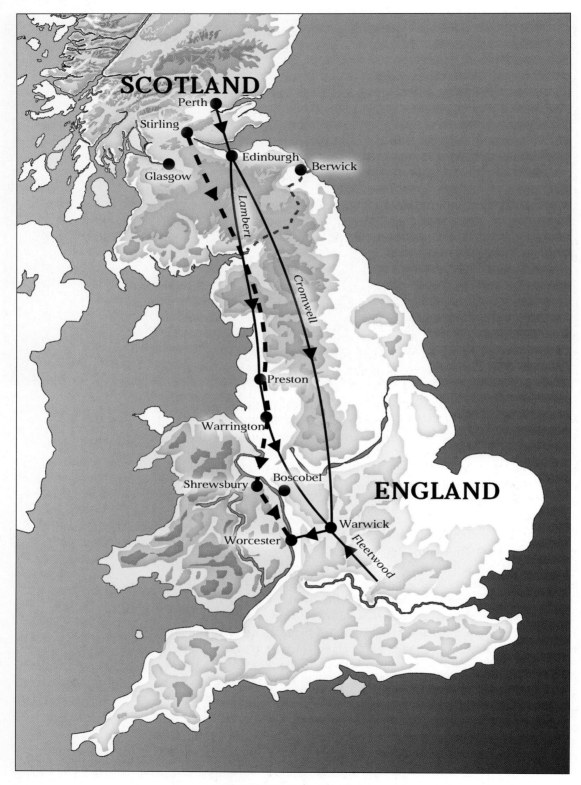

Map 11. The Worcester Campaign.

shadowing the Scottish advance. The king, unable to cut across towards London as he had planned, took his 16,000 men into the walled city of Worcester on 22 August and dug in. He called on his subjects to rise up and join him. Cromwell's soldiers burned the proclamation at the head of each regiment. They outnumbered the royal army nearly two to one.

Under the command of Robert Montgomerie, the Scottish resistance along the Teme was stubborn and effective. Even when the weight of numbers pushed them back from the river, the Scots made use of the hedgerows and lanes to mount a grinding defence reminiscent of Langdale's in the early phases of Preston. Meanwhile, Cromwell had sent a strong force out as his right flank two cut the road north, whilst his main body lined the ridgeline of Perry Hill and Red Hill which overlooked Worcester from the east. The Scots were almost completely cut off, dependent on their dwindling magazines and now with no hope of relief or resupply. It was almost a reverse of the situation of Dunbar. The Scots fought with the desperation of men with their backs to the wall.

Around 3pm Cromwell launched three brigades west across the Severn to break the deadlock north of the Teme. He led them over his bridge of boats in person, bringing an overwhelming force against Pitscottie's men and forcing them back. But still the Scots fought, as Cromwell himself put it, 'from one defence to another.'[3] Montgomerie was now no longer holding but fighting a dogged rearguard northwards towards the St John's suburb of the city. Behind him was a reserve under Tam Dalyell of the Binns, a veteran of the Scots campaigns in Ulster who had refused to shave since the execution of the late king in 1649. Further back, and on the other side of the river and covering the north side of the city, was a further reserve supported by a large body of cavalry under no less a commander than David Leslie.

Worcester was ringed by medieval stone walls which had been strengthened with projecting earthen bastions. Most of the defences had been there before the Scots arrived, giving the defenders a head-start in their preparations. The most significant work undertaken had been the construction of a substantial redoubt situated on a high bluff overlooking the London road. Named Fort Royal, it was connected by earthworks to the town walls, creating a projection on the south-eastern side of the city. Just inside the walls here was an old medieval hospital complex known as the Commandery. The River Severn ran along the city's western side, a long wharf creating a thin corridor between the waterside and the town walls. The dominant feature of the townscape was the vast cathedral at its heart, and from its tower the king looked on as Cromwell and Lambert pushed Pitscottie and Montgomerie back towards Dalyell.

The king then made a valiant decision. To turn the tide on the left, Cromwell had weakened his centre; the narrow pontoon bridge over the Severn and a considerable distance of open ground separated the two. Faced with almost insuperable odds, Charles sensed that this gave him a window of opportunity which was unlikely to be repeated. Accordingly, he launched

---

3 Letter from Cromwell to Speaker Lenthall, 4 September 1650; Carlyle, p. 458.

'ESSENTIAL AGONY'

57. View from a corner bastion of Fort Royal, looking towards Worcester Cathedral. The replica cannon faces towards the English at Red Hill. Interpretation panels and a bronze memorial sit within the redoubt, which is now a park, just a short walk from the Commandery museum.

'a very bold sally' against the English centre. Two Scots columns surged out of Worcester and onto the offensive: the first, led by the Duke of Hamilton, stormed up the considerable slopes of Perry Hill; the second attacking along the road to Red Hill was led by the king himself. Both attacks came out of the protection of the defences and had to cover open ground before ascending towards the enemy lines, under artillery and then musket fire all the way. On reaching the English lines, the ferocity of the Scottish assault seemed as if it might almost prove enough. 'It was a very fierce and sore battle, and long fought *in dubio*,' but the news carried to Cromwell and he acted with decisive speed.[4] Returning across the bridge, the general was able to drive his wearying troops on into the flank of the king's attack.

Charles' heroic gamble had failed. The English centre had suffered 'a very hot salute, and put to a little retreat and disorder,' but the line had not broken.[5] Cromwell had then reinforced it with such mass as to bowl the Scottish attack back towards Worcester. As they attempted to fall back, disorientated by the lingering fog of the crashing salvoes, flashing on all sides with banks of orange flame, the Scottish lines began to break up. Troops of horse crashed through and around the fragmenting battalia, friend and foe almost impossible to discern. As the fighting flowed back down the slopes Hamilton's men mingled with the king's, all cohesion collapsing. Soon the retreat became a rout, the pounding thunder of great guns opening up once more now that

---

4 Row, *Robert Blair*, p. 283.
5 Stapleton, in Whitelocke, p. 346.

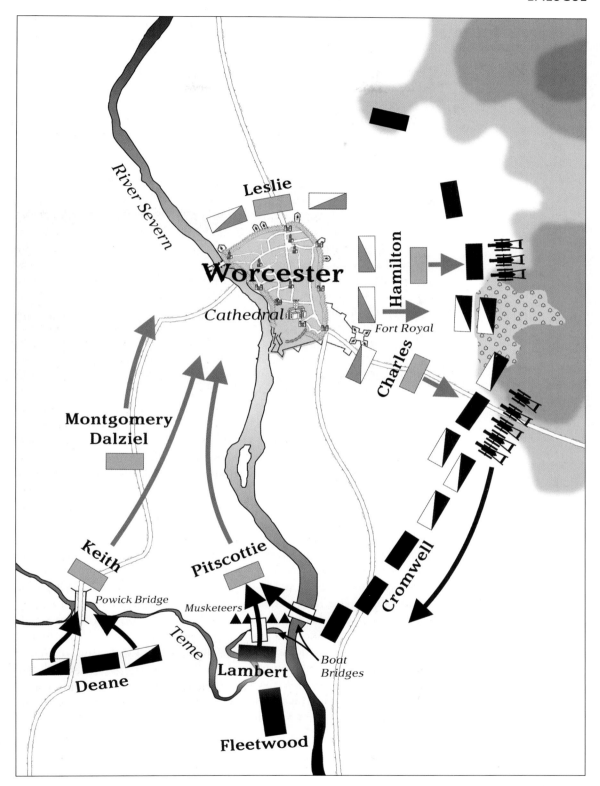

Map 12. The Battle of Worcester, 3 September 1651.

the ridge was clear. The Scots spilled back over their earthworks and into Fort Royal, but the routing soldiers blinded their own guns and there could be no support. William, Duke of Hamilton, was flung to the ground as his leg was smashed by cannon-fire. Cromwell's men stormed through the fleeing Scots, and in such confusion the defences were overrun with unimagined ease and the parliamentarians rushed towards the city gates.

On the other side of the river the picture was similar: even after Cromwell had withdrawn part of his forces there the Scots had been too hard pressed to hold. Robert Montgomerie was struck, falling as the line at last began to crumble. Dalyell, who had been reluctant to advance in support for fear of being cut off from Worcester, now took up the fighting retreat across the Severn. But as the Scots withdrew into one end of the city it became clear that the defences had faltered at the other. On both sides then the Scots were tumbling into Worcester with their enemy in unstoppable pursuit. Some were funnelled into the gap between the walls and the river, hopelessly hemmed in. Meanwhile Cromwell ordered a general assault from all possible approaches from the east, west and south. The Scots guns on Fort Royal were turned against the city they had been mounted to protect.

The king was driven back into the city, where he attempted to rally what men he could. But the chaos had become general and Worcester had become a death trap. The fighting continued 'in the streets,' but it was soon clear that the king could achieve no more. Discarding his breastplate and helmet, he made a final attempt to draw a cavalry force together and then pressed through the throngs towards St Martin's Gate to the north-west. Here he was able to break out around 6pm. Unengaged Cromwellian horse spotted the exodus and set off in pursuit, but they were too far to intercept the king. Besides, coming around on the north side of Worcester was the only part of the Scots army which was completely intact. David Leslie's brigade had contributed nothing to these momentous events, but now they joined the flight. 'A great part of the Scots horse flies homeward,' reports Hodgson.[6] Behind them, thousands of Scottish foot-soldiers fought on through the evening. By 10pm the battle was over.

The Battle of Worcester had cost the Scots army almost the same losses as it had suffered at Dunbar. Around three thousand had fallen; more than three times that went into captivity. Most would face transportation, although they were spared a repeat of the tragedy at Durham. Cromwell's losses were considerably higher at Worcester, several hundred, and the fighting had clearly been severe and protracted. The Duke of Hamilton died of his wounds in Worcester Commandery a few days later; there is a plaque in his honour inside the cathedral. Whether Cromwell had intended Worcester to fall that day or just to tighten the noose around it ahead of a subsequent assault will never be known. It was a decisive victory, achieved by an army with a massive numerical and psychological advantage. It was, at least in terms of the great battles, the end of the Wars of the Three Kingdoms.

---

6   Original Memoirs, p. 347.

Back in Scotland, Stirling Castle had already surrendered to Monck; Dundee had been stormed with unaccustomed brutality. Aberdeen would soon capitulate and by December the last Scottish field forces had surrendered or disbanded. Sporadic fighting would continue to break out in pockets around the country, but none of the attempted uprisings could gain traction against Monck and his army of occupation. Immense fortresses were constructed in Inverness, Perth, Ayr and Leith to overawe the population. Nothing is visible at Perth, and only a single gate survives in Leith, but the remains of Ayr Citadel stand as a remarkable testament to the expense and efforts taken to subdue Scotland. A parliamentary union was proclaimed, and Scotland was annexed by the new republic. From 1653, the Commonwealth of England, Scotland and Ireland was governed by Oliver Cromwell as Lord Protector.

Oliver Cromwell died on the eighth anniversary of his triumph at the Battle of Dunbar. The loss of the strong man which held it together set the republic tottering. The attempt to pass power to his son Richard was a false starter, and it fell to veterans of Dunbar to determine the fate of the British nations. Charles Fleetwood moved to bring down Richard Cromwell, and then John Lambert was sent north to intercept George Monck. The latter's designs were impenetrable, but his long governance of Scotland had kept him away from the intrigues of the Westminster. By 1659 he knew that he had an opportunity to play a decisive role in determining the outcome of the crisis. Lambert's march against Monck was a humiliating end to a glittering military career: the whole army deserted. Monck marched on London unopposed and summoned all the MPs who had been excluded by Pride's Purge more than ten years before. Lambert attempted to rally the parliamentarian cause, but he was taken back into captivity before he could make a beginning. Parliament opened negotiations with Charles II.

The escape of the young king after Worcester has entered popular legend, particularly the episode of the royal oak at Boscobel House. After considerable danger, the like of which would be shared by another Charles Stuart seeking the throne ninety-five years later, the king escaped into an increasingly taxing exile. Charles II entered London as king on his thirtieth birthday, 29 May 1660. He was pragmatic enough not to be immediately vindictive, understanding the need to rebuild consensus. But his crown's greatest enemies were not to escape: Cromwell was exhumed so that he could be punished for his treasons. Lambert would remain in prison for the rest of his life.

The king had not forgotten those who had bartered with him over the terms of his kingship in 1650 either. The Marquess of Argyll, despite having crowned Charles at Scone, was executed for supporting the Protectorate government against attempted royalist uprisings. A funerary monument in the High Kirk of St Giles' in Edinburgh commemorates his significance, mirrored by one on the opposite aisle for his great enemy Montrose, whose body was reinterred with dignity on the king's orders. Johnston of Wariston, author of the National Covenant, was hanged in 1663. When Charles II was finally restored to the throne, it was by English hands not Scottish: there was no need to honour the notion of the covenanted king. The surviving Covenanters held no cards in 1660.

'ESSENTIAL AGONY'

To those who served him in arms, Charles was more generous. John Middleton, excluded from the Dunbar campaign only be the paranoia of the Kirk Party, was rewarded for his service at Preston and Worcester with an earldom. He died in 1674 whilst commanding the English garrison at Tangier, Morroco. James Turner, who we had last met in the chaos of the retreat to Warrington in 1648, had returned to Scotland the day prior to Dunbar and in 1651 had been admitted back into the army. He served on the staff at Worcester and was captured, before escaping and eventually making his way into exile. Turner fought in continental service, but also returned to Scotland to test the potential for royalist uprisings. The king knighted him at the Restoration and Turner went on to fight against the latter day Covenanters during the so-called Killing Times. He retired after being accused of provoking the Pentland Rising in 1666, which pitted a veteran of Dunbar (James Wallace) against a veteran of Worcester (Tam Dalyell) at the Battle of Rullion Green.

Alexander Leslie, Earl of Leven, had played a relatively passive part in the campaign of 1650 and had been captured by dragoons in the summer of 1651. After a spell in the Tower of London he had been released on bond, with the Queen of Sweden intervening on his behalf in recognition of his former service to her country. Leven was eventually able to return to Balgonie Castle, where he remained in retirement until his death in 1661. David Leslie had been languished in the Tower since his capture in the days following Worcester, and fined £4,000. Captivity had saved him from any risk of collaboration in the intervening years, and so despite his failure at Dunbar and his inexplicably inadequate performance at Worcester Leslie

58. Statue of King Charles II in Edinburgh's Parliament Square, erected following the Restoration. It shows the king in the armour of a Roman emperor, having overcome his enemies to recover his kingdoms.

was elevated at the Restoration as Lord Newark. He retired to his home at Newark Castle on the Fife coast, the ruins of which perch precipitately over the bay west of St Monans. Leslie died in 1682, his grave now lost.

In a strategic sense, Inverkeithing and Worcester in 1651 were more decisive engagements, but the English army could probably have survived defeat at either. it is the Battle of Dunbar which defines the struggle between Cromwell and the Covenant in the popular imagination today. It did in 1650 too, as the *Act of Pardon and Grace to the People of Scotland* passed in 1653 and proclaimed at the cross of Edinburgh, specifically identified Dunbar as the watershed moment. Those who fought in the Scots army up until that point were included in the terms of the indemnity; those who fought after 3 September were excluded from it. Dunbar had been the last stand of the Covenanter revolution and the truly independent government which it had created; it marked the end of the brilliant decade of Scottish military capacity which had begun with Leven's defiance of Charles I at Duns Law in 1639. The defeat split the Covenanter movement and ensured it would never again be able to form a national consensus. Dunbar, as a devastating and unexpected defeat, on home soil, of an army led by men in whom the state had complete confidence and who had done all possible to secure the support of their God, was a psychological blow far heavier than the subsequent failures. That is clear still today, from the way it is still spoken off in Scotland with that strange sense of self-flagellation and regret: the Scots came down the hill and presented themselves for defeat.

But the real significance of the Battle of Dunbar may in fact lie in what did *not* happen. If the battle had turned out different, in even a partial defeat,

59. The Battle of Dunbar Monument, erected in 1950.

evacuation or surrender for the English, what then becomes of the Oliver Cromwell so beloved of Thomas Carlyle? The 'essential agony' of the Battle of Dunbar would then no longer be the casting down of the Covenanters, but the constraining of the arrogance of the Independents; the sacrifice of *their* godly army, and the humbling of their champion. Whether the wound would have proved fatal to the career of Cromwell will never be known, but his rise to pre-eminence was far from inevitable and Dunbar could have been a significant stumble. At the very least we can speculate that the name of David Leslie would be recognised across the length and breadth of Scotland as the man who broke both Montrose and Cromwell, one of Scotland's greatest commanders since Bruce. But it is not.

Before the Battle of Dunbar, Cromwell was losing; the outcome changed the course of British history.

Colour Plate Commentaries

Figures

A1 Scots Officer
Officers marched to war in their own personal attire. This one wears straight-cut breeches which are open at the knee and enhanced with expensive trim. Officers' doublets could be of fine quality also, like the velvet coats ordered in Edinburgh. Here the doublet is covered by a sleeveless leather buff-coat which provides protection not only from sword blows but also from the elements. Around his neck the officer wears a steel gorget. The 'scarf' (sash) is the only formal identification of an officer and although the Scots probably favoured blue the colour may have varied at the discretion of the senior command or the individual wearer. A portrait of David Leslie depicts him wearing a silvery-coloured scarf. This officer wears a round hat, although some officers preferred the blue bonnet.

A2 English Infantry Officer
This officer has chosen to reflect the fashion of the professionalised forces of the English parliament by wearing a suit of scarlet. Following the latest trend, the breeches are open at the knee and, like his Scots counterpart, the officer is wearing a sleeveless buffcoat. They had become something of an unofficial badge of rank for the officer class in both armies. This officer has opted to wear back-and-breast armour over his however, as a result of which he has chosen to wrap the scarf around his waist rather than from his shoulder. By 1650 most of Cromwell's officers were highly experienced and motivated, and could operate without the fear of political purges which bedevilled their opponents.

B1 Scottish Musketeer
The most common colour for uniform issued to Scottish soldiers in the civil wars was hodden grey. This refers to cloth woven from undyed wool from both black and white fleeces, making it an inexpensive option for large scale orders. Pre-industrial production meant that there would have been a variety of different tones achieved, ranging from shades of grey to earthy browns. The result was probably a less homogenous appearances to the Scottish soldiery than is commonly imagined, although it also gave the Covenanters a sense

of uniformity which English armies had not matched until red coats became pre-eminent in the new-modelled parliamentarian army. This musketeer has no secondary weapon, relying entirely on the matchlock musket.

B2 English Musketeer

This musketeer wears his uniform coat of Venetian red buttoned up over his doublet. A warm knitted cap, similar to a "Monmouth cap", keeps his head warm despite the persistent rain. Like his Scottish counterpart, this soldier has wrapped the lock of his musket and plugged the barrel with cloth to give it protection from the elements. A length of match-cord can be seen sticking out of his pocket; other good places to keep match dry included underneath bonnets and armpits. The collar of bandoleers contains the powder for each charge, the ball being held in a pouch on the hip. A cheap hanger on the left hip gives the musketeer a secondary weapon in the melee.

C1 Scottish Pikeman

This pikeman is wearing an issued grey coat over his personal doublet and breeches. In the crisis of 1650 the Scottish levies were provided with coats rather than full suits. This one has a large number of small cloth buttons, similar to that worn in the famous "Jockie" print. Although browns and greys were also common, blue was the most popular colour for bonnets and these became something of a national identifier. Although the pikeman wears no armour, the rolled tartan plaid will provide a degree of protection in the push of pike. He has a short sword at his side so that he can drop his unwieldy pike and fight at close quarters when required.

C2 English Pikeman

As simple four-tailed red coats became standard across the regular regiments, coat colour could no longer be used to identify individual units. Contrasting linings, visible when the cuffs of the coat were turned back, provided a means to differentiate between regiments. This was the beginning of a process which would see tape and lining colours used as the primary means to identify regimental identities for generations. Although back-and-breast armour was no longer as common amongst pikemen as it had been earlier in the civil wars, this soldier is still provided with a morion helmet to protect his head during combat. The rim, peak and crest were shaped to deflect bladed weapons.

D1 English Trooper

The cream of the Commonwealth army was its heavy cavalry, equipped almost universally as harquebusiers. A stiff leather buff-coat with full overlapping skirts is reinforced in this instance with back-and-breast armour. The latter were particularly useful when facing lancers, who penetrating power was greater than that of the sword. The iconic 'pot' helmet with its articulated neck-guard and three-bar face protection is invaluable in the close fight, and as Cromwell orders replacements for his troopers in the post-Dunbar campaigns they are clearly put the test in the fray. Pistols are holstered on either side of the saddle, and a heavy-bladed sword hangs on the troopers left side. A buff leather sling holds the carbine, shorter barrelled than a musket but giving greater range than a pistol.

D2 Scots Lancer

The Scots cavalry were generally lighter than their counterparts, both in the size of their mounts and in their equipment. In contrast to the thick heavy buff-coat of the harquebusier, this lancer wears a simple leather jerkin over his coat. On his head he wears a steel cap to protect him particularly from sword blows, and it was not uncommon for pistols to be stuffed into the tops of the stiff riding boots. Carbines were less common amongst Scottish troops than English, although some were certainly present as one was used against Cromwell personally near Corstorphine. The lance was cheaper to supply than firearms, and Scottish cavalry tactics had evolved to exploit its effectiveness at disrupting enemy formations.

Flags

PRESTON AND CARBISDALE, 1648-9
E1 & E2 Engager Foot Regiments
E3 Royalist Colour: The Return of Montrose

Armies required recognisable flags, known as colours, to identify individual units and act as rallying points in battle. Unlike later armies which would have regimental colours, in this period each troop or company within a regiment should have its own. The Engager army of 1648 considered itself to be no different to the Armies of the Covenant which had fought in Scotland, England and Ireland since 1639. They therefore followed the established conventions for most of their colours, basing them on the national emblem: the saltire cross of St Andrew. It was the combination of the colours used for the background and the cross which marked out the different regiments. Lord Home's Regiment (**E1**) from the eastern Scottish Borders used the green colour of their commander's heraldic arms, a throwback to the feudal nature of earlier armies. Tullibardine's Regiment (**E2**) from Atholl in Perthshire re-used an existing flag from previous campaigns, which bore one of the older Covenanter mottos. The red cross on white was a colour scheme used again nearly a hundred years later by the Atholl Brigade of 1745.

Unconstrained by the conventions of the Covenanters or the judgements of local committees of war, Scottish royalist colours could be more diverse. In 1650 James Graham, Marquess of Montrose returned to Scotland to raise the north in the name of Charles II. Appreciating that Scottish public opinion was generally outraged at the English Parliament's execution of the king, Montrose chose to march under a gruesome but emotive banner bearing the late king's severed head (**E3**). But the Covenanters were more moved by an almost pathological fear and hatred of Montrose than they were by the fate of the king, and they moved to crush his uprising quickly whilst maintaining their own negotiations with Charles II.

'ESSENTIAL AGONY'

ENGLISH ARMY COLOURS
F1 Charles Fairfax's Regiment, Colonel's Colour
F2 Charles Fairfax's Regiment, 5th captain's Colour
F3 Monck's Regiment, Lt-Colonel's Colour

In 1649, Charles Fairfax's Regiment ordered a new set of colours of 'the best taffety of the deepest blue'. As was the norm the Colonel's Colour (**F1**) was the most distinctive, bearing a Latin motto meaning *Faithfully and Gladly*, surrounded by a 'handsome compartment', the interpretation of which is speculative and usually missed out of reproductions. The Lieutenant-Colonels colour was the same blue but with a simple St George Cross in the canton, from which trailed a wavy white tail (known as a pile, or stream blazant) on the Major's Colour. Company colours followed the normal practice of identifying the company by the number of devices, in this case stars (**F2**). By the Restoration George Monck's regiment was marching under green colours, matched by the cuffs of their coats. They may well have marched under green colours in 1650 therefore, as show in this reconstruction of a Lieutenant-Colonel's Colour (**F3**). As coat colours had become standardised for regular regiments, the regimental flags were all the more important for identification.

SCOTS ARMY COLOURS
G1 Campbell of Lawers' Regiment, Captain's Colour
G2 Stewart's (Edinburgh) Regiment, Captain's Colour
G3 Douglas of Kirkness' Regiment, Colonel's Colour

For the Dunbar campaign the Covenanter motto had been standardised as *Covenant for Religion, King and Kingdom(e)s*, reflecting the added emphasis on the king's interests. The fact that kingdoms was plural was an acknowledge of Charles II's claims in England. Campbell of Lawers' Regiment had been in service almost continuously since the wars began, however, and they do not seem to have updated their colours (**G1**). Other than the new motto however, the basic design of the flags remained as they had been throughout the civil wars, using a variety of colour combinations for the saltire and background. An exception was the Edinburgh Regiment, which used a style much more like the English colours, with a saltire in the canton (**G2**). It may have been one of these company colours which was carried at the surrender of Edinburgh Castle in December 1650. Scottish Colonels' colours tended to be white with heraldic devices: the Edinburgh Regiment's bore the city arms; Sir James Douglas of Kirkness' Regiment shows the famous crowned heart of the Douglases, a feature of their heraldry since the Black Douglas took the heart of Robert the Bruce on crusade.

COLOUR PLATE COMMENTARIES

H1 Colonel's Colour, Charles II's Lifeguard Regiment
H2 Reverse side, Colonel's Colour, Charles II's Lifeguard Regiment
H3 Brown's Regiment of Horse, Cornet

No flags amongst the Scots army of 1650-51 better exemplified the confusion of the times than those of Charles II's Lifeguard of Foot. The Colonel's Colour (**H1**) was a dark blue field bearing the Royal Arms of Scotland (meaning, unlike in some reconstructions, the Lion Rampant appeared in two quarters, as evidenced in contemporary painted panels). The reverse of the flag however was devoid of royal imagery and bore simply the Covenanter motto (**H2**). The other colours followed the same pattern, but rather charmingly using images from the royal arms for each company, starting with the traditional heraldic supports: a silver unicorn and gold lion for the Lt-Colonel and Major; the *fleur de lis* of France; the lion rampant of Scotland; the three leopards of England; and the harp of Ireland. As the lieutenant-colonel was captured at Dunbar, it is likely that at least part of the regiment was present at the battle, presumably after the king's departure from Leith. Some of the companies may not yet have been formed, and drafts from other regiments were used to bring the regiment to full strength after the battle. The regiment is believed to have bucked the trend in the Scots army by wearing red, possibly a legacy of its founders' former service under English supply arrangements in Ulster. The Lifeguard was destroyed at Worcester, wearing brand new coats.

Unlike infantry colours, cavalry cornets were about a third smaller and often fringed. They could be extremely complex in design or very simple, as with this one belonging to Brown of Fordell. The regiment supported the Whiggamores in 1648, served on the right at Dunbar in 1650, and later in that year was beaten up in its quarters by the royalists under Middleton. It suffered badly at Inverkeithing and dispersed thereafter.

Appendix I

Instructions from the Scottish Parliament to the commissioners going to the King's Majesty, 8 March 1650

You shall show his majesty that immediately after the receipt of his letter all possible expedition was used for your dispatch before the parliament, but the meeting thereof having drawn near before you could be in readiness, it was thought necessary that you should receive your directions and approbation.

1. You shall show his majesty that this kingdom was not satisfied with his majesty's letter, and that the sending of commissioners to treat with his majesty was not upon the grounds of the said letter but in prosecution of their former desires and upon the grounds cleared to his majesty by their commissioners in the former papers.

2. You shall desire that his majesty recalls and disclaims all commissions issued forth for acting any thing by sea or land to the prejudice of the covenant or of this kingdom or of any who shall adhere to the Solemn League and Covenant and to monarchical government in any of his other dominions, and all declarations made by any in his name or by his warrant against the same. And further you shall desire his majesty to disallow and disclaim or declare null and void all treaties or agreements whatsoever with the bloody rebels in Ireland, and to declare that he will never allow nor permit the liberty of the popish religion in Ireland or any other part of his dominions.

3. You shall desire that his majesty would acknowledge the authority of this and the former parliaments that have been since the time of his royal father or commissioner were present therein, and particularly you shall demand from his majesty such an allowance and approbation of the acts made in this and the two last immediately preceding sessions of this current parliament as the commissioners of this kingdom obtained

APPENDIX I

from his royal father in answer to their first demands in the large treaty of 1641.

4. You shall remonstrate to his majesty the motives contained in the 11th article of the former instructions sent in March 1649 and prosecute the same with all the arguments you can, especially from the straits this kingdom may be put to after so many ineffectual addresses to his majesty.

5. You are to demand from his majesty that so soon as he shall come to Scotland and before his admission to the exercise of his royal power he shall swear, subscribe and seal the National Covenant and the Solemn League and Covenant in the words following to be subjoined to both:

> I, Charles, king of Great Britain, France and Ireland do assure and declare by my solemn oath in the presence of almighty God, the searcher of hearts, my allowance and approbation of the National Covenant and of the Solemn League and Covenant above-written, and faithfully do oblige myself to prosecute the ends thereof in my station and calling. And that I, for myself and successors, shall consent and agree to all acts of parliament enjoining the same National Covenant and the Solemn League and Covenant and fully establishing presbyterial government, the directory of worship, confession of faith and catechisms in the kingdom of Scotland as they are approved by the general assembly of this kirk and parliament of this kingdom, and that I shall give my royal assent to acts of parliament enjoining the same in the rest of my dominions. And that I shall observe these in my own practice and family, and shall never make opposition to any of these or endeavour any change thereof.

6. You shall likewise acquaint the king's majesty with the oath of coronation, which according to the acts of parliament he is to take. And you shall desire his majesty to consent and agree that all matters civil be determined by this and the subsequent parliaments of this kingdom and such as are and shall be authorised by them, and matters ecclesiastical by the ensuing assemblies of this kirk and such as shall be authorised by them, as was formerly condescended and agreed to by his majesty's royal father.

7. If his majesty shall grant the desires contained in the second, third and sixth articles and shall faithfully and clearly promise and assure in the first word to give the satisfaction desired in the last article, so soon as his majesty shall come to Scotland and shall deliver to you under his hand and seal the grant and assurance aforesaid directed to the parliament (and they not sitting, to the committee of the estates of parliament and to the commissioners of the church), you shall, in their name, invite his majesty to come to this kingdom and give him assurance that he shall be received and entertained with all the duty and respect which can be demanded or expected from loyal subjects who are tied to him by so many bonds and oaths, and that upon giving the satisfaction as

is aforesaid, his majesty is freely to exercise his royal power. But it is rather our advice and earnest desire that his majesty should give the satisfaction aforesaid in Holland, that he may at his first arrival enter to the full exercise of his royal government to the great contentment of all his good people.

8. If there shall be any question about the meaning of the oath and assurance which his majesty is to give for security of religion, that it be declared to his majesty that it does not only import that the National and Solemn League and Covenant be taken by his subjects, but also his approbation of all the heads and articles thereof in his own particular judgment.

9. If his majesty upon these grounds resolves to come here, you shall desire that his majesty would be pleased to leave all these persons who were excluded by the proposition of both kingdoms or against whom this kingdom has just cause of exception, and to consent and declare that he will in matters civil follow the counsel of his parliament and such as shall be or are authorised by them, and in matters ecclesiastic the counsel of the general assembly and such as are or shall be authorised by them, which is declared by this parliament to be the only meaning of the general clause in the act of 7 February anent the king's giving satisfaction in what further shall be found necessary for the settling of a happy peace, preservation of the union between the kingdoms and for the good of the king, his own honour and happiness.

10. You shall observe a good correspondence with the commissioners of the church according to their former instructions.

11. You shall observe a good correspondence with the English presbyterians and encourage them to be constant in the cause and covenant.

12. After meeting with the king and the first day of the treaty, you are not to continue the treaty any longer than 30 days, which is the time affixed to you for closing unless you find good cause to stay longer, in which case you are allowed to stay 10 days longer and to return.

Appendix II

Orders of Battle for the Armies at Dunbar

The Army of the Commonwealth of England

Foot
Colonel George Monck's Brigade:
George Monck's Regiment, John Mauleverer's Regiment, George Fenwick's Regiment (5 companies)

Colonel Thomas Pride's Brigade:
Thomas Pride's Regiment, Oliver Cromwell's (Lord General's) Regiment, John Lambert's Regiment

Colonel Robert Overton's Brigade:
Alban Coxe's Regiment, William Daniel's Regiment, Charles Fairfax's Regiment

Horse
Major-General John Lambert's Brigade:
Charles Fleetwood's Regiment, John Lambert's Regiment, Edward Whalley's Regiment

Colonel Robert Lilburne's Brigade:
Robert Lilburne's Regiment, Francis Hacker's Regiment, Philip Twisleton's Regiment

Reserve:
Oliver Cromwell's (Lord General's) Regiment
John Okey's Regiment of Dragoons (six companies)

Each foot regiment was supported by two field guns; and there were up to ten heavier guns.

'ESSENTIAL AGONY'

The Army of the Kingdom of Scotland

The allocation of individual regiments to brigades is not possible with absolute confidence, but Furgol (1990), followed by Reid (2004), has assembled a convincing Order of Battle. A list identifying likely areas of recruitment and possible unit strengths, also based on Furgol, is published as Appendix G in Pugh (2003). Some smaller units may be missing, having been temporarily absorbed into larger regiments to balance the battalia numbers. For example, the capture of Lt-Colonel James Wallace of Auchans strongly suggests some companies of the King's Lifeguard of Foot were present at Dunbar, presumably after remaining with the army after the king's visit to Leith.

Foot

Lieutenant-General James Lumsden's Brigade:
James Lumsden's Regiment, General of Artillery's Regiment, William Douglas' Regiment

Colonel James Campbell of Lawers' Brigade:
James Campbell's Regiment, George Preston's Regiment, John Haldane's Regiment

Major-General Colin Pitscottie's Brigade:
Colin Pitscottie's Regiment, David Home's Regiment, John Lindsay's Regiment

Colonel John Innes' Brigade:
John Innes' Regiment, John Forbes' Regiment, Master of Lovat's Regiment

James Holborne's Brigade:
James Holborne's Regiment, George Buchannan's Regiment, Alexander Stewart's (Edinburgh) Regiment.

Horse

Robert Adair of Kinhilt's Regiment	Robert Hakett's (Halkett's) Regiment
Charles Arnott's Regiment	Gilbert Ker's Regiment
Lord Brechin's Regiment	David Leslie's Regiment
John Browne's Regiment	Earl of Leven's Regiment
Earl of Cassillis' Regiment	Lord Mauchline's Regiment
Thomas Craig of Riccarton's Regiment	Robert Montgomery's Regiment
Arthur Erskine's Regiment	Walter Scott's Regiment
Master of Forbes' Regiment	William Stewart's Regiment
James Hakett's Regiment	Archibald Strachan's Regiment

Appendix III

Scottish Officers taken at the Battle of Dunbar

Two lists of captured officers were drafted within days of one another sent to London, both of which are presented here for comparison. The names have been transcribed as published, retaining the phonetic errors of the original authors.

LIST ONE

The Lord Liberton
Lieut. Gen. Lumsden, Sir James (lieut. gen. of horse)
The Lord Grandison
Brown, Sir John
Colonel Douglas, Sir William
Colonel Gurdon
Lieut. Col. Hamilton, Walter
Lieut. Col. Wallis
Lieut. Col. Lesley
Lieut. Col. Murray
Lieut. Col. Malwin, Henry
Lieut. Col. Forbus
Lieut. Col. Walthrop (of horse)
Lieut. Col. Dunbarre
Lieut. Col. Hamilton, William
Lieut. Col. Dundasse
Lieut. Col. English, Alexander
Lieut. Col. Craford

Majors
Carmihil, Henry
Cranston, James (of horse)
Moat, George
Forbus, George (Reformado)
Jeremy, William
Steward, George
Bickerton, James (adjutant-gen. of horse)
Cample, George (scout-master-general)
Mr. Gallespy (Minister)
Mr. Wangle, John (Minister)
Mr. Jeffery, Alex, of the committee of estates
Mr. Jeffery, Tho.

Captains of Foot
Belon
Sterline, James
Nue, Francis
Agree
Sibbald
Montegreff, Alex.
Halliburton, George
Brown, Tho.
Bonner
Murray, William
Scot, James
Rutherford, William
Macubray, James
Montgomery, Hugh
Aiken, James
Smith, George

'ESSENTIAL AGONY'

Mackihellan, John
Madole, Hugh
Pingle, George
Scot, Robert
Wood, Alexander
Hamilton, Robert
Gray, Tho.
Adamson, Robert
Duncan, Robert
Mancaula, Robert,
Scot, Walter
Creshton, Matthew
Steward, James
Douglas, William
Lesley, Walter
Wauchop (of horse)
Borthock, James
Murray, Daniel
Murray, John
Burton, William
Camil, James
Capt. Hamilton, Roger
Capt. Wood, Robert
Blayre, William
Capt. Anderson, Rob.

Lieutenants of Foot
Cunningham, James
Blackwood, James
Marnal, Patrick
Cunningham, Henry
Car, Lancelot
Macknight, John
Hume, John
Gourdon, John
Cunningham, George
Weare, Geo.
Eston, Henry
Cowston, Nicholas
Steward, Alexander
Petre, William
Lesly, Norman
Gladston, William
Hamilton, Robert
Mackburn, Gen.
Strahan, Robert
Allen, Richard
Mackbey, James

Disset, George
Nichols, James
Car, John
Mennib, Thomas
Sims, William
Car, Alexander
Twede, James
Leich, William
Suiers, James
Moor, John
Kenner, Andrew
Baily
Rich, John
Camel, John
Knocks, William
Anderson, Thomas
Car, Lancaster
Monnorgome, James
Car, Thomas
Twede, James
Armer, James
Smer, James
Kenner, Andrew
Camel, Jo.
Steward, John
Osborn, Allen
Wilson, John
Wanhop, Walter
Warberton, Patrick
Ingles, William
Gourdon, Alexander
Gourdon, Samuel
Harkenson, Lancaster
Rankin, Robert
Colemine, Cha.
Rawson, John
Guiler, Andrew
Totterson, Geo.
Hutchen, Thomas
Emnes, John
Skew, John
Hunter, John
Markdoughal, John
Drummon, Andrew
Moale, George
Scot, Francis
Kiff, Alexander
Markdoughil, John

APPENDIX III

Lesley, George
Livery, William
Denant, John
Elliot, William
Windram, George (Cornet)
Collerwood, Thomas (Cornet)
Lindsey, Patrick (Cornet)
Captain Brisbon, William (of horse)
Cunningham, William (Cornet)
Maxwel, James (Cornet)
Denham, Jam. (Cornet)
Lieut. Bruse, James (of horse)
Magel, John (Cornet)
Steward, Walter (Cornet)
Hay, John (Cornet)
Captain Danrimple, William (of foot)
Captain Kerkpatrick, Charls
Lawson, C. Nich.
Magavile, Ja (Cornet)
Brown, John (Cornet)
Michel, Alex. (Cornet)

Quartermasters of Horse
Richinson, Tho.
Fabus, William

Ensigns of Foot
Kilpatrick
Mac Doghal, Walter
Sanckle, William
Jack, George
Gud, Hartley
Carnetuss, William
Wallis, Thomas
Myan, Andrew
Bennet, James
Linsey, John
Hanna, Andrew
Pringle, Thomas
Hamilton, Robert
Delap, James
Gunny, John
Edwards, John
Camel, Col.
Heatly
Ray, Robert
Hurral, Gilbert

Musket, James
Simple, William
Ogleby, Robert
Williamson, Robert
Lesley, William
Shields, Ersbield
Habern, Robert
Scot, William
Edmaston, James
Lawson, Robert
Newen, James
Bathick, Andrew
Elphenson, Gorge
Hindise, John
Whittle, Henry
Donnalson, Andrew
Kenede, David
Camel, John
Kemel, Dunkin
Engles, Cornelius
Calion, Patrick
Mawod, William
Kerkebrik, Henry
Calmers, Alex.
Crime, George
Rede, James
Somervil, John
Abenille, John
Clark, John
Breme, Alexander
Chapman, William
Muckin, John
Spence, Alexander
Mark, John
Thompson, Thomas
Dixon, John
Smith, John
Johnson, Alexander
Egger, William
Grant, David
Guyle, George
Wallis, John
Kemen, John
Anderson, Thomas
Brewse, James
Mamblan, William
Carmihil, James
Walsin, William

'ESSENTIAL AGONY'

Anderson, William
Dunbarre, James
Calderwood, James
Rey, Hugh
Bayde, Thomas
Beed, David
Craw, Robert
Calley, George
Ruherford, James
Scot, Walter
Steward, Walter
Henne, Robert
Facquer, James
Marmath, James
Ackman, Henry
Weare, John
Brown-Lee, John
Bisket, David
Hinderson, George
Blacketter, John
Michel, Alexander
Baily, Alexander
Wallwood, Robert
Watson, John
Greere, William
Crawford, John
Wilson, William
Dunbar, John
Gurdon, Samuel
Munins, John
Cunningham, John
Staolm, William

Guthery, Alexander
Hunter, John
Luckey, Adam
Mayrey, Andrew
Macktellon, Robert
Gerne, Robert
Mackews, John
Brotherson, James
Gentry, William
Sincler, Edward
Brede, Andrew
Hunter, Robert
Gray, John

Serjeants
Muckerry, Henry
Sibbet, Alexander
Gray, Gilbert
Ellis, James
Gardner, Collin
Axenhead, John
Hogg, John
Watson, William
Mackwel, John
Lyel, James
Coddel, James
Morris, John
Kerk, Adam
Captain Rutherford, Robert (of foot)
Captain Car, John (of foot)

The whole number of officers and private soldiers taken, ten thousand.
Four thousand slain.
Thirty-two pieces of ordnance, of all sorts.
Two hundred colours, horse and foot.
All their arms, tents, bag and baggage.

LIST TWO

Lomsden, Sir James (lieut.-gen. of foot)

Colonels
Col. Douglas, Sir Will.
Col. Lomsden, Will.
Colonel Gurdon

Lieutenant-Colonels
Lieut. Col. Wallis
Lieut. Col. Lesley
Lieut. Col. Murray
Lieut. Col. Malvin, Henry
L. Col. Forbis, Arthur
Lieut. Colonel Wanhap (of horse)
Lieut. Col. Dunbarre
Lieut. Col. Hamilton
Lieut. Col. Crawford

APPENDIX III

Lieut. Col. Ingles
Lieut-Colonel Montgomery, John
Bickerton, James (adjutant-gen. of horse)

Majors
Carmihil, Henry (of foot)
Cranster, James (of horse)
Moat, George (of foot)
Scringer, Will. (of foot)
Steward, John (of foot)
Forbes, George (Reformado)[1]
Moor
Oagle
Freesle

Captains of Foot
Sterlyn, James
Agnue, Francis
Sibbald
Monpreff, Alex.
Holliburton, George
Brown, Tho.
Murray, William
Scott, James
Rudderford, William
Macularoy, James
Montgomery, Hugh
Aken, James
Smith, George
Maclellan, John
Mackellum, Robert
Madole, Hugh
Pringle, George
Scot, Robert
Wood, Alexander
Hamilton, Robert
Gray, Tho.
Adamson, Robert
Beton

Captains of Horse and Foot
Duncan, Robert

Maccaulla, Robert
Scot, Walter
Creshton, Matthew
Steward, James
Douglas, William
Lesley, Walter
Manhop, Wil. (of horse)
Borthick, James
Murray, David

Captains of Horse
Murray, John
Burton, William
Camil, James
Bresbon, William (of horse)
Daurlmple, William
Kerkpatrick, Charls
Lawson, Nicholas
Rudderford, Robert
Car, John
Dundass
Ogleby
Gourdon
Bonner
Lieut. Bruse (lieutenant of horse)

Cornets of Horse
Cunningham, William
Maxwel, James
Denham, James
Magil, James
Steward, Walter
Hay, John
Macdoer, Anthony
Brown, John
Michel, Alex.
Collerwood, John
Winderum, George

Captains-Lieut. of Horse and Foot
Monnergain, John
Emery, William
Blayer, William
Anderson, Robert
Holden, Roger
Wood Robert

---

1   A reformado could be a volunteer of officer status but without an active commission, or an officer serving despite the absence of his regiment.

'ESSENTIAL AGONY'

Lieutenants of Foot
Cunningham, James
Blackwood, James
Macknab, Patrick
Cunningham, Henry
Car, Lancelot
Macknight, John
Heume, John
Gourdon, John
Cunningham, George
Weare, James
Eston, Henry
Gun, William
Coston, Nicholas
Steward, Alexander
Petre, William
Lesley, Norman
Bailey, William
Gladston, William
Hamberton, Robert
Mackburney, Geo.
Straughan, Robert
Allen, Richard
Mackbey, James
Bisset, George
Nichols, James
Mennis, Thomas
Sinnis, William
Car, John
Car, Alexander
Twede, James
Leich, Philip
Armor, James
Sayers, James
Meer, John
Pennere, Andrew
Bailey, Patrick
Camil, John
Rich, John
Steward, John
Camil, John
Osborn, Allen
Knocks, William
Wilson, John
Anderson, Thomas
Wanhap, Walter
Holliburton, Patrick
Car, Lancelot

Engley, William
Car, Thomas
Gourdon, Alexander
Forguson, Lancaster
Rankin, Robert
Coleman, Cha.
Lewson, John
Guiler, Andrew
Patterson, George
Hutchen, Thomas
Ennis, John
Sken, John
Hunter, John
Mackdoughal, John
Drumon, Andrew
Lesley, George
Moat, George
Scot, Francis
Elliot, William
Ciff, Alexander
Denguit, John

Quartermasters of Horse
Richman, Tho.
Forbis, William

Ensigns
Kilpatrick
Macdoughel, Walter
Sinclare, William
Jack, George
Gadley, Hartley
Carnecuse, William
Wallis, Thomas
Rolston, James
Myn, Andrew
Bennet, James
Linsey, John
Hanna, Andrew
Pringle, Thomas
Hamilton, Robert
Delop, James
Gray, John
Edward, James
Camel, Collin
Heatley, --------
Roy, Robert
Harral, Gilbert

APPENDIX III

Musket, James
Sample, William
Ogleby, Robert
Williamson, Robert
Lesley, William
Shields, Ersby
Haborn, Robert
Scot, William
Edminston, Ja.
Lawson, Robert
Neicen, James
Barthick, Andrew
Elphenston, George
Fairdise, John
White, Henry
Dunalson, Andrew
Camide, David
Camil, John
Engles, Cornelius
Camil, Duncan
Canburn, Patrick
Mannord, William
Craw, Robert
Calley, George
Rudderford, James
Scot, Walter
Steward, Walter
Heume, Robert
Forquer, Jas.
Macknath, James

Ackman, Henry
Wayer, John
Brown, John
Chapman, William
Macuo, John
Spence, Alexander
Black, John
Thompson, Thomas
Fryer, Robert
Thompson, John
Dixon, John
Smith, Geo.
Johnston, Alexander
Egger, William
Grant, David
Gayler, George
Wallis, John
Kemmen, John
Enderson, Thomas
Brewse, James
Maclan, William
Carmihil, John
Watson, William
Anderson, William
Dunbar, James
Elderwood, James
Roy, Henry
Boyd, Thomas
Reed, David

Appendix IV

Letter from David Leslie to the Marquess of Argyll

May it please your Lordship, this morning, coming to Stirling, I received your Lordship's letter desiring me to send his Majesty my advice (which is but of small value), only being commanded by your Lordship, my opinion is that he stay in St Johnston [Perth], and that your Lordship, with my Lord Lothian, were by our Committee of Estates to give your best advice for the better managing of affairs. Concerning the Misfortune of our Army I shall say nothing; but it was the visible hand of God, with our own laziness, and not of man, that defeat them, notwithstanding of orders given to stand to their arms that night. I know I get my own share of the fault by many for drawing them so near the enemy, and must suffer in this as many times formerly, though I take God to witness we might have as easily beaten them, as we did James Graham at Philiphaugh, if the officers had stayed by their troops and regiments; which is all, but that I long to see your Lordship here (without whom there will be little done), and remains, your Lordship's most humble and faithful servant,

David Leslie
Stirling, the 5 September 1650.

Appendix V

Cromwell's Proclamation Concerning Wounded Men

The Lord General's Proclamation concerning the Wounded Men left in the Field.

Forasmuch as I understand there are several soldiers of the enemy's army yet abiding in the field, who by reason of their wounds, could not march from thence: these are therefore to give notice to the inhabitants of this nation, that they may and have free liberty to repair to the field aforesaid, and with their carts, or any other peaceable way, to carry the said soldiers to such places as they shall think fit; provided they meddle not or take away any the arms there; and all officers and soldiers are to take notice that the same is permitted. Given under by hand at Dunbar.

O. Cromwell.
Sept. 4, 1650.
To be proclaimed by beat of drum.

Bibliography

Primary Sources

A Large Relation of the Fight at Leith; also a Perfect Account of Every Day's Transactions and Engagements between the Armies', in *Original Memoirs written during the Great Civil War; being the Life of Sir Henry Slingsby and Memoirs of Captain Hodgson*, (Edinburgh: Archibald Constable & Co, 1806).

Anon, *The several speeches of Duke Hamilton Earl of Cambridge, Henry Earl of Holland, and Arthur Lord Capel upon the scaffold immediately before their execution*, (London: Cole, Tyton and Playford, 1649).

'Articles of the Rendition of Edinburgh Castle to the Lord-General Cromwell', in *Original Memoirs written during the Great Civil War; being the Life of Sir Henry Slingsby and Memoirs of Captain Hodgson*, (Edinburgh: Archibald Constable & Co, 1806).

'A True Relation of the Proceedings of the English Army now in Scotland', in *Original Memoirs written during the Great Civil War; being the Life of Sir Henry Slingsby and Memoirs of Captain Hodgson*, (Edinburgh: Archibald Constable & Co, 1806).

'A True Relation of the Daily Proceedings and Transactions of the Army in Scotland', in *Original Memoirs written during the Great Civil War; being the Life of Sir Henry Slingsby and Memoirs of Captain Hodgson*, (Edinburgh: Archibald Constable & Co, 1806).

'A True Relation of the Routing of the Scottish Army near Dunbar', in *Original Memoirs written during the Great Civil War; being the Life of Sir Henry Slingsby and Memoirs of Captain Hodgson*, (Edinburgh: Archibald Constable & Co, 1806).

'A True Relation of a Second Victorie over the Scots at Hamilton', in *Original Memoirs written during the Great Civil War; being the Life of Sir Henry Slingsby and Memoirs of Captain Hodgson*, (Edinburgh: Archibald Constable & Co, 1806).

Baillie, R. *The Letters and Journals of Robert Baillie* (3 Volumes), (Edinburgh: Bannatyne Clube, 1841)

Brereton, W, *Travels in Holland, The United Provinces, England, Scotland, and Ireland*, (Manchester: Chetham Society, 1844).

Brown, K. M. et al (eds), *The Records of the Parliaments of Scotland to 1707*, (St Andrews: University of St Andrews, 2007-2019).

Bryant, A (ed). *The Letters, Speeches and Declarations of King Charles II*, (London: Cassell, 1935).

Carlyle, T. *Oliver Cromwell's Letters and Speeches*, 2nd Edition, (Glasgow, 1846).

Carte, T. (ed), *A Collection of original letters and papers, concerning the affairs of England, from the year 1641 to 1660: Found among the Duke of Ormonde's papers*, (London, 1739).

Gardiner, S. R. (ed), *Letters and Papers Illustrating the Relations between Charles the Second and Scotland in 1650*, (Edinburgh: Scottish History Society, 1894).

Green, M. A. E. (ed), *Calendar of State Papers, Domestic Series, 1649-50*, (London: Longman & Co, 1875).

Hodgson, J. *Memoirs of Captain John Hodgson of Coalley-Hall, near Halifax*,

Johnston, A. Sir, *Diary of Sir Archibald Johnston of Wariston, Volume II 1650-54*, (Edinburgh: University Press, 1919).

Laing, D. (ed), *Correspondence of Sir Robert Kerr, First Earl of Ancrum, and his son William, Third Earl of Lothian*, Volume II, (Edinburgh: Roxburghe Club, 1875).

'Letters from the Head-Quarters of our Army in Scotland', in *Original Memoirs written during the Great Civil War; being the Life of Sir Henry Slingsby and Memoirs of Captain Hodgson*, (Edinburgh: Archibald Constable & Co, 1806).
'Letter from Sir Arthur Haselriggee to the Honorable Committee of the Councel of State', in *Original Memoirs written during the Great Civil War; being the Life of Sir Henry Slingsby and Memoirs of Captain Hodgson*, (Edinburgh: Archibald Constable & Co, 1806).
Row, W. *Life of Mr Robert Blair, Minister of St Andrews*, (Edinburgh: Woodrow Society, 1848).
Rushword, J. *A Declaration of the Army of England, Upon Their March Into Scotland*, (Newcastle: Husband and Field, 1650).
'Several Letters from Scotland, relating to the Proceedings of the Army there', in *Original Memoirs written during the Great Civil War; being the Life of Sir Henry Slingsby and Memoirs of Captain Hodgson*, (Edinburgh: Archibald Constable & Co, 1806).
Steele, W. *Duke Hamilton Earl of Cambridge his case, spoken to, and argued on the behalf of the Commonwealth, before the High Court of Justice*, (London, 1649).
'The Lord General Cromwell, his March to Sterling; being a Diary of all Proceedings in the Army', in *Original Memoirs written during the Great Civil War; being the Life of Sir Henry Slingsby and Memoirs of Captain Hodgson*, (Edinburgh: Archibald Constable & Co, 1806).
Turner, J. *Memoirs of His own Life and Times*, (Edinburgh: Bannatyne Club, 1829).
Walker, E. *Historical Discourses, Upon Several Occasions,* (London, 1705).
Whitelock, B. *Memorials of the English Affairs, from the Beginning of the Reign of Charles the First to the Happy Restoration of King Charles the Second*, Volume 3, (Oxford: University Press, 1853).
Wishart, G. *A Complete History of the Civil Wars in Scotland under the Conduct of the Illustrious James Marquis of Montrose, in two parts*, 2nd Edition, (Edinburgh: William Adams, 1724).
Wood, M. (ed), *Extracts from the Records of the Burgh of Edinburgh 1642-55*, (Edinburgh: Oliver and Boyd, 1938).

Secondary Sources

Adamson, J. *The Noble Revolt: the Overthrow of Charles I*, (London: Weidemfeld & Nicolson, 2007).
Archibald, S. *English Civil War Flags: English & Scots Foot Regiments*, (Hemel Hempstead: Redcrest, 2018).
Asquith, S. *New Model Army 1645-60*, (Oxford: Osprey, 1981).
Atkin, M. *Worcester 1651*, (Barnsley: Pen and Sword, 2008).
Barratt, J. *Cavaliers: the Royalist Army at War 1642-1646*, (Stroud: Sutton, 2000).
Blackmore, D. *Arms & Armour of the English Civil Wars*, (London: Royal Armouries, 1990).
Bull, S. & Smeed, M. *Bloody Preston: the Battle of Preston 1648*, (Lancaster: Carnegie, 1998).
Corsar, K. 'The Surrender of Edinburgh Castle December 1650', *Scottish Historical Review* 28, no. 105 (1949): 43-54.
Edwards, G. *The Last Days of Charles I*, (Stroud: Sutton, 1999).
Furgol, E, *A Regimental History of the Covenanting Armies 1639-1651*, (Edinburgh: John Donald, 1990).
Firth, C. 'The Battle of Dunbar', *Transactions of the Royal Historical Society*, Vol. 14, (Cambridge: University Press, 1900), p. 19-52.
Firth, C. *Cromwell's Army: a History of the English Soldier during the Civil Wars, the Commonwealth and the Protectorate*, (London: Greenhill, 1992).
Fraser, A. *Cromwell, Our Chief of Men*, (London: Hatchette, 2011).
Fraser, M. *The Rivals: Montrose and Argyll and the Struggle for Scotland*, (Edinburgh: Birlinn, 2015).
Gerrard, C. et al. *Lost Lives, New Voices: Unlocking the Stories of the Scottish Soldiers from the Battle of Dunbar 1650*, (Oxford: Oxbow, 2018).
Grainger, J. *Cromwell Against the Scots: the Last Anglo-Scottish War 1650-1652*, (East Linton: Tuckwell, 1997).
Graham, A. 'Archaeology on a Great Post Road', *Proceedings of the Society of the Antiquaries of Scotland*, 96 (Edinburgh: Society of the Antiquaries of Scotland, 1963), p. 318-47.
Louth, W. *The Arte Militaire: the Application of 17th Century Military Manuals to Conflict Archaeology*, (Solihull: Helion & Company, 2016).
Lyon, C. J. *A Personal History of King Charles II from His Landing in Scotland to his Escape from England*, (Edinburgh: Stevenson, 1851).
Macleod, J. *Dynasty: the Stuarts 1560-1807*, (London: Hodder & Stroughton, 1999).

McGavin, W. (ed), *The Scots Worthies*, (Oxford: University Press, 1839).
Martine, J. *Reminiscences and Notices of Ten Parishes of the County of Haddington*, (Haddington: Sinclair, 1894).
McGavin, W. (ed), *The Scots Worthies*, (Oxford: University Press, 1839).
McNally, M. *Ireland 1649-52: Cromwell's Protestant Crusade*, (Oxford: Osprey, 2009).
Miller, J. *The History of Dunbar from the Earliest Records to the Present Time*, (Dunbar: Downie, 1859).
Murdoch, A. *Scotland and America c1600-1800*, Macmillan (), 2009.
Parker, G. *The Military Revolution: Military Innovation and the Rise of the West, 1500-1800*, Second edition, (Cambridge: University Press, 2016).
Paterson, R. *A Land Afflicted: Scotland and the Covenanter Wars 1638-1690*, (Edinburgh: John Donald, 1998).
Peachey, S. *The Soldier's Life in the English Civil War: Organisation, Food, Clothing, Weapons and Combat*, (Bristol: Stuart, 2016).
Peachey, S. and Turton, A. *Common Soldier's Clothing of the Civil Wars 1639-46, Volume I: Infantry*, (Bristol: Stuart, 1995).
Plowden, A. *Women all on Fire: the Women of the English Civil War*, (Sutton: History Press, 2004)
Pollard, A. (ed). *Tudor Tracts 1532-1588*, (New York: E P Dutton, 1903).
Pugh, R. *Dunbar: the Battles of 1296 and 1650*, (Dunbar: 2014).
Pugh, R. *Swords, Loaves & Fishes: a History of Dunbar*, (Balerno: Harlaw Heritage, 2003).
Purkiss, D. *The English Civil War: a People's History*, (London: Harper Perennial, 2007).
Rankin, W. *St Helen's Church, Old Cambus*, (Scottish Church History Society, 1938).
Reese, P. *Cromwell's Masterstroke: Dunbar 1650*, (Barnsley: Pen and Sword, 2006).
Reid, S. *Crown, Covenant and Cromwell: the Civil Wars in Scotland 1639-51*, (Barnsley: Frontline, 2012).
Reid, S. *Scots Armies of the English Civil Wars*, (Oxford: Osprey, 1999).
Reid, S. Scots Armies of the 17th Century 1: the Army of the Covenant 1639-51, (Partizan: 1988).
Reid, S. Scots Armies of the 17th Century 2: Scots Colours, (Partizan: 1990).
Reid, S. Scots Armies of the 17th Century 3: the Royalist Armies 1639-46, (Partizan: 1989).
Reid, S. *Dunbar 1650: Cromwell's Most Famous Victory*, (Oxford: Osprey, 2004).
Roberts, K. *Matchlock Musketeer 1588-1688*, (Oxford: Osprey, 2002).
Roberts, K. *Pike and Shot Tactics 1590-1660*, (Oxford: Osprey, 2010).
Roberts, K. *Cromwell's War Machine: the New Model Army 1645-1660*, (Barnsley: Pen and Sword, 2005).
Rowland, A. *Military Encampments of the English Civil Wars 1639-59*, (Bristol: Stuart, 1997).
Royle, T. *Civil War: the Wars of the Three Kingdoms 1638-1660*, (London: Abacus, 2006).
Scott, D. *Politics and War in the Three Stuart Kingdoms, 1637-49*, (Basingstoke: Palgrave Macmillan, 2004).
Stace, M. (ed), *Cromwelliana: a Chronological Detail of Events in which Oliver Cromwell was Engaged*, (London: Machell Stace, 1806).
Spencer, C. *Prince Rupert: the Last Cavalier*, (London: Weidenfeld & Nicolson, 2007).
Stevenson, D. *The Scottish Revolution, 1637-44*, (Edinburgh: John Donald, 2003).
Stevenson, D. *Revolution and Counter Revolution, 1644-51*, (Edinburgh: John Donald, 2003).
Tincey, J. *Marston Moor 1644: the Beginning of the End*, (Oxford: Osprey, 2003).
Wanklyn, M. 'Some Further thoughts on Oliver Cromwell's Last Campaign', *New Approaches to the Military History of the English Civil War*, (Solihull: Helion & Company, 2016).
Wanklyn, M. Reconstructing the New Model Army, Volume II 1649-63,
Warwick, L. *The Second Battle of Stirling? Or When is a Battlefield not a Battlefield?* (unpublished, 2018).
Wedgewood, C. The King's Peace 1637-1641, (London: Folio Society, 2001).
Wedgewood, C. The King's War 1641-1647, (London: Folio Society, 2001).
Wedgewood, C. The Trial of King Charles I, (London: Folio Society, 2001).
Williams, R. *Montrose*, (Colonsay: House of Lochar, 2001).
Wilson, D. *The King and the Gentleman: Charles Stuart and Oliver Cromwell 1599-1649*, (London: Hutchinson Random House, 1999).
Woolrych, A. *Britain in Revolution: 1625-1660*, (Oxford: University Press, 2002).